Domesticating Resistance

*The Dhan-Gadi Aborigines
and the Australian State*

EXPLORATIONS IN ANTHROPOLOGY
A University College London Series
Series Editors: John Gledhill and Bruce Kapferer

Jadran Mimica, *Intimations of Infinity: The Cultural Meaning of the Iqwaye Counting System and Number*

Tim Ingold, David Riches and James Woodburn (eds), *Hunters and Gatherers*
Volume 1. *History, evolution and social change*
Volume 2. *Property, power and ideology*

Barry Morris

Domesticating Resistance

*The Dhan-Gadi Aborigines
and the Australian State*

BERG

Oxford / New York / Munich

Distributed exclusively in the US and Canada by
St Martin's Press, New York

First published in 1989 by
Berg Publishers Limited
Editorial offices:
77 Morrell Avenue, Oxford OX4 1NQ, UK
165 Taber Avenue, Providence, RI 02906, USA
Westermühlstraße 26, 8000 München 5, FRG

British Library Cataloguing in Publication Data
Morris, Barry
   Domesticating resistance: the Dhan-Gadi
   aborigines and the Australian state –
   (Explorations in anthropology)
   1. New South Wales. Dhan-Gadi, history
   I. Title II. Series
   994.4'0049915

ISBN 0–85496–271–9

Library of Congress Cataloging-in-Publication Data
Morris, Barry.
   Domesticating resistance: the Dhan-Gadi
aborigines and the Australian state / Barry Morris.
      p.   cm. — (Explorations in anthropology)
   Bibliography: p.
   ISBN 0–85496–271–9 : $45.00 (est.)
   1. Dangadi (Australian people) 2. Australia—Native races.
   I. Title. II. Series.
   DU125.D35M66 1988
   305.8'9915—dc19   88–39473

Printed in Great Britain by Billings of Worcester

In Memory of
John D. Quinlan
Ellen M. Davis
James Kelly
Sadie Miranda

Philosophic discourse has always been essentially related to law, institutions, and contracts which, taken together, constitute the subject matter of sovereignty and have been part of the history of sedentary peoples from the earliest despotic states to modern democracies . . .

It is common knowledge that nomads fare miserably under our kinds of regime: we will go to any lengths in order to settle them, and they barely have enough to subsist on . . . But the nomad is not necessarily one who moves: some voyages take place *in situ*, are trips in intensity. Even historically, nomads are not necessarily those who move about like migrants. On the contrary, they do not move; nomads, they nevertheless stay in the same place and continually evade the codes of settled people. (Deleuze 1977: 148–9)

Contents

Tables, Maps and Diagrams

Tables

Maps

Diagrams

Acknowledgements

This book has been generally supported by many people. I am foremost in the debt to Chris Morris who shared with me the period of fieldwork and the writing up and has supported and encouraged this project throughout, often at her own inconvenience. I also extend my thanks to Terry Widders who was instrumental in my original decision to go to the Macleay Valley and whose initial personal introductions to a number of people were to be of invaluable assistance during my fieldwork.

To the Dhan-gadi people, I owe a unique debt. There is no doubt for me that they are responsible for what limited insights I have gained into the social and political world of the Dhan-gadi. They permitted me to observe, and patiently and tolerantly instructed me, in many matters which, when all things are considered, they might well have wished to keep to themselves. I thank them for this and value the friendships that developed in the process. There are many people who helped me. My special gratitude I wish to express to Mr John D. Quinlan, Mrs Ellen Davis, Mrs Carlene Davis, Mr James Kelly, Mrs Daphne Kelly, Mrs Sadie Miranda, Mr Len de Silva, Mr Ray Kelly, Mr Letton Smith, Mr Alfie Drew, Mr Colin Campbell, Mr Robert Campbell, Mr Bill Duroux, Mrs Mary Duroux, Mrs Maisie Mason and Mrs Victoria Archibald. In general, I owe the Dhan-gadi people a great debt for their hospitality and acceptance.

I wish to thank Jeremy Beckett, Andrew Lattas and Gillian Cowlishaw for their encouragement and detailed and constructive criticisms. I also owe an intellectual debt to Bruce Kapferer, Douglas Miles, Sue Barham, Tom Ernst, Geoff Bagshaw, Michael Roberts and Lee Sackett. The Anthropology Department of Adelaide University provided a stimulating environment for the intellectual nurturance of this book.

I gratefully acknowledge the financial assistance given to me through the Greenwell Bequest (Anthropology Department, University of Sydney) and the Australian Institute of Aboriginal Studies.

I would like to acknowledge the research assistance given by the Macleay Historical Society, Mitchell Library, NSW State Archives, NSW Museum Library and the Australian Institute of Aboriginal Studies.

Abbreviations and Acronyms

AAM	Australian Aborigine Mission
AAPA	Australian Aboriginal Progressive Association
ABS	Australian Bureau of Statistics
AHR	Historical Records of Australia
AIAS	Australian Institute of Aboriginal Studies
APA	Aborigines Progressive Association
APB	Aborigines Protection Board
AWB	Aborigines Welfare Board
AWO	Area Welfare Officer
B	Brother
CWA	Country Women's Association
D	Daughter
F	Father
f. b.	full blood
FF	Father's father
FFZ	Father's father's sister
FZ	Father's sister
FZD	Father's sister's daughter
FZS	Father's sister's son
HC	Housing Commission
h.c.	half caste
HFA	Homes for Aborigines
M	Mother
MA	*Macleay Argus*
MB	Mother's brother
MBD	Mother's brother's daughter
MBS	Mother's brother's son
MC	*Macleay Chronicle*
MDWC	Macleay District Welfare Committee
MF	Mother's father
MFZ	Mother's father's sister
MHS	Macleay Historical Society
ML	Mitchell Library
MM	Mother's mother
MMB	Mother's mother's brother

MP	Member of Parliament
NPWS	National Parks and Wildlife Service
NSW	New South Wales
NSW Leg. Ass.	New South Wales Legislative Assembly
PSB	Public Service Board
S	Son
SA	New South Wales State Archives
SRNSW	Statistical Registrar of New South Wales
TAB	State government betting agency
USA	United States of America
V and P	Votes and Proceedings
Z	Sister
ZD	Sister's daughter
ZS	Sister's son

Introduction

This book is an attempt to interpret the social history of the Dhan-gadi Aboriginal people from the Macleay Valley in northern New South Wales (henceforth NSW), Australia. I explore the changing relations between the Dhan-gadi and the state between the mid-nineteenth century, when Europeans first occupied the valley, and the present. The analysis focuses on how changing configurations of power partly structured Dhan-gadi responses and how, in turn, continuous attempts by the Dhan-gadi to resist incorporation into an encompassing state system subverted and modified the power of the state. The study seeks to explore the forms of power that have oppressed the Dhan-gadi and convey something of the stubborn creativity of their resistance.

Because the Macleay Valley has been long colonised and intensively settled by Europeans, it provides an ideal setting in which to study the development and transformation of colonial relations between an indigenous population and the state. The Dhan-gadi people's formerly traditionally-held lands in this rural part of NSW were expropriated by Europeans and used predominantly for small-scale dairy, agricultural and beef production. Being of overwhelmingly British descent, the local European community was highly uniform in character and, until recently, remained relatively stable socially and economically and in much the same form since the late nineteenth century. Throughout most of this period, relations between Europeans and Aborigines were based on varying degrees of racial separation and social exclusion, somewhat reminiscent of the stark simplicity of Fanon's (1976) construction of the colonial world as a Manichaean universe. The Aborigines experienced their Manichaean universe as a racial dichotomy between the coloniser and the colonised, expressed in the categories of white/black, superior/inferior and civilised/primitive. Social interactions at the local level, as well as political relations with the state, determined these social and political categories.

Many of the problems and issues discussed here have been examined elsewhere in a number of studies on peasants and slavery by the anthropologists Wolf (1971, 1982), Mintz (1974), Sider (1980) and Taussig (1980, 1987) and the cultural marxist historian, Genovese (1974). What I share with these authors is a concern with capitalism in its colonial form, in

1

which colonialism is viewed not simply in terms of a particular set of exploitative relationships, but as the implementation of a distinctive cultural system with specific features which differ from other cultural and social systems. My concern is to delineate the historical specificities of the Dhan-gadi people's cultural encounter with colonial capitalism.

These substantive issues provide the starting point for my analysis of the profound changes which have affected the social life of the Dhan-gadi during the twentieth century. The major dynamic for these changes came, however, not from the economic coercions of capitalism, but from the extra-economic coercions of the state. As part of a policy to transform Aborigines into autonomous, self-regulating individuals as a precondition for citizenship, the authoritarian practices of the modern liberal state sought to extinguish existing familial and communal ties. In this respect I am particularly interested in the homology which exists between bureaucratic forms of state control and the social and ideological formations of capitalism. Certain policies, including the introduction of manager-supervised government reserves, as well as the various institutional forms of pedagogic intervention which pervade capitalist culture (i.e. norms of instrumental rationality and a culture of privatisation), were applied to break down existing kinship and communal ties.

The specific characteristics of this cultural domination emerged out of the particular form colonialism took in NSW. In the initial period of colonisation, there was no systematic attempt to conserve or control the indigenous population. This resulted in the destruction of the existing Dhan-gadi society and the marginalisation of its remaining members. The indigenous population was reduced to a landless minority and these Aborigines increasingly relocated on government settlements scattered throughout the state. As such they acquired the liminal status of colonial wards, in other words they were non-citizens. The impetus of government policy in resolving colonial contradictions has been towards negating one element – the indigenous population – and this mainly through policies of assimilation. Domination is constituted as a process of hegemonic incorporation. The state effectively attempts to control expressions of Aboriginal identity, i.e. to shape new constructions of identity and new patterns of sociality. I analyse the movement from limited forms of intervention to more totalising forms of state control.

Along the lines of Foucault's work I explore the specificities of how this group suffered domination and how it lost control of its communal existence. Foucault (1977, 1980, 1982) reformulates the concept of power in bourgeois society by expanding the focus of its analysis. He argues that the exercise of power in its negative and repressive role does not exhaust its manifestations in contemporary society. The dominance of such centralised and hierarchical forms of control, which 'repress and forbid', are identified with earlier configurations of power in western society. Foucault argues that the expressions and sites of power are more pervasive within contemporary society. The extensive forms of control are exercised through 'disciplinary power', which is 'positive and productive' as it seeks to transform the affective make-up of the individual through the disciplining of the body. Disciplinary power is exercised through a constant process of monitoring and surveillance of the subject population. It needs information for those in the strategic positions of authority to exploit. Such asymmetrical relations are based on a division between the observer and the observed, which establishes a hierarchy in terms of those who can participate in the constructions of knowledge. The subject group is turned into an object of knowledge over which others, as the dispensers of truth about the needs and requirements of the subject group, gain control. Correspondingly, there is a loss of control over communal identity as the group is called upon to fulfil the constructions of its identity created by those in authority.

My anthropological approach seeks to grasp the cultural logic of the reproduction of power relations. I am concerned with developing a critique of the specific forms of knowledge and interpretations of meaning which have sustained such relations of domination. The evidence is drawn from local newspapers, books, government publications and enquiries and the oral testimony of Aborigines and Europeans. The ideological construction of Aboriginality by state systems and in the circulation of various public texts is understood in terms of a process of interpretation. In this, I have primarily followed the discursive approach argued by Foucault (1970, 1978). My aim is to consider the regularity and consistency in the appearance of disparate statements about Aborigines within the framework of their historical specificity. The constructions of Aboriginality are seen not simply as a changing field of representations but as a sphere of social action which intersects and serves certain relations of power. Discourses about Aborigines pertain to the politics of race relations and in this they justify certain social relations and systems of power and control.

My study of the Dhan-gadi analyses the cultural politics of domestic dependency as it developed in the course of the state's attempt to domesticate the indigenous population. The institutional regimes attempted to impose bourgeois ideas and practices on individual, familial and community relations in terms of a cultural logic associated with instrumental rationality and the calculative reason of an autonomous, sovereign individual. The implementation of this form of cultural and political hegemony occurs through attempts to break down the sites of collective activity and associated forms of collective identity. Such hegemonic processes seek to alter radically the cultural expectations of interpersonal relations embodied in the particular forms of kinship obligations which characterise Dhan-gadi sociality. The importance of a Foucauldian approach is its concern with 'disciplinary power', the exercise of continuous and systematic forms of power, which function at the level of everyday gestures and activities. This form of power underpinned the administrative policies of institutional dependency and domestication.

The successive deployments of state power conditioned the social existence of the Dhan-gadi and generated specific forms of resistance. The forms of resistance that emerge were/are neither direct nor violent, but discrete and indirect resistance to those in authority who seemingly have unlimited power. Resistance in this sense refers to the indirect ways in which oppressed groups gain some degree of relative autonomy by limiting or frustrating the controls those in authority exercise over their lives. Such resistances are defensive strategies which do not change the relations of oppression, but contain them and remain contained by them. The modes of resistance respond to the immediate demands imposed upon them by the changing deployments of state power.

Such resistance is not, however, simply a matter of limiting and frustrating repressive state control. Resistance is conditioned and emerges in response to the immediate effects of domination because power is exercised over their most intimate activities as individuals and as a social group. Resistance is manifested in cultural struggles against the immediate effects of the power that seeks to separate individuals, to reconstitute their social relations, to fragment communities and to 'produce' new forms of social individuality. The forms of struggle are not necessarily expressed in terms of an overt political consciousness or actions but more specifically as a culture of resistance: that is as cultural practices which develop as a 'way of life' in opposition to the specific structures of domination.

Oppositional struggles are inscribed at the level of culture. The forms of *collective* activity and expressions of *collective* identity sustain the continuity of the Dhan-gadi as a social group *vis-à-vis* the dominant society. My concern is to reject such reified views of culture as existing outside time and space. The core of collective identity is internally constituted not simply in terms of how the Dhan-gadi conceptualise their relationships to each other but also in terms of the significance they gain from the predominantly oppositional and antagonistic interpretations of relations with the dominant society. My focus is on the politics of identity as part of a process of sustaining cultural distance from the dominant society which seeks their incorporation.

My interpretation of the politics of identity is focused on both public and private utterances combined with a consideration of the more general social circumstances in which they occur or describe. Oral testimony is dealt with here not simply as a means of communicating information but as a cultural practice and, hence, as an expression of identity. Following Thompson's suggestion, my focus on social utterances will be to see language as 'not simply a structure which can be employed for communication or entertainment, but [as] a social phenomenon which is embroiled in human conflict' (Thompson 1984: 2). Furthermore, speech is doing something inasmuch as the social world is in part given meaning through the naming of objects and the categorising of experience within that world. Memory condenses the past through language, in summary and metaphor, into representations of experience. As Murphy (1986: 165) argues, it is tropes rather than 'facts' that provide the basis for an interpretive reading of 'how the past is remembered and presented' as 'oral sources are asked not so much what happened but what their experience was like'. In the case of the Dhan-gadi my concern will be to interrogate the oral testimony for its social and cultural meanings through which the Dhan-gadi create for themselves an image of themselves as a group. My focus on the politics of identity is less concerned with the political rhetoric of lobby groups than with the mundane utterances of the everyday world, articulated at the level of casual encounters.

My concern with the social character of language is not associated with individual strategies of the various actors or their alleged intentionality. The subjective motivations of the authors, whether in public texts or oral testimony, are unimportant to my analysis. Instead, my approach aims to understand speech acts and public texts via their integration into a wider socio-historical field of circumstances, events and institutions which provides for a more complex interpretative process. The importance of the oral testimony of the Dhan-gadi is that it reveals active, critical evaluation of our own social processes and institutional forms. The critical insights that emerge not only express the experience of domination, but also reveal the limitations and historically finite nature of our own interpretative traditions.

Chapter 1

Colonial Domination as a Process of Marginalisation

It is a truism to say that colonialism belongs to the domain of politics and economics. By its very nature, colonialism involves political conquest and economic exploitation. Yet it is more than this. Colonialism is also a cultural process. The colonial process in Australia, which decimated the original inhabitants, expropriated their traditionally-held lands and segregated them on small reserves, has only recently received attention. Previously, colonial discourse, masquerading as history, had insinuated the Aborigines' complicity in their own demise; they had simply faded away (see Ward 1958; Blainey 1966; Mulvaney 1975).[1] In correcting this impression, much of the recent material has revealed a great deal about Aboriginal resistance to colonial expansion. Indeed, new research reveals a complex and widespread pattern of Aboriginal resistance (see Reynolds 1981; Ryan 1981; Loos 1982). Yet, given the evidence of this more active rather than passive response by Aboriginal groups, there has been very little analysis, either of the savage culture that prolonged the process of conquest and dispossession, or of the distortions of human relations that the social processes of colonialism unleashed.

The frontier culture of terror is an important dimension in this anthropological interpretation of the Australian colonial process. The questions asked have been largely formulated in Taussig's (1987) significant work on colonialism in South America. The clues to this colonial process are found in the political and economic forces gener-

---

1. The general consensus until recently has stressed the cultural unpreparedness of Aborigines to come to terms with 'modern' Australia. Mulvaney's statement illustrates this approach, 'the unexpected challenge of the Europeans evoked no response in Aboriginal society because it overwhelmed all three factors of man, land and animals in a balanced economy' (1975: 242). Blainey refers to the 'relatively mild threat of attack from Australian Aborigines' (1966: 132), while Ward suggests that 'one difficulty the Australian pioneers . . . did not have to contend with was a warlike native race . . . They [Aborigines] were amongst the most primitive and peaceable people known in history' (1958: 21). Such characterisations effectively wrote Aborigines out of colonial history.

ated by capitalism in its colonial form and in the colonists' cultural representations of their own experiences. Few clues remain of the experience from the other side of the frontier, for those other voices were either dismissed or silenced. Their silence brings its own pained awareness of how successfully the colonisers have implanted their own images of the colonial process. In analysing this colonial discourse about Aborigines it is important to remember that the only knowledge we have of the 'other', of the object of the colonising process, was produced as part of the political act of colonialism. The remaining knowledge (official records, private letters, autobiographies) was manufactured in alliance with the forces of colonial oppression as malleable forms of understanding lending themselves to legitimating the process.

1.1. The Political Economy of Settler Colonialism in New South Wales

The political economy of the colonisation of NSW generated a number of distinctive features. What differentiates it from Wolpe's (1975) 'normal colonialism' is the virtual absence of exploitative relations associated with trade, labour and/or the production of specific raw materials. The colonising powers in NSW were not concerned with establishing trade relations or labour relations but, as Hartwig (1978) points out, with expropriating Aboriginal land, which was not seen as anyone's, for European settlers. The latter is, of course, a distinctive historical feature of colonisation in the Americas and, more particularly, the United States and Canada (see Bee and Gingerich 1977; McNickle 1973; or Lithman 1978). As the colonisers exercise control over the colonised peoples while occupying the same territory, settler colonialism is by definition associated with internal colonialism (Wolpe 1975). This is the case whether the coloniser remain a minority with exploitation of indigenous labour as the predominant relationship, as for example in South Africa, Kenya and Rhodesia (Zimbabwe), or whether the indigenous population is reduced to a territorial minority and the expropriation of indigenous land is the major basis of relations, as for example in Australia, New Zealand, Israel, the United States and Canada.

Emergent colonial relations in NSW during the early nineteenth century were characterised by the absence of any formal administrative control over the indigenous population. (It was not until the 1880s that a systematic policy of intervention was developed and rudimentary forms of control were applied to the surviving Aboriginal populations.) These specific features of the colonial process in NSW were directly related to the rapid expansion of the wool industry from the 1820s, which provided the basis of the European economy, and the integration of the colony into the world economy as a supplier of raw materials.

The generative aspect of this economic relationship between the settler colony and its metropolis, Britain, was based on capital investment in the land-extensive production processes of pastoralism. The economy of NSW developed as a supplier of raw materials for the British Empire. It rapidly expanded through its ability to attract British capital. The wool industry attracted a considerable amount of capital investment for most of the nineteenth century. For example, whereas in 1822, 172,000 pounds of wool were being exported for use in the expanding English woollen industry, by 1830 this figure had risen to 899,750 pounds (Morrissey 1970: 50). As Butlin (1968: 225) puts it, 'The decade between 1830 and 1840 was a period of *extraordinarily rapid economic growth* in which immigration and capital import furnished the material for a *vast geographical expansion* of the wool industry.' (Emphasis added throughout unless otherwise stated.) The extent of this 'extraordinarily rapid growth' in wool exports to Britain is shown in the following figures. Between 1830 and 1836 wool exports to Britain increased fourfold to 3,693,800 pounds (Roberts 1964: 359). Over the following years the spectacular rise in wool production continued and by 1844 had again quadrupled to reach 13,542,000 pounds (ibid.). By 1834 wool had become the colony's single most important export.

The rapid expansion of the pastoral industry depended on the growth in commodity production in the English textile industry. From the early 1800s the textile industry started to industrialise, with hand weavers progressively being replaced by power-driven machinery. Between 1820 and 1850, steam-driven looms became firmly established in the textile industry (Jeans 1972: 98). The use of new techniques revolutionised commodity production, for it made possible the mass production of 'cheap cloths using coarse wool' as well as 'finer cloths of softness to appeal to expensive tastes' (Morrissey 1970: 60). The effect of industrialisation was to lower the cost of production and to increase output through the establishment of a wider market for the English woollens industry.

In the search by British capital for cheaper sources of raw materials, Australian wool increasingly replaced that of Germany and Spain (Roberts 1964; Fitzpatrick 1969; Morrissey 1970; Jeans 1972). In 1834 Germany had 50 per cent of the English market, the Australian colonies 12 per cent and Spain 10 per cent (Roberts 1964: 46). In the 1840s the Australian share doubled to 25 per cent (1841) and had reached 50 per cent by the end of the decade (Fitzpatrick 1969: 85) Over the same period, the increase in wool exports to England grew from 12 million to 39 million pounds and the English market expanded from 49 million to 77 million pounds (ibid.). As he puts it, 'the English woollens industry had increased its consumption by half but the Australian contribution to it of raw material had been multiplied by more than three' (ibid.). This remarkable development continued throughout the nineteenth century.[2] Such expansion occurred not through some naturally occurring process of expansion, but through the logic of capital, i.e. the calculated, ordered administration of commodity production. However, as I will show below, pastoral expansion was regulated and given impetus by the state (see also McMicheal 1979). The state scrupulously recorded and, hence, controlled the economic factors involved in the remarkable rate of increase and expansion of the fledgling economy. The only unquantified 'factors' were the amount of Aboriginal land and the number of Aboriginal dead that secured each spectacular incremental increase.

The market rationality regulating pastoral expansion was not simply based on regularised investment of capital in wool production, but also on the transformation of profits from the wool industry into capital goods for consumption within the settler colony. It was European immigration that provided the basis for consumer demand and, hence, a broadly-based domestic market. In effect, the land-extensive production of the wool industry performed a double role in maintaining both the level of capital investment and the flow of capital-intensive goods. Expansion into the major part of NSW occurred in a compressed period of some 15 to 20 years as a result of what is called the 'pastoral boom' of the 1830s. This 'pastoral boom' was funded by British capital, overseen by British owners, serviced by British labour and based on the expropriation of Aboriginal land.[3]

The colonial economy of NSW was characterised by a strong demand for manufactured goods. It was this market, as Cochrane (1980: 5) argues, that provided the impetus for continued investment. 'Colonial demand for imported manufacturing goods was a condition of capital investment. *Australia's export earnings in Europe were transformed into import demand.* From the British standpoint, continued investment was contingent upon the sale of its manufactured goods in Australia and meeting its debts on the City of London.' The economy was doubly tied

2. In the period between 1875 and 1880, the Australian (New Zealand included) market held 64 per cent of the British market of imported raw wool (Fitzpatrick 1969: 135). In terms of sheep numbers in NSW this can be translated as; 1861: 5.5 million sheep; 1871: 16 million sheep; 1881: 37 million sheep; and 1891: 62 million sheep (ibid. p. 137). Throughout the nineteenth century, the pastoral industry in NSW increasingly became the major supplier of wool to the English market.

3. The close links with British capitalism, generated by the pastoral boom, led to dependent development rather than underdevelopment. As Clark (1975: 51) defines it, '"Dependent development" described a situation where the development of one economy is influenced if not conditioned by the development and expansion of another. In the Australian case we see a situation where at times growth is impressive but at other times is clearly limited by our links with Britain; thus although we develop, the development process is only comprehensible in terms of our dependence in respect to Britain and to the timing and needs of her development process.' Significant 'metropolis' control did not retard the development of this colonial economy (cf. Brenner 1977; Amin 1973).

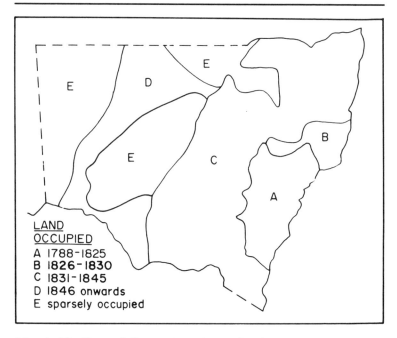

LAND
OCCUPIED
A 1788-1825
B 1826-1830
C 1831-1845
D 1846 onwards
E sparsely occupied

Map 1. The Pastoral Occupation of New South Wales

to the wool industry. The structure of NSW's economy provided the basis for capital investment in the pastoral industry and a growing domestic market for manufactured goods. The stimulus for internal consumer demand was generated by settler migration and the pastoral boom.

Central to the colonisation of the indigenous population of NSW was the connection between the inflow of capital investment and capital intensive goods, and the rapid development of a land-extensive economy. As Butlin (1968: 226) puts it, the 'vast geographical expansion' in NSW occupied 'roughly half the total area' in the 15 years between 1830 and 1845. Such rapid pastoral expansion swiftly expropriated the land from the indigenous population by removing or peripheralising them. This dramatic change was due to some extent to the ever-increasing numbers of Europeans, but more importantly to the large numbers of livestock, especially sheep, which radically transformed the physical environment of the region. Some 1,214,575 hectares were alienated for the use of European colonists by 1830 (see, for example, Table 1). This pattern of expropriation of Aboriginal land accelerated during the pastoral boom. Between 1830 and 1848 another 16,599,190 hectares were expropriated (Roberts 1964: 362; see also Map 1). On these

Table 1. Rapid Growth of Initial Pastoral Expansion (1821–1828)

District	Year	Land Utilised Hectares	Stock Run	
			Cattle	Sheep
1. Bathurst Plains	1821	1,020	5,884	27,848
	1825	37,100	21,906	92,067
	1828	119,225	49,290	165,786
2. Hunter Valley	1821	258	236	376
	1825	27,449	4,495	8,909
	1828	622,465	46,805	119,391
3. Argyle and St Vincent Districts	1821		4,464	6,063
	1825	15,259	22,028	31,864
	1828	147,205	73,670	125,649

Source: Adapted from Perry 1966: 130–2

pastoral leases some 2,358,000 sheep and 644,000 cattle were depastured (Roberts 1964: 362).

By contrast, the use of Aboriginal labour had never, in any systematic or sustained way, been seen to have had a role in the economic development of the colony.

In 1814 Governor Macquarie (1810–1821) set up the Native Institution, a school for training Aborigines, because he saw a useful potential for Aborigines as labourers and mechanics in the lower orders of society (Reynolds 1972: 109). This remained the only attempt by the state to 'civilise' the Aborigines in the early nineteenth century. After repeated 'failures' the Native Institution closed in 1829. There were two further attempts before 1850 through private church ventures to set up missions to 'civilise' Aborigines. Protestant missions were set up at Lake Macquarie (1825–1841) (in the Hunter Valley area) and Wellington (1831–1842) (in the Bathurst Plain area). Both folded in the early 1840s. The first coordinated and systematic attempt by the state to deal with Aborigines was in the 1880s (see Chapter 5). The aim by then was not to create a viable labour force, however, but to 'protect the remnants' of what was seen as 'a dying race'.

Throughout the pastoral boom (1830–1850) there was no attempt to conserve or to control the indigenous population. Furthermore, the impact of pastoral expansion, with the conflicts it created, brought about a significant depopulation of Aboriginal groups in NSW (see Chapter 3). The scale and rapid expansion of colonial occupation meant that the Aborigines became obstacles to rather than resources for colonial exploitation. Australian pastoral industry differed from other colonial enterprises in that it was serviced, not by indigenous labour or by transplanted black slave labour, but by British convict and immigrant labour.[4] In other words, the white 'slave' labour of convicts initially provided that other essential ingredient of a rationalised capitalist enterprise, a disciplined labour force. The convicts transported to NSW between 1788 and 1840 (when transportation was abolished) numbered some 80,440 (67,980 men and 12,460 women) (Robson 1965: 4). At the beginning of the pastoral boom the population of NSW numbered 36,598 Europeans, of which 16,442 were male convicts and 1,554 were female convicts (Clark 1984: 69). Convict labour in the 1820s had been sufficient to meet the needs of the pastoral industry because convicts were sent to country areas on assignment. Emancipists (ex-convicts) also made up a significant proportion of the population on the pastoral frontier in the 1820s. The three areas of extensive pastoral development (Bathurst, Argyle and St Vincent, and the Hunter Valley) were founded on convict labour in 1828. This sector, which included emancipists, pardoned convicts and assigned convicts, comprised 90.6, 83.8, and 84.4 per cent of the populations respectively (Perry 1966: 136).

By the 1830s the demand for convicts had exceeded the supply. Of the 8,452 requests for assigned convict labour in 1830, only 3,827 were fulfilled (Dunn 1975: 37). By 1838, the gulf between assigned labour (some 5,454) and applications (between 10,000 and 12,000) had further widened (Fitzpatrick 1969: 59). The Select Committee established by the New South Wales Legislative Assembly Council (in 1838) assessed that in terms of the labour shortage it could 'not assume that the want of labour in the colony can be supplied by the introduction of a smaller number than 3,000 adult males every year' (ibid. p. 58). Contemporary estimates of the Aboriginal population were far lower than this. It is worth noting that the explorer Thomas Mitchell, whose government-sponsored expeditions of 1830/31, 1835 and 1836 traversed the major areas of future pastoral expansion, estimated that the entire Aboriginal population of eastern Australia was less than 6,000 (Mitchell 1839: 345).[5]

The expansion of the pastoral industry in the 1830s and the 1840s continually suffered from labour shortages, yet there was no attempt to incorporate indigenous labour. Instead, during this period the inflow of convicts increased. Between 1820 and 1829, some 21,956 convicts arrived in NSW and over the following ten years another 31,661 convicts were transported (Robson 1965: 170). This was well over half

4. The availability of convict labour resulted from the unique origins of NSW as a penal colony. It received approximately 82,000 convicts between 1788 and 1840 when transportation was abolished (Robson 1965: 4). By comparison, the initial recipients of transportation, the American colonies, received 30,000 of the convicts transported from Britain between 1717 and 1776 (Bowle 1974: 314). The difference between America and Australia in this context was that the former was privately controlled and the latter state controlled.

5. This figure undoubtedly underestimates the population numbers in south eastern Australia. Radcliffe-Brown (1930: 690) estimates the pre-colonial population of NSW at between 40,000 and 48,000 inhabitants and Victoria's population at 11,500 inhabitants. Both populations are included in Mitchell's observations.

the number of convicts transported to NSW. In addition, in the late 1830s the convict population was augmented by free immigration to the colony, funded by government revenue from land sales/leases. Between 1838 and 1848, another 44,028 British immigrants arrived in NSW (Roberts 1964: 329). Land was for the colonial administration the essential element in underwriting such immigration policies. The £850,000 collected for land revenue between 1838 and 1840 funded the arrival of some 48,000 immigrants over the same period (Jeans 1972: 171). In overall numbers, between 1830 and 1850 the vast majority (some 75,689 of 101,914) were 'free' immigrants assisted by land revenues (Shaw 1973: 45; Fletcher 1976: 88).

The colonial administration sought to use British labour to overcome the 'labour crisis' in the pastoral industry. The colonial administration's dependence on land revenues to pay for the assisted passages of the major inflow of British labour reinforced the significance of land to this expanding settler colony. By contrast, the use of Aboriginal labour was given only ephemeral consideration. In 1841, the Immigration Committee circulated a letter seeking information on the use of 'native labour' (Roberts 1964: 335). According to Roberts, only one land commissioner out of the nine appointed to exercise government control over the pastoral districts saw a potential use for Aborigines (ibid.). Furthermore, five-sixths of the squatting witnesses regarded Aborigines as an unreliable labour supply (ibid. p. 336). As Roberts records, 'some squatters, like Ryrie of Yering (Port Phillip), Walker of Castlereagh, and Rouse of Mudgee, had experimented with them, but they were undependable in every case, and would readily desert their flocks for any chance excursion into the bush' (ibid.). Thus, it would appear that only a small number of Aborigines were employed on pastoral properties. The Australian Agricultural Company, for example, permanently employed 22 Aborigines (ibid.), but also, however, employed some 350 convicts and 150 freemen throughout the 1830s to develop its extensive cattle and sheep properties on the Liverpool Plains to the north-west of the Hunter Valley (ibid., p. 141). In the same year as the Immigration Committee sent its circular letter, 11,343 assigned convicts formed the 'bulk of the squatter's labour supply' (ibid., p. 360).

Evidence from the Immigration Committee in the late 1830s and early 1840s indicates that in the previous decade pastoralists had made some attempts to incorporate Aboriginal labour, but had usually given up on the grounds that Aborigines could not be induced to become rural labourers and to adopt European patterns of work discipline. These assessments were quite uniform and this attitude was probably derived from the Europeans' experience of the 'endless bush' of the new frontier. As a result, in the 1830s and early 1840s, the Aborigines made up an insignificant proportion of the total labour supply in pastoral capitalism.

The colonial assessment of Aborigines was guided by the pro-ductionist ethos of capitalist culture, in which, under the gaze of this market mentality, people were valued according to their instrumental worth. Aborigines had no real instrumental worth and, in addition, failed to meet the requirements of a disciplined work-force. Signifi-cantly, the belief that Aborigines could 'work neither hard nor steadily' or were unable to resist ' the many calls of the bush' sustained the division between Aboriginal and European labour throughout the nineteenth century.

The 'common sense' of this market-price appraisal of labour under-pinned the differential treatment of Aboriginal labour. In 1841 it was conventional to pay Aborigines in rations rather than wages (Roberts 1964: 336), which was the first step in transforming Aboriginal groups into what were called 'station blacks'. 'Station blacks', who usually resided on a squatter's property, consisted of a number of men and their dependents (see Hardy 1976; Mathews 1977; Goodall 1982). They formed a useful part of the squatter's property, for the Aboriginal men and women formed a pool of cheap labour to be drawn upon when required to perform menial jobs. When they were not required they sustained themselves through their own forms of subsistence. What emerged in these contexts were *de facto* forms of control over Aboriginal groups exercised by private interests on a number of pastoral proper-ties. Such forms of control developed before the introduction of government policies and controls.

Throughout the nineteenth century the indigenous population was marginal to the colonial process. Aborigines existed on the edges of the capitalist economy which had supplanted them. The process of margin-alisation reflected the rapid totalising of political and economic he-gemony which was established in NSW. The economic development of colonialism, significantly involving the state, also played an important part given the absence of administrative political controls. The encap-sulation and control of Aborigines within the expanding capitalist economy was located at the level of civil society, i.e. in the private interests of squatters.

As 'station blacks' Aborigines were incorporated at the margins of the European economy and in non-capitalist relations of exchange, such as rations. Such relations, generated by the expansion of capital-ism in its colonial form, were reinforced by the colonists' view of Aborigines as a defective commodity in the labour market (who were unable to work either hard or steadily), and by the non-separation of Aborigines from indigenous forms of subsistence and social interaction – 'the many calls of the bush'. On pastoral properties this 'impediment' to their 'dependability' provided the basis for semi-private forms of control of Aboriginal labour. And, given that 'station blacks' comprised such a small part of the labour force and that an ever decreasingly proportion of the population was being affected by directly or indirectly violent forms of usurpation, such controls were relatively easy to sustain.

1.2. Secondary Elaborations: Colonial Occupation of the Macleay River Valley

The colonial occupation of the Macleay River Valley was a historical precipitate of the pastoral advance into northern NSW in the 1830s. Pastoral expansion was proceeding in all directions throughout the colony, and the northern frontier had overtaken most of the inland plains adjacent to the river valleys of the northern coast. The Awabakal and Worimi peoples of the Hunter Valley had been dispossessed of their lands in the 1820s. From the Hunter Valley the frontier spread north-west to the Liverpool Plains inhabited by the southern Gamilraay who were violently dispossessed in the 1830s (see Reece 1974). By the mid-1830s the New England Tablelands, occupied by the Anewan peoples, had become the new frontier (see Walker 1962; Campbell 1978a; Blomfield 1981). The government recognised the occupation of the Tablelands in 1839 when it appointed a land commissioner to supervise pastoral matters (Roberts 1964: 144). By 1843 sheep numbers there had reached 425,201 (AHR, vol. XXIII: 764).

The occupation of the northern river valleys occurred concurrently with the advance into New England. By 1840 settlements had been established at Armidale, Guyra and Tenterfield (Fletcher 1976: 108), which directly overlooked the coastal valleys of the Macleay, Clarence and Richmond rivers respectively. The introduction of the Crown Lands Occupation Act (1836) officially began the pastoral penetration of the northern rivers. In that year, the Port Macquarie Pastoral District was established (which included the three river valleys) and this signalled the necessity for the state to regulate pastoralism on the coastal belt.[6] Many pastoralists had moved their stock over the steep escarpment of the Tablelands and down into the river valleys. By 1842, the rate of pastoral advance into the Clarence and Richmond river valleys necessitated the establishment of the Clarence River Pastoral District to provide a minimal government presence in these river

---

6. Squatting outside the 'limits of settlement' of the original 19 counties was officially sanctioned with this Act. Prior to this, crown land outside the counties could not be leased or purchased, and those who used it for pastoralism did so illegally. Many pastoralists had made increasing use of the 'vacant' crown land for such purposes. The regulations of the Act recognised this reality and were designed to strengthen government control over them. Following the Act, the colony was further divided into pastoral districts and placed under the control of the commissioners of crown land. The duty of the commissioners was to collect an annual fee for occupancy and to settle disputes between squatters and Aborigines.

valleys.[7] The extent of the penetration into the valleys is revealed in the government's stock returns for the following year. On the Macleay River, cattle and sheep numbered 16,162 and 19,734 head respectively, whilst in the Clarence and Richmond river valleys the figures were 12,457 and 122,599 respectively (AHR, vol. XXIII: 764). In the initial stages the close developmental relationship between the coastal belt and the high plateau country of New England, reflected in the excessively high figures for sheep, reproduced the pattern of rapid expansion that occurred elsewhere.

The initial exploitation of the Macleay River Valley by Europeans, however, was not through pastoralism but through the cedar trade. Forestry grants given to a number of Europeans saw incursions into the valley in 1835 (Thorpe 1968: 7). The major exploitation of the timber stands of cedar, found in the rain forest areas of the Macleay and the sub-tropical environments of the other northern river valleys, did not occur until 1839.[8] In that year some 39 licences were issued to traders (Neil 1972: 31). In the short period of intensive cedar cutting and logging some 200 Europeans were engaged in the trade (ibid.), but by 1842, with the removal of the most accessible cedar, the cutters had moved further north (Sullivan 1978). It was a familiar pattern, which occurred in all the river valleys along the east coast. The incursions of the cedar cutters into the Macleay Valley were brief and would appear to have had a limited impact on the Aboriginal population. The economic interests of the cutters simply involved plundering the environment of a singular and limited resource and moving on.[9]

By contrast, the direct effects of pastoral expansion and exploitation of the environment generated a more sustained form of conflict with Aborigines. The commercial imperatives of pastoralism required extensive land, permanent European settlement and the 'domestication' of the environment. By 1841, 206,293 hectares of land from the coast to the western boundary of the escarpment had been taken up (Thorpe 1968: 8; Campbell 1968: 36). The number of pastoral properties increased throughout that decade: 30 in 1843; 37 in 1844; 42 in 1845 and 45 in 1846 (SA 4/5458–9). By the following decade, the European economy had

---

7. The rapid expansion of the colonial frontier ensured that both topographical information and the exact boundaries remained incomplete. The official description cited below was given in the *Government Gazette* of 21 May 1839: 'No. 1. – Port Macquarie District: Bounded on the west by a line north, by compass, from the top of Werrikimber Mountain, on the south by the range extending from Werrikimber Mountain to Crescent Head, a point on the coast; on the east by the sea coast; on the north the boundary is indefinite' (cited Campbell 1968: 15).

8. According to Henderson's account (1851, vol. I: 122), the valley contained much red cedar: 'For the most part, in the bends of the river, at the embouchure of creeks, and in many places along the banks, thick and luxuriant brush is found, matted together with vines, and abounding in the red cedar.'

9. See Rowley (1974: 108–24) for an account of the colonial conflict in the Clarence River Valley.

stabilised, but at lower numbers than at the height of the pastoral occupation. This reduction is unusual in early pastoralism. The figures available for 1855 and 1856 reveal that the number of pastoral properties had fallen to 29, sheep had declined to 180 head and the pastoral production of cattle fluctuated between 16,300 (1855) and 12,838 (1856) (SA 4/5472; see Map 2). The number of hectares leased to station owners had been reduced considerably to 385,120 (1855) and 353,240 (1856) (SA 4/5472; see Table 2 for 1855 figures). Numbers stabilised at this level and remained constant for the next two decades.

Unless these specificities are considered, an adequate understanding of minutiae of Aboriginal/European conflict is lost. The unsuitable nature of the environment for sheep production meant that the development and consolidation of European occupation of the Macleay Valley differed from the helter-skelter nature of colonialism in the inland regions. The Macleay Valley was a marginal area in terms of its importance or contribution to the overall economy of NSW. In regions where pastoralism was itself marginal, the dynamics of interaction differed.

Both economic and environmental factors were responsible for the predominance of cattle in the Macleay Valley. The growth of beef production was based on provisioning the colony's expanding urban markets, which significantly increased in the 1840s and 1850s. In this, the coastal areas had the advantage of closer and easier access to the Sydney meat market than other inland areas. Rather than droving cattle long distances over land, fattened cattle in the coastal regions were shipped to Sydney without loss of condition (Jeans 1972: 147). The high rainfall and moist terrain of the northern coastal valleys were regarded as less suitable for sheep than cattle (ibid.). The deep ravines, gorges and steep mountain ranges, as well as the heavily timbered woodlands and dense rain forest, were more suitable for cattle than sheep. Unlike sheep cattle usually formed 'camps' near water-holes, which made them easy to find when needed for branding or sale (ibid., p. 149). Cattle runs required less supervision and had limited labour needs. However, the high percentage of hilly land covered with rain forest and woodlands and the extensive swamplands of the lower Macleay Valley also restricted the pastoral occupation. Pastoralism in the nineteenth century only utilised the land within a few miles of the river and creek frontages. Even by 1865, the land held by squatters amounted to 170,298 hectares out of a possible 1,124,060 hectares of the Macleay catchment area. The limited labour needs and restricted development of pastoralism ensured that the European population of the valley remained small. In 1848, the population had reached 429 (SA 4/5459). It was not until 1861 that the population reached 1,963 (Neil 1972: 49).

Aborigines retained a large degree of autonomy in relation to European

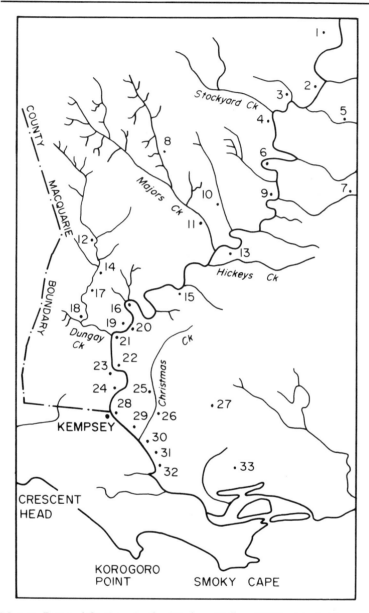

Map 2. Pastoral Stations in the Macleay Valley (1855). *Adapted from Neil (1972)*

occupation of the valley partly because of the environmental particularities of this coastal region. As the following land commissioner, Massie, observes in his annual report of 1842, 'They [Aborigines] appear harmless and inoffensive, although totally disinclined to work. This partly arises *from subsistence being so easily obtained from the quantity of fish in the river* and partly *from the indolence of disposition peculiar to their race.*' (AHR, vol. XXII: 652) and again in 1843, 'From the great facilities the river and coast afford them [Aborigines] for obtaining fish as an article of food, *the natives of this district have less intercourse with the White people resident at the different stations, than is generally the case in the interior [of NSW].*' (ibid. vol. XXIII: 764) The autonomy associated with the limited interaction between Europeans and Aborigines reflects regional particularities in the early period of colonial expansion.

The abundance of food resources is corroborated in the evidence available from early settler colonists in the valley. According to Hodgkinson (1845: 220), the extensive food resources enabled 'each tribe to subsist on a small tract of land'. More specifically, Henderson (1851, vol. II: 108) observes that each 'tribe' had a 'beat' of 'not more than twenty miles in diameter from which they never move, unless on certain occasions, when they visit the territory of a neighbouring tribe for the purpose of a fight, or a ceremony'. Estimates of the pre-conquest population vary significantly, which attests to a lack of familiarity with the terrain and its peoples. The land commissioners' estimations were 150 in 1842 (AHR, vol. XXII: 65), 200 in 1843 (vol. XXIII: 489); and 500 in 1850 (vol. XXX: 2). Hodgkinson, who was the government surveyor for the north coast region, provides the most systematic estimate of the Aboriginal population and its location within the valley. He states that:

> On the immediate banks of the Macleay River alone, there are six distinct tribes; viz. the Yarra-Hapinni, and Clybucca tribe, the Calliteeni or Kempsey tribe, the Yarra–Bandini, Munga, Wabro, and Conderang tribes, *besides several others near the sources of the river among the mountains.* Each of them contains on an average from eighty to one hundred men and women, exclusive of children. (Hodgkinson 1845: 222)

These estimates would give us a population on the immediate banks of the Macleay River alone of some 480 to 600 men and women.

The spatial distribution of these Aboriginal groups throughout the valley can be judged from government officials and squatters, such as Massie (AHR 1842), Hodgkinson (1845) and Henderson (1851). The larger concentration of groups on the lower Macleay (see Map 3) would seem to reflect the limited knowledge about the 'several others' located on the upper reaches of the river. The pattern of exploitation of the resources throughout the valley involved 'small parties of eight or ten men, with their women and children' (Hodgkinson 1845: 222).

Table 2. Pastoral Stations in the Macleay Valley (1855)

Station	Number of Hectares	Head of Cattle
1. Kunderang	Outside Map	
2. Long Flat	7,255	950
3. Towal Creek	12,956	750
4. Stockyard Creek	6,219	450
5. Five Day Creek	8,292	750
6. Pee Dee Creek	4,664	450
7. Nulla Nulla Creek*	4,453	Not Assessed
8. Toorumbee	6,996	640
9. Elsineur*	4,858	Not Assessed
10. Warbro	8,810	1,300
11. Innes Creek	7,255	1,100
12. Booningii	6,478	640
13. Toorooka	5,960	640
14. Dungee	4,664	700
15. Corrungala	6,219	600
16. Moonaba	2,316	300
17. Yessaba	3,109	640
18. Dondingalong	1,036	150
19. Sherwood	1,814	300
20. Yarrawal	5,182	500
21. Border Police Station	—	—
22. Fattorinni's Wharf	—	—
23. Callatini	4,259	640
24. Euroka	1,012	200
25. Warwick	1,555	200
26. Yarrabandinni	9,328	600
27. Tanban	8,292	400
28. Scotchtown (Shipbuilders)	—	—
29. Glenrock	1,036	150
30. Klywooticka (Shipbuilders)	—	—
31. Bellimbopinni	3,887	500
32. Seven Oaks	2,591	600
33. Klybucca	6,219	800

* Based on 1857 statistics
Source: SA 4/5472

Hodgkinson provides extensive details of the numerous resources exploited by these small groups who 'roam over any part of the country within the prescribed limits' (ibid.). On the coastal beaches, he states, groups gathered clams, oysters, cockles, crayfish and crabs, while the estuaries were exploited for 'several kinds of fish, large eels', lobsters and freshwater mussels. On the densely forested terrain of the upper Macleay Valley, they exploited kangaroos, pademelons, possums, brush turkeys, snakes, fish, mussels and a variety of vegetable foods

MACLEAY RIVER VALLEY

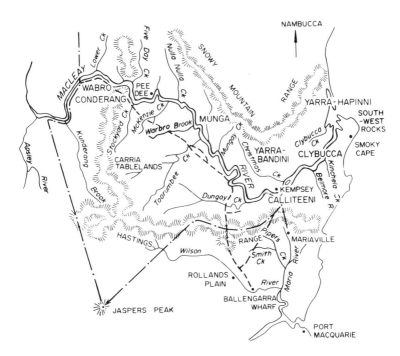

Map 3. Aboriginal 'Tribes' of the Macleay Valley (1845)
  Early tracks _ _ _ _ _ _
  Macleay River Squatting District — · — · —

Adapted from Neil (1972)

(see ibid. pp. 222–9).[10] The Aborigines who inhabited the valley used these rich resources to maintain both their social distance and their economic autonomy from the small European population that settled there.

  The Europeans' initial occupation and development of the valley was slower and less comprehensive than in the pastoral regions engaged in wool production. Its development was marginal to the wool-oriented mainstream economy. Under these circumstances, conflict between Aborigines and Europeans took longer to occur than in other regions and longer to suppress. The contingencies of the local conditions thus

10. Rudder (1925) gives a similarly detailed account of the abundance of food sources. Campbell (1978) has provided the most comprehensive reconstruction of the subsistence food sources of Aborigines in the Macleay Valley by drawing together a number of European sources.

produced certain particularities in the emerging relations between the two groups. Nevertheless, they also gave expression to the more general phenomenon of the colonial encounter. In the Macleay Valley, the familiar dynamics of colonial violence and conflict were played out, ordering social relations, if not always producing the same outcomes as other regions.

From the mid-1840s, Aboriginal resistance to pastoralism and permanent European settlement was to harden attitudes and relations towards Aborigines. There developed a prolonged and systematic pattern of direct resistance to pastoralism. The social and economic autonomy and superior knowledge of the terrain possessed by the Dhan-gadi was, however, insufficient to make their resistance to the European presence in the valley effective. It was characterised by sporadic attacks on isolated squatter stations, the more remote outstations of such squatters' runs, and the spearing of livestock. The conflict was not marked by epic battles but by sporadic depredations on the most immediate and conspicuous aspects of the European presence, the squatters' cattle. The land commissioner reports in 1846 that 'the tribes resident on the upper part of this river have been pursuing a constant and systematic plan of cattle spearing, which I have been unable to effectively suppress for the small number of troopers (two) at my disposal' (AHR, vol. XXVI: 56) and again in the following year that:

> the natives have for some time past systematically been in the habit of spearing and destroying cattle at four or five stations to the great loss and consequent complaint of the owners . . . It is almost impossible to catch them as they have been cunning enough never to kill any cattle except in most remote situations, and at times when, for circumstances of which they make themselves fully aware, there is no chance of their being discovered by stockmen or seen by the police (ibid., vol. XXVII: 393)

This pattern of resistance inflicted considerable losses on the stock populations of the local squatters. Letters for protection began in 1847 (ibid.) and were followed by petitions in 1849, signed by 29 of the 30 leaseholders (Neil 1972: 42) and, in 1854, by a request specifically for Native Police protection (Robinson and York 1977: 17). The resistance ended between the years 1856 and 1858 when the Native Police were stationed at Nulla Nulla Creek.[11]

Before the arrival of the Native Police Force, the station owners and

11. The Native Police Force was established, as Rowley (1974: 39–40) points out, to act as a 'military force' to come to the aid of squatters on the extreme limits of the pastoral frontier. In NSW their activities were restricted to the northern coastal region, the Clarence Pastoral District and the Macleay Pastoral District in the 1850s (ibid. p. 39). The pastoral frontier had passed NSW and had spread north to Queensland. The most effective and ruthless use of the Native Police Force occurred on the Queensland frontier (see Evans, Saunders and Cronin 1975).

their employees were kept in a constant state of alarm by the attacks of Aborigines. Attacks on the stations and outstations were regarded as treacherous and murderous acts, encouraged by the offender's ability to escape retribution. As Henderson, an up-river squatter, records:

> It is true that a good many have been shot, both at Towal Creek and Warbro when they attacked those stations. On the latter in particular, they made a resolute assault, and had suffered severely. On this occasion, they displayed great courage, rushing up even to the muzzles of the muskets, and seizing hold of the barrels which had been thrust out between the slabs in taking aim, endeavouring to bend them. Many treacherous murders, however, have been committed without suffering the punishment due to their misdeeds, for, from the state of the laws, the difficulty of catching them, and the almost impossibility of identifying the guilty, they could seldom be brought to justice, or even summarily punished. (Henderson 1851, vol. II: 4–5.)

Henderson expresses concern about Aboriginal immunity from punishment due to the absence of effective policing of the pastoral frontier by the state. This was a major grievance of the pastoralists. The establishment of the Border Police in 1839, paid from a tax on squatter stock (Shaw 1973: 48), had been largely ineffectual in exercising control over Aborigines. In the Macleay District there were only two such policemen throughout the 1840s.

Henderson depicts this colonial frontier in *Excursions and Adventures in New South Wales* (1851), which is drawn from his own experiences as a pastoralist on the upper Macleay in the early 1840s. He, like many other squatters, was an ex-army officer who sold his commission to become a grazier. His brief stay reflected a fluctuating pattern of ownership of pastoralism in the valley. Pastoralism for many was another means of plundering the land before moving on or retiring with their wealth. In practice, this capitalism was more akin to the 'speculative adventures' of the 'capitalistic adventurer' with their pursuit of pecuniary gain (see Weber 1976: 19–20) rather than regularised investment and the rational ordering of production towards increasing economic efficiency. Henderson's account reflects these social conditions and illustrates many of the pastoralists' sentiments on the frontier.

Henderson's writings demonstrate the kinds of explorations of Aboriginal humanness that were drawn from the colonial encounter. He depicts Aborigines as inhuman, morally degraded people who had neither dignity nor virtue, and this is particularly evident in his descriptions of them as people who engaged in treacherous and murderous attacks on outstation employees (known as 'hutkeepers'). He describes one incident, in which, after a previous altercation:

> The blacks gradually began to show themselves at the station on the creek in

friendly guise. Jamie was thrown off his guard, and one day, while sawing down a tree, assisted by a black, several others standing about him, he received a blow from a tomahawk on the temple, which must have been sufficient to kill him. He was horribly mauled, having his head nearly cut off. (Henderson 1851, vol. II: 50)[12]

The land commissioner, Massie, reporting on the incident, emphasised 'the invariable kindness he [the hutkeeper] had shewed [sic] the natives' (AHR, vol. XXIII: 488). He went on to generalise that this would be the possible outcome of 'any great intimacy between Black and White' as it led to 'a want of caution' on one side [Europeans] and a proportionate degree of boldness and treachery on the other [Aborigines] (ibid.). In effect, a psychological portrait emerges of the Aborigine as an amoral being completely lacking the essential 'human' feelings of sincerity or gratitude. In his depiction of this particular incident, Massie evokes a widespread image of Aborigines as 'ignoble savages' – a category thrown up by colonialism (see, for example, Smith 1984; Lattas 1986; Taussig 1987).

In such colonial discourse, Aborigines are synonymous with treachery. But this was not simply the playing out of the interactions of a localised context; it was also part of a wider cultural signification of categories thrown up in the broader colonial context. The theme is present in other contemporary accounts of massacres of Europeans by Aborigines in Australia. Although only few, they received widespread newspaper coverage, the four most notorious ones being the Faithfull massacre in Victoria in 1830 (see Andrews 1979), the Maria massacre in South Australia in 1840, the one at Hornet Bank in 1857 and that of

12. Such 'treachery' resembles the revenge killing commonly observed in kinship-based or 'stateless' societies. Here killing and counter killing are among the obligations of close kin, who commonly exercise stealth and surprise in such attacks. Hodgkinson (1845: 236–7) had earlier recorded one such revenge killing on the Macleay River: 'It seems to be a regular principle with the Australian Aborigines that blood must be shed for blood, and as an example will better illustrate the warfare of the natives than a general description, I will give a short account of a quarrel among some Macleay River tribes during my stay here. Three young men, belonging to the Yarra–Bandini tribe, which was also the name of our cattle-station, (as that locality was the headquarters of this tribe), had descended the river in a canoe to Verge's station, which is within the limits of the boundaries of the Calliteeni or Kempsey tribe. The object they had in view, was to kill a Tryal Bay native, whom the sawyers had nicknamed Cranky Tom, from his comical hilarity: for it would appear one of the relations of these men had been killed in a fight, and they now determined to revenge his death. Poor Tom, who was my earliest acquaintance among the Tryal Bay natives, was stopping with his 'gin' Dilberree near Verge's, without any suspicion of treachery, when he was suddenly confronted by his enemies. Having endeavoured in vain to protect himself with his shield, he soon fell pierced with wounds, and his head was then cut off by his savage enemies, one of whom, named Henry, also took possession of the woman. This act of treachery roused the indignation of two tribes, the Kempsey or Calliteeni blacks, on whose grounds the outrage had been committed, and the Tryal Bay blacks to whom the murdered man belonged. On speaking to the chief men of the Yarra–Bandini tribe about this cowardly attack, they merely told me in reply that Henry and the other men were "murry stupid" to act as they did, but that Cranky Tom was a "murry saucy fellow," and deserved what he had got.'

Cullinaringoe in Queensland in 1861 (see Reynolds 1981). In each of these incidents, the reports emphasised that the Europeans who had been killed had been unsuspecting of their fate. They had been initially helped or had previously had friendly relations with the Aborigines involved. All the accounts efficiently demonstrated that Aborigines were treacherous and murderous.

Although this 'colonial frontier' image of the Aborigine as a morally degraded human being effectively irredeemable to civilisation was fairly widespread, it was not the only view in circulation at the time. There were other counter representations competing with it. Hodgkinson's *Australia from Port Macquarie to Moreton Bay* (1845), for example, emphasises the Aborigine's humanity and even land commissioner Massie's earlier (AHR 1842) reports describe a more benign 'romantic savage'. Like Henderson, Hodgkinson had settled in the valley for a few years in the early 1840s. His account, which is both a geographical and an ethnographic report of the north coast, was commissioned by the surveyor-general of the colony and carried out by means of careful and detailed empirical observation. As a man of natural science, Hodgkinson places the natives on the same level as the other aspects of the natural world – the plants, animals, landscapes, or any other of nature's oddities or wonders.

His depiction of the Macleay Aborigines is empathetic and seeks to correct misconceptions about their cleanliness and intelligence and to modify views about their inherent treachery. Hodgkinson saw the Aborigines' simple life with nature as a virtue which had been lost to civilisation:

> What great inducement does the monotonous and toilsome existence of the labouring classes in civilised communities offer, to make the savage abandon his independent and careless life, diversified by the exciting occupations of hunting, fishing, fighting and dancing. It is certainly not from want of intelligence that the Australian Aborigines have hitherto proved so irreclaimable. The mental faculties of the Australian savage have been too much underrated, except by those authors who have had the best opportunity of witnessing their manners and customs in their purely wild state. (Hodgkinson 1845: 242)

In effect, Hodgkinson depicts Aborigines as the repository of the pristine virtues of manliness and freedom identified with the hard and simple life of the romantic savage.

Smith (1984: 326) shows how this romantic savage epitomised 'the virtues of the natural man of the enlightenment', which emphasised, amongst other things, 'a great love of personal freedom' and 'a temperament which reacted violently and immediately to experience, courage, great emotional depth, and a childlike warmth and generosity of feeling'. Hodgkinson explicitly employs 'romantic savage' representations to counteract the pastoralist image of Aboriginal savagery. His themes of freedom, intelligence and courage are a simple reversal of those of the degraded humanity of the ignoble savage. Both representations are essentially European fictions.

There was no singularly construed reality of the colonial frontier. The importance of such representations is *not* their illustration of cultural relativity, nor, as Taussig (1987: 75) argues, is there a necessity for some meticulous winnowing of 'truth from distortion, reality from illusion, fact from myth'. In effect, as he says, such attempts seek to impose a singular reality, some unity passing for transcendental truth, which ultimately desensitises and distorts our understanding of the terror and chaos of the colonial frontier. The importance of these colonial works, he argues, lies in their attempts to 'create uncertain reality out of fiction, giving shape and voice to the formless form of the reality in which an unstable interplay between truth and illusion becomes a phantasmic social force' (ibid. p. 121). The problem of depicting the past is not so much the selective representation of reality contained in the various writings, but the constitution of reality: the relationship or complicity between knowledge and power. These representations were therefore part of wider discourses that did not simply reflect, but actively created, that colonial reality.

Both Henderson's and Hodgkinson's assessments of the humanness of the 'savage' – their representations of Aborigines' radical otherness – are inferiorising mythologies. As Taussig (ibid. pp. 85–9) states, the perception of the 'child in the savage' provided the mediating principle on which power feeds in the 'patronising mythology' of the romantic savage. This is evident in the allegedly progressive and benevolent accounts of the Aborigines on the Macleay found in land commissioner Massie's early reports. Indeed, he was most concerned with the cedar cutters' 'aggression against the blacks' and the necessity to find some 'neutral ground . . . they may occupy without molestation' (SA 5458). Nevertheless, like Hodgkinson, guiding Massie's perceptions was a view of their vulnerability if not left in a 'purely wild state'. The Aborigines in the valley were perceived by Massie basically as 'grown up children' who were harmless and inoffensive but with indulgent and undeveloped characters – allegedly expressed in their unwillingness to work and a general vulnerability associated with their childlike innocence and simplicity. The source of corruption was found in the 'lawless and unprincipled men' of civilisation personified by convicts, ex-convicts and cedar cutters. As Massie puts it, 'in exchange for their simplicity they [Aborigines] merely get acquainted with every kind of profligacy and vice that can disgrace the human species' (AHR, vol. XXII: 263). The patronising image of the romantic savage effectively denies them the ability to control their own existence. The corollary that follows from this is that any attempt to civilise them must take place under the custodial protection of the state and that they must accept the authoritarian pedagogy of the church and/or state. Thus, the image of the romatic savage is as disempowering as that of the ignoble savage (or any other image created by the colonisers).

However, as we have seen, quite a different image emerges from the pastoralists' accounts (see also McMaugh 1931). For Henderson (1851, vol. I: 296), the Dhan-gadi were 'great, strapping, and ferocious-looking fellows' whom he regarded as 'a most dangerous and trouble-some race' (ibid. vol. II: 4). The psychological portrait of the Aborigine was not that of the primitive simplicity of the 'grown up child' but of a murderous, treacherous and cunning being, devoid of feelings of sincerity or mercy. The Dhan-gadi are presented by Henderson as corporal beings with a human form, but lacking a human interior. They are presented as a primordial form of terror and cruelty, unrestrained and irredeemable to civilising virtues. Such characterisations gave legitimacy to the culture of terror, to use Taussig's term, that developed on the upper Macleay in the form of the pastoralist redemptive viol-ence. It was violence that was needed to tame or nullify the 'savagery' in Aborigines (see Fredrickson 1985). Such an inferiorising mythology relied upon the empowering of Aboriginal otherness with a destructive efficacy. Treachery signified a power to wreak disorder and destruction because its efficacy lay in its seemingly undisciplined, unpredictable and arbitrary nature. Such representations reflected the deeper strain of fear, hatred and aggression which legitimated much of the redemp-tive violence produced on the colonial frontier.

The pattern of conflict in the Macleay Valley shares features in common with those recorded in other areas of the pastoral frontier. These are revealed in the more general histories by Robinson and York (1977) and Reynolds (1981), as well as in the more specific regional studies of Hartwig (1965), Reece (1974), Ryan (1981) and Loos (1982). They show the extent to which attacks on hutkeepers, the spearing of cattle and attacks on pastoral stations were common Aboriginal re-sponses to the pastoral occupation. Similarly, they establish the extent to which the punitive expedition was used, officially or unofficially, to annihilate 'troublesome blacks'. The Macleay Valley retained the charac-ter of a new frontier for a longer period than other areas. The prolonged period of conflict there was associated with specific economic, demo-graphic and environmental factors, which differentiated it from other areas in which the pastoral advance had been much more rapid and decisive.

The settling of the Macleay Valley was a secondary elaboration of the pastoral economy of the colony of NSW. Yet, the inexorable logic of colonial dispossession ensured that conflict was not so much reduced as extended. The guerrilla tactics which characterised Aboriginal resist-ance determined that, for the settler colonists, it was not a matter of securing control through a major and decisive battle but surviving the seemingly arbitrary hit and run attacks of the Dhan-gadi. As Henderson (1851, vol. II: 56) states, 'There is a necessity for constant vigilance on the part of the settler, and for reliance upon himself alone for defence, or redress; the police being for these purposes, and more specially for the former, totally ineffective.' In effect, the circumstances were such that control was precarious and attempts to secure control equally precarious. Aborigines were perceived to be dangerous to have around stations because of their treachery.

Aboriginal resistance consciously or unconsciously began to generate its own form of terror, which was sustained by the perceived isolated vulnerability of the pastoralists themselves. This did not derive simply from Aboriginal/European relations but also from the competitive economic relations colonialism produced between Europeans themselves. Henderson (ibid. vol. I: 295–6) provides a clear account of these competitive relations:

> My nearest neighbour dwelt at the station called Warbro, on the creek ten [to] twelve miles down river. I could therefore have no society, even if he had been inclined to be social. But the fact was that, like most other squatters, though at some distance from him he thought I had encroached on his run by coming so near. This of course led to a rupture and finally to adjustment of our differences by the Commissioner of Crown Lands.

In fact adjudicating boundary disputes and alleged incidences of trespass was one of the land commissioner's regular duties in the Macleay Valley.[13] Thus, I would argue that it was not only the relations with Aborigines, but the more general social relations spawned by capitalism in this colonial form that intensified the Aboriginal terror.

Much of the evidence of the killing of Aborigines on the frontier is found at the level of local history published in the accounts of local squatters or in the oral traditions of Aborigines and Europeans in the area. The punitive raids to ensure that Aborigines were, as Henderson put it, 'summarily punished', were carried out not only by official state apparatuses but also and mostly by unofficial groups of squatters. Henderson (1851) and McMaugh (1931) give a number of accounts of massacres of Aborigines in the valley. Henderson recounts how Aborigines, who cut loose 500 sheep and made away with them, were finally tracked down and 'two or three dozen men were slaughtered' (1851, vol. II: 6) and how the 'Yarraharpny blacks, a tribe notorious for their savage dispositions' were 'dispersed with some slaughter' (ibid. pp.

---

13. The land commissioner's reports reveal that in the 1840s the incidence of conflict over boundaries was a common one. As Massie states in 1845, 'Numerous complaints . . . that stock of other licenced parties are constantly in the habit of trespassing upon their respective runs.' (SA: 7/524)

115–16).[14] McMaugh describes in more detail the retribution dealt out to Aborigines for the killing of 'two shepherds and their wives' and about 800 sheep:

> They found a large number of them [Aborigines] camped under a cliff . . . they immediately showed fight and a battle ensued but the white men were well armed and a great number of blacks were killed but the only casualty on the other side was a horse, the men took cover behind the trees and fired at the murderers, a few sheep were found but the blacks were so numerous that they killed and ate twenty a night. (cited Blomfield 1981: 37.)

Local oral tradition provides evidence of another three massacres, which occurred in the upper Macleay region at Sheep Station Knob, at Majors or Innes Creek and to the south around Walcha. These accounts largely correspond to those of Blomfield (1981) who records massacres at Sheep Station Bluff, Stockyard Creek and at Boozers respectively with the addition of another massacre at Durallie Creek (Kunderang). In each of the accounts a large number of Aborigines were said to have been killed.

The whites achieved control over the valley through a series of local skirmishes and punitive raids undertaken by local squatters and, in a brief period, by the Native Police Force. Given the nature of the conflict, small family groups bore the brunt of the squatters' redemptive violence, the victims being groups of men, women and children rather than armed parties of men. These punitive expeditions against the 'guilty mobs' in the valley inevitably turned into indiscriminate attacks on small unsuspecting groups of often sleeping Aborigines. Henderson (1851, vol. II: 109–10) explains how, 'They sleep more soundly towards the morning, and when expeditions have been made against them by the whites, they have always endeavoured to surprise them in the grey light of dawn. At this time, they never attack each other. They are afraid to move about in the dark.' Colonial culture's distortion of human relations is shown in 'the unreal atmosphere of ordinariness' contained in these accounts.

Human relations and the cultural meanings they expressed were shaped by the social forces of colonialism and, following Taussig's argument (1987), they also contained within them the historical

14. What is significant here is that the Dhan-gadi did not only resist pastoral expansion through the systematic spearing of cattle and sheep but also took advantage of this new food source. As Henderson (1851, vol. II: 6) states, prior to their massacre, 'The natives had managed wonderfully well, one of the gins taking them out to graze every day, and penning them up at night in bush-yards, made by the tribe of stakes and boughs of trees. The remains of the unfortunate muttons had been very cunningly disposed of, the bones being placed under the skins, which were spread out with the wool uppermost, at small distances from each other, and looked like patches of yellow withered grass.' This response by Aborigines to European cattle and sheep was widely recorded along the pastoral frontiers (see also Reynolds 1981: Ch. 6).

conditions that made the 'fictional realities' that constituted Aboriginal 'otherness' possible. The representations of 'otherness' impose a truth which attributes to Aborigines an essential being and, in effect, denies the social reality of their existence. This 'essential' rather than 'social' being is confined within a singular reality which exists outside time and space. Fiction and reality were inexorably intertwined in the killing and maiming of Aborigines during their early history in the Macleay Valley. The terror and massacres of the punitive expeditions were authorised by the fictional reality of Aboriginal treachery. Pastoralist propaganda established knowledge and imposed truth which was inseparable from the exercise of power on the colonial frontier. In effect, such representations of reality sought to explain the problems which the very existence of colonial society had caused.

There was a drastic population decline. One can safely presume from analogous evidence relating to the contact history of Aboriginal groups that the Dhan-gadi suffered from introduced diseases which reinforced massacres in reducing the population. The remaining Dhan-gadi, it would appear, continued to provision themselves from the remaining bushland that had been formally, but not yet physically, expropriated because of its inaccessibility. Thus, 30 years later, in 1886, the telegraph master at Bellbrook observed that, 'Although there are about 50 in this locality, they live principally by hunting and fishing and the government through the supply of the old and infirm ones with weekly rations. They are a very lazy race and will do anything other than work.' (MHS Toose file.) His observation suggests that in the immediate post-conflict period (1870s and 1880s), the vastly reduced numbers of the Dhan-gadi continued to retain their social distance and economic autonomy from Europeans. Thus Aborigines and Europeans would appear to have lived as separate communities once the threat to European lives and property had ceased as a consequence of the drastic reduction and subjugation of the Dhan-gadi.

Chapter 2

The Economic Incorporation
of the Dhan-gadi

The process of destruction of existing Dhan-gadi society did not mean that they were totally dispossessed. Marginalisation provided possibilities for the perpetuation of cultural forms which provided sites of resistence to their cultural and ideological incorporation. In the post-conflict period, the Dhan-gadi lived in two worlds, one Aboriginal and the other European. Social distance remained a distinctive feature of Aboriginal/European relations. The single point of interaction occurred as a result of their increasing economic incorporation in the early twentieth century. Across the social divide, there was a frequent movement of Aborigines between the reserve and the pastoral stations, between ceremonial life and pastoral work, and between the pastoralist's rations and bush food.

Furthermore, this partial incorporation was not simply in terms of labour and goods. The Dhan-gadi were not simply passive fodder in the cycle of rural capitalist production. Our understanding has to extend beyond the one-sided determinism that considers such relations only in their exploitative dimension. The Dhan-gadi had their own expectations and priorities which determined their involvement. Similarly, in the movement between the two worlds they found new possibilities, new skills and new bases of self-esteem. This can be drawn from the prominence given to such work by the participants in this study. For the men, especially, pride in the work they performed on European stations was as significant a feature of their historical self-representations as having been 'put through the Rule'. Indeed, for the Aboriginal participants, men and women, such work was seen as an important aspect of their identity. On their own terms, they were successfully innovative and yet powerless to control many of the factors which conditioned their daily lives. This inequality of power was manifested in the fact that whilst Dhan-gadi society had been reshaped by the colonial encounter, their European counterparts were not.

2.1. The Seasonal Rhythm of Rural Employment

Opportunities for the economic incorporation of the Dhan-gadi did not occur until the late nineteenth or early twentieth century when the labour requirements of the local economy increased through diversification and expansion. Changes occurred at the lower end of the economy when there was a major influx of smallholders, supported mainly by maize production, into the Macleay Valley in the 1880s. Between 1880 and 1889, the amount of land brought into maize production increased from 6,000 to 10,000 hectares and output from 23,000,000 to 36,000,000 kilograms (SRNSW figures). Much of this land was in the Hickeys Creek area of the upper Macleay Valley. The average size of a smallholding was eight hectares, although some were as large as 16 hectares. While returns for maize were high, so too were the overheads (often as much as 50 per cent of the returns), and life for the smallholders was never easy – theirs was very much a hand-to-mouth existence. Their farms were not self-sufficient and, once the corn was planted, they often had to seek other forms of employment to survive, usually working for the larger property owners or engaging in fur trapping.

Over the same period the pastoral economy of the Macleay Valley also expanded and, throughout the 1880s, stock numbers generally increased to around 30,000 head of cattle (SRNSW figures for 1880 to 1890; cf. Table 2). Similarly, the cattle stations also increased significantly in size (see Table 3). The general rise in beef production was related to the new access to British markets for dairy and beef cattle through technical advances in refrigerated transportation (Cochrane 1980: 19). This emergent economic expansion was forestalled in the 1890s through a general economic depression, and it was not until the early decades of the twentieth century that the pastoral economy once again began to expand.

The expansion of the pastoral industry in the upper Macleay Valley in the 1880s provided the preconditions for the incorporation of the Dhan-gadi into the European economy. In the early twentieth century the clearing of the heavily timbered woodlands and the rain forest provided a basis for Aboriginal employment. (The labour history of the Dhan-gadi began during this period.) By the early part of the twentieth century, there were already three major Aboriginal camps in the upper Macleay Valley.

The spatial distribution of these camps corresponded to the labour requirements of the European economy. They were located at Bellbrook, Lower Creek (37 kilometres away) and Georges Creek (a further 7 kilometres up river). A number of Aboriginal families lived in these camps more or less permanently, while many other families came and went as they desired. The men and women of these separate camps

Table 3. Pastoral Properties on the Upper Macleay River (1865, 1885)

Station	1865	1885
	Hectares	
Long Flat	6,998	N.A.
Stockyard Creek	5,441	10,122
Towal Creek	12,956	24,899
Five Day Creek	7,773	30,769
Pee Dee Creek	4,664	6,524
Nulla Nulla Creek	4,664	13,684
Toorumbee	6,478	19,028
Elsineur	N.A.	4,146
Warbro	8,810	19,433
Innes Creek	19,433	26,316
Toorooka	6,478	11,741

Sources: 1865: *Fussell's Squatting Directory* (ML 630.991F)
1885: Land Occupations Branch-Tracing of Runs (SA 4/7058–67)

provided the labour for the local European properties, especially at Lower Creek and Georges Creek.

Elkin (1951) portrays these camps as being in the more marginal areas of European settlement where European encroachment was neither rapid nor intensive and this, consequently, gave the Aborigines the time and space within which to adapt, at least minimally, to the new situation. As I have previously argued, however, historically, this was not the case in the Macleay Valley. The Dhan-gadi adapted minimally after the period of colonial conflict and not in the absence of frontier violence. It would appear that during the period of adaptation and incorporation, dating approximately from the late nineteenth century, rations of tea, flour and sugar were exchanged with Aborigines for their labour in locations where European labour was scarce. A reciprocal relationship developed between the property owner and a number of Aboriginal men and their dependants, where food and a place to stay were exchanged for a stable pool of cheap labour. The camps were the focus of these labour pools.

The camp at Georges Creek survived until the 1930s. The people there were not Dhan-gadi, like those at Lower Creek and Bellbrook, but Gumbaingirr people from Grafton. The men provided labour for one station, Kunderang, at the head of the Macleay River. This station covered some 36,423 hectares of rough mountainous country and carried an estimated 500 breeding cattle and between 3,000 and 5,000 wild cattle. The men of two families, called Duroux and Hilton, were employed full time. During the peak periods of the weaner muster and branding in the spring and the bullock muster in the winter, more Aboriginal men, usually Dhan-gadi, were also hired. Mustering lasted between six to eight weeks. The men from the other family at Georges Creek, the Naylors, did bush work for the surrounding stations. All the families in this community, which was well established on the banks of the creek, had bark huts and grew lemon and orange trees (still growing today), as well as vegetables and corn for domestic use. 'Bush tucker' provided the main source of meat. The closure of the school at Georges Creek in the early 1930s meant that the Duroux family had to leave to seek schooling for their children. Eventually only the Hiltons remained, and they maintained strong links with the Kunderang station.

At Lower Creek Aboriginal labour was used exclusively on pastoral properties, either for clearing land or stock work. One major property holder, on whose land the Aboriginal camp was located, was the chief employer. One of his employees told me that 'He was good to us goories . . . in drought time one mate of his said, "Why don't you hunt 'em off the flat?" [and he replied] "I wouldn't do that . . . if they see a cow down, or a bullock, they'll lift it up and walk it around." He knew we were useful in lots of ways.' One Aboriginal man, Quinlan, had an annual contract to clear land. His large family lived in a bark hut at Lower Creek, to which other families from the lower Macleay, Nymboida and especially Bellbrook were constant visitors. The families at Lower Creek were all related by kinship or marriage, and the Bellbrook and Lower Creek people were said to 'belong to one mob'. The pattern of interaction with Europeans was similar to that of the 'station blacks' referred to earlier. The continuing occupation of the site at Lower Creek was based on a personalised rather than a contractual relationship between the Dhan-gadi men and the local European station owners – a relationship that endured because the Aborigines were 'useful in lots of ways'.

The Dhan-gadi at Lower Creek also worked on other properties in the area. When the men had work some distance from Lower Creek, the families moved and set up bush camps near the work sites. As one woman put it, 'we was free then'. They simply picked up their blankets, and they were off. For the most part, the Lower Creek people lived and worked around this area. The exception was the once a year trip to Armidale for the agricultural show. When the show was over, the families travelled in a wide arc, as far north as Ebor, working where they could, and then down the Styx River back to Lower Creek. The charter for this temporary pattern of residence was provided, in the main, by the economic tie which existed between the labourers and the station owners.

This way of life among the Dhan-gadi had many features in common with the patterns of subsistence described earlier by Hodgkinson (1845). A number of families were involved at a particular work site. As one man put it, at Lower Creek 'they would go, you know, and take a lot of men over there and they'd do that ring barking or grubbin', go up into scrub all over the place. Made huts all around, no school.' This labour-intensive work brought large numbers of people together for considerable periods of time and, for a large contract, this could sometimes be for up to three months. As one of the workers described it, 'We went to Carroll Creek (we ate) 22 wallabies in a week and eight (bags) 50 (pound) flour. We had a big mob about 50 or 60 of 'em. We all camped together, working together, about 10–15 men.' Although the Dhan-gadi characteristically lived in small kin-based groups which were flexible in composition, mobile and relatively autonomous, their mobility was tied to the rural economic cycle rather than to their own subsistence needs, as had been the case in the past. This allowed them to supplement their bush tucker diet with European goods such as flour, tea and sugar (this will be discussed below). The particular way in which the Europeans used Aboriginal labour allowed the Dhan-gadi to maintain their relatively autonomous way of life and to continue their indigenous forms of subsistence.

The pattern of Aboriginal employment was significant as at this early stage it reflected the development of a rural capitalist economy based on segmentation in a situation in which race provided a conspicuous marker. Aboriginal labour was predominantly employed on the up-river properties, for example, Lower Creek and Georges Creek. The availability of smallholder labour in the Hickeys Creek area ensured that the middle Macleay Valley was worked predominately by Europeans. Smallholders competed with Aborigines for employment around the Hickeys Creek area, because of the close proximity to their own properties. Conditions of work·on the upper Macleay stations were, however, less than desirable for Europeans: long periods away from their families and properties and bush camp life were major disincentives. Aboriginal employment was concentrated on the remote upper Macleay stations, where the Aboriginal patterns of employment had a great deal of continuity with earlier patterns of subsistence. Even so, Aboriginal labour had a marginal place in the local economy.

In the second phase of Dhan-gadi incorporation, the pattern of scattered camps on the upper Macleay River was replaced by their increasing concentration on the government reserve at Bellbrook. In 1901 the population of the two camps was 89 people. By the end of the 1930s, 213 were resident on the reserve (AWB Report, 1941: 5). In part, this related to the reformulation of state power with regard to Aborigines brought about by the Aborigines Protection Act (1909). (This will be fully discussed in Chapter 5.) The most immediate affect for Aborigines in the upper Macleay was the introduction of compulsory and segregated schooling for children on the reserves. Both recruitment and teaching operated at an elementary level. Missionaries functioned as teachers to combine religious and secular education. As the local school inspector's report (1911) stated, 'The pupils show considerable aptitude for art work . . . singing is a very good subject, as is also scripture . . . Much interest is shown in sewing and gardening.' (ML Q572 9901 A) It was not until 1916, however, that a special syllabus for Aboriginal children, emphasising manual training (sewing and gardening) was formalised and introduced. Reading, writing and arithmetic were included in the syllabus, but only up to third-grade primary school standard (i.e. at the level of eight-year-old European students). The introduction of compulsory education effectively ended existing work patterns and restricted Aboriginal mobility. Women and children could no longer accompany their men to the various work sites, and the Aboriginal families at Lower Creek had to move back to Bellbrook reserve to live. As a consequence Aboriginal men and their older sons would spend more time away from their families when they were working.

At first the policy formulated by the Aborigines Protection Board (APB) had only a limited influence on the lives of the Aborigines on the upper Macleay River. The most significant aspect of the creation of the reserve had been the setting up at the turn of the century of four small (1.2 hectare) farms run by Aboriginal men, on which maize was grown for sale at the city markets. A missionary report in 1911 stated that 'Those who had corn in, are busy, pulling, husking and threshing. There were some fine examples of corn grown by our people here. We are hoping to see a larger area under cultivation next season.' (ML Q572 9901 A) Once the corn had been planted, these farmers, like other smallholders, went off to seek other employment – in bush work, fencing, corn pulling or farming. When government policy changed again in the 1930s, this pattern was destroyed (see Chapter 5), but the educational policy continued to draw the Aboriginal population onto the reserve.

The changing economy of the upper Macleay Valley also affected the concentration of Aborigines. By the early 1920s the Dhan-gadi no longer used the camp at Lower Creek. The bankruptcy of the station owner with whom they had had close relations may have been a factor, but the main reason for the population shift was the involvement of smallholders in the growing dairy industry. The emergence of dairying in the lower Macleay Valley in the 1890s brought about a dramatic change in the rural economy, especially for smallholders (see Table 4). During the 1890s three butter factories were established on the lower Macleay, followed by another in Kempsey, in 1905, and a butter factory on the upper Macleay in 1906. By 1916 the valley's new industry had become stabilised. There were two cooperatives, two proprietary butter factories and four cheese factories. In that year, the number of dairies registered was 1,200 (Neil 1972: 78). The rural landscape that had existed prior to 1890 had been significantly transformed.

Table 4. Dairying Account: Initial Four Years' Production: Macleay River (1894–1897)

Year 1894	Number of Gallons	Monies £	s	d	Year 1896	Number of Gallons	Monies £	s	d
January	290	2	5	8	January	1,417	21	3	5
February	304	2	11	1	February	1,299	15	5	4
March	60		9	0	March	1,566	17	17	5
April	270	2	3	0	April	1,303	16	3	0
May	360	3	2	4	May	1,076	16	10	0
June	318	3	12	9	June	849	13	0	0
July	302	4	11	7	July	768	11	12	0
August	360	5	5	0	August	699	10	10	0
September	324	4	0	0	September	898	12	0	1
October	464	4	10	0	October	1,302	14	6	0
November	630	5	6	2	November	1,404	15	10	0
December	707	7	7	0	December	1,901	20	0	0
Total	4,389	45	3	7	Total	14,482	183	17	3

Year 1895	Number of Gallons	Monies £	s	d	Year 1897	Number of Gallons	Monies £	s	d
January	646	5	5	0	January	1,918	15	18	3
February	610	3	5	0	February	1,608	12	15	7
March	648	4	8	0	March	1,511	13	8	5
April	571	4	17	6	April	1,476	18	0	11
May	528	5	0	0	May	1,323	26	7	6
June	630	9	6	3	June	1,228	28	14	2
July	589	10	2	2	July	1,528	29	16	5
August	541	8	5	6	August	1,922	32	0	3
September	578	10	11	7	September	2,155	31	0	3
October	949	14	7	0	October	2,345	28	6	9
November	1,062	14	8	9	November	2,678	28	14	0
December	1,297	19	4	3	December	2,994	31	18	7
Total	8,649	109	1	0	Total	22,686	297	1	1

Source: MHS files

The setting up of a cooperative in 1906 caused dairying to spread from the lower to the upper Macleay and to become established around Hickeys Creek, on Nulla Nulla Creek at Bellbrook and on the large properties further up the river. For the smallholders this was a much needed boost, for, instead of only the annual return from maize, they now earned a monthly return from dairying (see Table 4). In effect it had enabled them to diversify. The smallholders could combine the now more important dairy production with maize and pigs, while the medium and large pastoral concerns could combine beef with dairy, pig and maize production. Pig raising had always been combined with maize crops, but it really expanded with dairying. The growth of dairying in the Macleay Valley was based on manufacturing butter and cheese rather than milk production (although pigs did provide a profitable means of disposing of skimmed milk). Dairying and diversification basically formed the basis of the Macleay region's greater prosperity and self sufficiency.

This had significant consequences for the employment of Dhan-gadi men. As I mentioned earlier, smallholders competed with Aborigines on the job market, but the sale of their labour was concentrated around Hickeys Creek. This situation changed with the introduction and growth of dairying. Smallholder participation in dairying had the effect of reducing the labour supply, for it was now moving into more secure and profitable areas of the economy. The demand for Aboriginal labour therefore increased in the areas the smallholders vacated. At the same time, the greater prosperity of the valley created more employment opportunities as medium and large landholders sought to bring more land into production. As one smallholder put it:

> There was a period about the twenties to the Second World War when actually the land holders depended on them [Aborigines] for their annual suckering and ring barking and any of the subsequent work that was necessary. . . . From the twenties when things became more prosperous I think people did start on the bigger holdings doing probably 100 acres each year. For three or four years anyhow it had to be followed up to have the regrowth treated. The Aborigines did a lot towards that.

This was borne out in 1938 when the APB decided to close down the reserve and move the Dhan-gadi out of the valley to another location further south. The local Europeans objected to this proposal, claiming that they would be deprived of their work force. The Dhan-gadi consequently remained at Bellbrook.

In the second phase there was a consolidation of the trends evident in the first phase, with the labour market becoming more and more racially segmented. Although Aboriginal labour had become important in the upper Macleay River area, it was in occupations that were marginal to the European economy. The Aborigines were generally in lower status, lower paid, physically more strenuous jobs than the Europeans, in which conditions were worse and underemployment rates higher than in the other sectors of the economy.

There were four main types of work for Aboriginal men on the upper Macleay – bush work, fencing, corn pulling and stock work. Bush work, which involved clearing large tracts of land on the upper Macleay during the winter months (when sap activity in the trees was low and frost could kill off any regeneration) was the mainstay of Aboriginal employment and was carried out almost exclusively by Aboriginal men. Their employers tended to be the middle and large property owners, for the smallholders simply had insufficient capital to employ outsiders and had to rely on family labour for the various tasks.

Some subtle changes were introduced to contracts for bush work which were in keeping with the altered circumstances brought about by compulsory education. As one Aboriginal man who had been a contractor at the time put it, he 'wouldn't take on a big job but try to do it in a week'. This was primarily so that he could 'come home every weekend'. The contractor required a degree of skill to assess the amount of work in a particular job. The usual contract was calculated by the acre, 'one chain wide and 10 chains long' (0.4 hectare). A 'good man' could clear 0.8 hectare in a day, but 0.4 was the norm. The largest contract was 168 hectares, given in 1918 at Elsineur. This was a notable exception, and long contracts were rare. The conditions on the job, however, did vary so that it was always possible that the men might have to work at weekends. As the following quotation indicates, this was something that they strenuously avoided: 'Me and Johnny and a brother, George, and somebody else, [we got] soakin' wet finishin' the work up there. We was comin' home on the Friday, we was finishing up in the mornin' and this rain started at night and we was in the wet all day finishin' the job.' Conditions of work were usually determined by some kind of compromise between what the Dhan-gadi men wanted and what was on offer. They tended to prefer contract work because it enabled them to work on their own, 'to be their own bosses', and to have control by Europeans limited to an inspection at the end of a job. One man would get a contract from a pastoralist and then take on a number of other men to do the work. Although regarded by others as exceptional behaviour, some individuals engaged in bush work as a form of self-imposed solitude, as a means of limiting all forms of sociality. They could work entirely by themselves and 'would stay out for weeks and months and never bother comin' in at all'. They would take some flour, sugar, tea and salt with them, as well as a shot gun or 'pea' rifle (.22) so that they could live off the land by eating wallaby, bush turkey and possum. For most contract gangs, in fact, 'bush tucker' was the primary source of subsistence. As one man stated:

> We was over in . . . gully falling the big black scrub. We only took bread with us and couldn't see anything when we were going and we had a pea rifle. We got out there workin' away and comin' towards dinner. Harpy was there then . . . 'No meat or anythin', he said. He said 'sool them dogs in down on the end of the scrub' see. I shot 'em in, this, Sue and Joe, and kept Baldy up on the edge and they went in round ahead barkin', barkin' up the side and I see Baldy running up the ridge. Then I see him comin' back chasin' this wallaby. You know he caught that nearly right where the fire was. Harpy come and he skinned him and we had 'im cooked on the coals in no time.

Contract work effectively combined European employment with traditional forms of subsistence. This marginal incorporation into the
European economy thus allowed the Dhan-gadi to maintain a degree of
autonomy from the Europeans.

When bushwork was available in the winter months it involved long
hours and physically strenuous work. As one man stated:

> I worked all the time with my father, we'd walk from Bellbrook right out up in
> them hills and work straight away ring-barkin'. Don't stop till you have
> dinner. Have dinner and a little bit of a sit down and you start again and you
> don't knock off till your comin' home. He'd never pull up, never stop when
> he's workin'. He's fallin' scrub there at Sauer's (gully), he chopped all day, no
> stop, and only gettin' 1/6 to 2/– an acre, see, for ring-barkin'.

Bush work involved four separate operations: grubbing, ring barking,
sucker bashing and burning off. They formed part of a unified process
which could be carried out in consecutive years. 'Sucker bashing', the
killing off of new growth, was the most labour intensive of these
operations. One man explained how 'You might have to do suckerin'
for nearly five years every winter, same paddock. You might grub the
seedlings out [with a maddock], he's finished. But the suckerin' comes
on all the time.' Bush work provided plenty of work for Dhan-gadi men
in strenuous, labour-intensive employment. At the same time, the
remuneration of this seasonal work remained low. There were two
types of bush cleared: woodlands and rain forest. For woodlands, the
pay around 1920 was 1/6d per 0.4 hectare; it rose to 2/6d in the 1930s
and later to 5/6d. For clearing rain forests on the steep slopes and
densely-covered gullies of the ranges, the pay was considerably higher.
Men would ask for 20/– and later 40/– for 'black' forest work. It was the
job of the contractor to assess and negotiate the rate with the land-
owner. In later years the exchange was in cash, not rations, and the
contractor was the only person paid. The use of Aboriginal labour for
clearing land, which enabled pastoralists to bring more land into
production, was both extensive and inexpensive.

Corn pulling provided the main source of work in the late summer/
winter months. It was carried out by a number of men who were paid
individually, but who were employed for a much shorter duration than
for other types of work. This work also involved intensive physical
labour, as the following quotation suggests:

> They had a horse with a dray and while your pullin' it [corn] see . . . poor old
> horse he'll go along never stop. You gotta keep pullin' all the time. He [horse]
> just put his foot here and he put his foot there and he know there's people
> with corn at the back throwin' it in. You gotta throw it in the dray until full
> then you take it up the barn. Then you come back and go again.

Most men were employed on surrounding farms during the harvest season. A missionary report states that 'Most of the men are away corn pulling all week, coming home Saturdays and going away again on Monday mornings.' (ML Q572 9901 A.) At Burraga, the only station that continued to specialise in corn production, six Aboriginal corn pullers were employed each year at harvest time for a period of six weeks. The men pulled corn all day, and then at night the corn was husked and threshed until about 9 p.m. As many as 50 bags (threshed) were loaded onto the bullock train and sent to Greenhill, from where they were shipped to the city markets. The round trip to Greenhill and back took a week to complete.

Fencing was a source of contract work that could be done at any time during the year. It was, however, a highly irregular form of work. One man described it as follows: 'Three good men and you'd go a long way (50 posts a day depending on terrain): a man to dig the post hole right, a man to line up the post and another boring the post holes (in the upright post) (6d a post) . . . but if you got four (men) on is no good then.' This work could either be contracted separately (the more usual pattern), or carried out by the few men employed as general hands, who in addition to fencing paddocks would build pig runs or stockyards and undertake general repairs. A number of the men were also involved in maize production on European properties. One man, who had previously been running a farm in the reserve until the APB's manager's residence was built on it, found daily employment in the market gardens at Nulla Nulla Creek.

Stock work was less reliant on Aboriginal labour than other kinds of work. Most properties employed only one or two men (usually the same men) on a regular basis during the peak periods of beef production. These men worked alongside the owners and European workers. Kunderang station was the exception, however, for it did rely on Aboriginal men for stock work. After the Georges Creek community dispersed, Gumbaingirr men, who had married into the Dhan-gadi, continued a close connection with Kunderang and supplied the extra workers, usually their sons or relatives, during the weaner and bullock musters. Contract work existed in droving but only for Europeans. Aborigines might be hired to assist, but were never given contracts. Most of the Europeans who did this contract work had smallholdings in the valley.

The employment of Aboriginal women was much more limited. They were employed by Europeans to do domestic work on the properties. This was a common practice regardless of the size of the properties. Washing clothes was the main activity. It was both monotonous and repetitive work. As one woman described it:

A day's work for 3 bob [shillings] a day, and that means that you gotta copper

standing over there, and you gotta put tins around it and then you gotta carry
water from the [river] bank to fill that copper up before you can boil the thing
and put wood under it; there wouldn't be any wood for you, you got to pick
your own wood up . . . and put it under there, and then you got to get the tub
and carry that away 3 bob a day, and you can feed outside. If there are foul
dogs or anything, you could still eat there.

This work was regular but only for a couple of days a week at most. A
number of women also did general housework, such as washing,
taking in the dried clothes, ironing, bedmaking, dusting and child-
minding.

An important source of autonomy and an additional source of income for Dhan-gadi men outside the local economy came from the
commercialisation of hunting. Most men on Bellbrook were involved in
the trapping of animals for their furs. While it lasted, fur trapping
provided a lucrative source of money to the Bellbrook community.
Possum pelts realised as much as £3 a pound. This work was carried
out all year, with the winter months, when the fur was thicker, being
the most profitable times. Men and boys would go out at night,

> They say to you come on we're going up here for Willai [grey possum], you
> might get half a dozen young fellows going up there, thinking they'd kill it. It
> was a real toy to get a torch like that . . . and hold it up in the tree like that,
> 'see one there, there he is! there he is,' bang! hit the ground, see.

For the Dhan-gadi, hunting and trapping possums provided a source of
food as well as of income. 'He'd bring the carcass home, carry the skin
in a bag, bring that home to give to the people . . . I used to watch for
him to come. If anybody wanted some he'd fetch 'em home.' When the
possums were 'cleaned out', rabbits and dingoes took their place, and
they too yielded profitable cash returns. As it was compulsory for local
landholders to eradicate rabbit infestations, this provided many Aboriginal people on Bellbrook with work. Rabbit pelts realised between
£2/10/0 and £3 per pound of pelts. Rabbit trapping differed from
possum hunting in two ways. First, women participated in the former
but not in the latter, and second, possums were eaten whereas rabbits
were not. For some men, the ease and profitability of trapping reduced
the incentive to do bush work.

Because it was much more specialised and required particular skills,
only a few men worked at dingo hunting. As one man described his
father at work:

> He'd bring 'em right up to 'im too, he'd howl 'em right up. I was watchin' 'im,
> we was ring-barking right at Gap Creek, we was right on top, we would hear
> this dingo howlin' right down, and he howled and he said 'wait here now and
> I'll go back and get the gun'. I sat down there and he come back and he waited

there where he was howlin' and I see 'im move over a bit, you know, he
musta noticed the dingo come up, well that dog came right up there till he
shot 'im, bang! . . . Yea he could bring 'em right up to 'im. He was good on
them. He'd just know when their gonna come too. He said 'they give that
little bark, yelp, . . . they [trappers] know their coming'. He was ready for
'em.

The returns for those who were successful were good. Local property
owners paid up to £1/10/0 a scalp for troublesome dingoes, and a
bounty of £1 was payable from the Pastures Protection Board as well.
One man, for example, reportedly 'bagged' 90 dingoes on one large
property in a year, although this was regarded as exceptional.

In the early decades of the twentieth century, Dhan-gadi men and, to
a lesser extent, women, established a niche for themselves within the
European economy on the upper Macleay Valley. Aboriginal labour
became qualitatively important to European pastoralists in marginal
occupations within the local economy. Through employment by Europeans and the commercialisation of hunting, the Dhan-gadi community re-established itself as a relatively autonomous social entity
concentrated on the Bellbrook reserve. What emerged in this context
was an economy in which Europeans and Aborigines *did not compete* for
jobs. Unlike the early 1900s, Aboriginal employment was no longer
concentrated largely within the area covered by the more remote
stations around the upper reaches of the Macleay River. Now they
were also employed on stations around the middle Macleay which
extended to Toorooka and Willy Willy.

The spatial segmentation of labour evident by the late nineteenth
century gave way to a pattern of segmentation based on occupation.
Europeans were property owners, whether large or small, while Aboriginal men and women began to sell their labour. In bush work, corn
pulling, fencing, stock work and domestic work, the Europeans were
always the employers and the Aborigines the employees. Where Aboriginal and European employment overlapped a range of subtle distinctions differentiated them. In stock work, for example, the Europeans
unofficially acquired exclusive rights to contracts for droving cattle and
would then employ Aboriginal stockmen. Similarly, when Aborigines
were employed as general hands which, amongst other activities,
involved ploughing, planting and harvesting maize crops, they were
paid a wage. Europeans, by contrast, would be employed as share-
farmers, which entitled them to 50 per cent of the profits from the sale
(see Table 5).

For aspiring smallholders (usually the sons of smallholders), share-
farming or share-dairying was an initial step towards accumulating
enough capital to purchase their own farm. For Aborigines, neither
share-dairying nor share-farming (except as labourers) was an option.

Table 5. Aboriginal Employment and Maize Production Costs

(a) Aboriginal Employment: Jolliffe Farm

1919				£	s	d
July 31	Ploughing	—	9 days @ 7/–	3	3	0
August 31	Ploughing	—	22 1/2 days @ 7/–	7	17	6
October 31	Ploughing	—	24 days @ 7/–	8	8	0
November 30	Ploughing	—	18 days @ 7/–	6	6	0
December	Farm Work	—	13 days @ 7/–	4	11	0
1920						
January 31	Farm Work	—	12 days @ 7/–	4	8	0
February 29	Farm Work	—	16 days @ 7/–	5	12	0
March 14	Corn Pulling			3	10	0
				43	15	6

(b) Maize Production Costs   (30.6.1920)

Pulling maize	1/– per bag
Husking and Threshing	2/6 per bag
Sacks	1/– per bag
Cartage to Kempsey	2/– per bag
Boat to Sydney	1/– per bag
Commission and Cartage	1/– per bag
	8/6 per bag

300 bags of maize @ 25/– per bag = £382.10s.0d.
        minus costs @ 8/6 per bag
equals 300 bags of maize @ 16/6 = £247.10s.6d.

Source: Private records.

What emerged, in effect, was a clear pattern of differentiation which restricted Aboriginal employment to a number of specific jobs. This pattern in the use of Dhan-gadi labour reveals a number of qualitative similarities with the exploitation of cheap, indigenous labour in other colonial contexts. It reflects what Meillassoux (1972) calls the 'super-exploitation' of indigenous labour, in which indigenous workers are paid token wages, and the cost of reproducing the indigenous population is borne by its own subsistence. In other words, super-exploitation refers (a) to the payment of low wages and (b) to the fact that employers are relieved of the burden of supporting such labour when it is not required. In this respect, the Dhan-gadi on Bellbrook reserve provided an ideal work-force, for it could be drawn upon when required, and the economy only required temporary, seasonal workers.

When their labour was no longer needed, the Aborigines could support themselves with traditional sources of subsistence. In fact bush tucker remained a significant part of the Dhan-gadi people's diet irrespective of whether or not they were working, and this meant that neither the employers nor even the rural economy ever had to bear the full cost of reproducing the population on the upper Macleay.

The pattern of Dhan-gadi incorporation into this rural economy involved more than simple exploitation of cheap labour. Segmentation also had an ideological function in that it provided a basis for the maintenance of hegemonic unity amongst Europeans. The structuring of authority relations between Europeans and Aborigines remained consistent with an ideology of European dominance, but perhaps even more significant was that this segmentation was based on an ideology of exclusion – it excluded Aborigines from dairying on the grounds that they were associated with disease and physical contagion. This view of them as a polluting and dirty race was also expressed in other practices, such as their exclusion from public schools and their segregation in hospitals and cinemas. (These points will be discussed more fully in Chapter 5.)

Another such practice was what the Aborigines called 'feedin' outside'. This referred to the practice of giving food to Aborigines working on the properties, but making them eat it away from the house, i.e. 'eatin' on the woodheap' or 'eatin' with the foul dogs'. 'Inside' in this context did not mean being invited into the kitchen or dining-room, but into the laundry which had a table to eat off and 'a copper to keep you warm', or even onto the verandah, which is where the European labourers were fed. 'Feedin' outside' was an expression of such notions of Aboriginal 'pollution' at the level of everyday interactions. It was a common practice, although there were exceptions, as one woman experienced:

> That old gentleman he was a very nice man him and his . . . she was a grumpy old thing, but she was nice. She always thought that our people wanted food and she'd say come here and sit down on the verandah and have a mug of tea or a piece of cake, even some dinner and yet her brother over the next place, oh, they would feed you outside, feed you outside where the dogs and fowls would be, but this old lady would be on the verandah. Sit down there, either he'd sit with you or she'd sit with you while you were eating and yarn away with you.

For Aborigines, 'feedin' outside' was equated with being classified as farm animals and was greatly resented. As one man replied to a station owner when asked to return his plate, 'a dog doesn't bring his plate back missus, does he?'. For Europeans such everyday practices affirmed Aboriginal inferiority.

The Dhan-gadi were not, however, passive dependents of the European economy but dynamic actors attempting to shape the world around them. While this marginal form of incorporation is an aspect of their domination into a set of exploitative relations, it paradoxically also provides opportunities to perpetuate sites of opposition to an encapsulating form of colonialism. Thus, although the historical conditions of Dhan-gadi existence were generated by capitalism, the ways in which their relations with the local economy were articulated were not in themselves capitalist. There existed a dialectical relationship between the Dhan-gadi and the local economy. Dhan-gadi workers cannot be reduced to facsimiles of European workers or members of an 'underclass' or 'lumpenproletariat' (cf. Castle and Hagen 1978). Theirs was not merely a shared structural position, it was a radically different historical creation. The rhythm and the pattern of their work reveal the existence of an interplay between their own priorities and meanings and the structural niche they occupied within the local economy.

At the level of production, the implications of this interplay are perhaps most clearly understood in terms of the distinction Thompson (1967:60) makes between task-oriented labour found in non-capitalist societies and time-measured labour found in capitalist societies. In the former, the demarcation between life and work is minimal, whereas in the latter, in which labour is timed by the clock, work and life are culturally constructed as separate realms of social experience. The significance of contract work for the Dhan-gadi has to be understood as a form of task-oriented social labour. It allows Dhan-gadi men to be their own bosses and to continue the pattern of intermingling life and work. It also allows their employers to fix wages to tasks rather than to time.

This is perhaps most apparent in the initial stage of Dhan-gadi incorporation into the European economy when work patterns and subsistence patterns were very similar. This was the time when Aboriginal groups moved from work site to work site and/or congregated in considerable numbers for lengthy periods at large contract sites. The second phase of incorporation corresponds less neatly to this pattern of work/life continuity in that it saw a significant change in the composition of the people at the work sites. It was no longer a case of 'we'd all shift there', men, women and children. Women and school children had to remain at Bellbrook reserve, and the work sites became the almost exclusive domain of the men. In some ways, however, this phase accentuated pre-existing cultural distinctions between Dhan-gadi men and women.

The work gangs were made up of 'fathers and sons and fellas who come out for help later', i.e. they were kinship based. Each gang was composed of a father (contractor) and his elder sons, and classificatory son's, brother's and sister's sons, or male siblings. The most distinctive thing about employment patterns during this period was that they became a separate male realm. Furthermore, as the continuity in the type of work ensured that the older men held the knowledge and work skills, it further accentuated adult male authority. As one man put it:

> They [fathers] used to take the boys out with them, to help 'em on the job, learn how to cook, what to eat and all that sort of thing. That's what they used to do them old people . . . You go out they learn you how to cook damper and all that, to cook wallaby, anythin' like that . . . They the first fella learn you all them things when you go out in the bush.

The work patterns that emerged tended to accentuate the division between men and women and reinforced the control that the 'older fellas' had over the young boys.

The incorporation of Dhan-gadi men into the European economy facilitated a certain continuity in social relations between men. The induction of young boys into working life occurred in the period when both gender differences and generational distinctions were given most cultural significance. Inclusion in the contract gangs coincided with the young boys' incorporation into the secret sacred world of 'men's business', the initiation ceremonies. As one put it, once initiated, he 'was goin' to be a man not silly anymore'. He further described the symbolic separation of young men from the work of children and women:

> They [initiates are] put on a big bundle of blankets, sit there in a row like that, about eight or nine boys. Men there ready to run away with you; hold you by the arm, and then your mother and sister have got the sticks ready and they throw sticks at you while you're goin' and they sing ya! ya! ya! Why they throw the stick is so you don't come back till you finish. That's the law.

Such ceremonies continually emphasise the distinctions between initiated men (as the possessors of secret/sacred cosmological knowledge) and women and children to whom such knowledge is never revealed.

The intrusion of European religious and secular education onto the reserve seemed to heighten further the distinction between Dhan-gadi and European ways of regarding gender. For a start, Christian and secular education were both taught by female missionaries, which effectively stood in opposition to the gender-specific forms of knowledge which underpinned the social and cosmological worlds of the Dhan-gadi. The authoritative position of the female missionary appeared to generate a response of avoidance by the men to her presence on the reserve. As the missionary's report stated, 'The missionary sees very little of the male part of her community just at present. Their consciences must be troubling them and consequently they give their missionary a wide berth.' (ML Q572 9901) When the report was written, the missionary had been in residence on the reserve for a relatively lengthy period, some 13 months.

Furthermore, the egalitarian access to Christian and secular knowledge cuts across the differential access to knowledge amongst the Dhan-gadi. This difference was manifested in the school context through the undercutting of established patterns of social interaction. There was brother/sister avoidance before, but as one woman put it, 'When they went to school like, we used to talk to our brothers. They were getting more the white man's way.' The differential patterns of social interaction associated with gender relations, expressed in this case through sister avoidance, are placed in conflict with the dominant society's egalitarian norms of interaction. What emerged in this conjuncture was a reconstitution of the significance of social space. There was a sharpening of the men/working sons – women/children distinction in terms of a differentiation between the reserve and the 'bush'.

Contract work was important not simply because it enabled Dhan-gadi men to be their own bosses, but also because the *bush* represented a specific social domain identified as an autonomous Aboriginal world. When men were 'put through the rule' what was emphasised was that they went *out in the bush* to which one man added, *'she (sister) don't go out in the bush, but I want out . . . I was put through'*. This view of the bush as a site for the collective reproduction of male cultural identity also extended to the work sites. As suggested earlier, the bush was where 'the first fella learn you all those things' to do with cooking and eating the right food. In addition, 'When they're out in the bush they sing the right song to suit the bush. You know, you wouldn't hear 'em when your home. They wouldn't sing the songs.'[1] In fact the work sites in the bush represented a distinctive world – a world quite separate from the Aborigines' living sites on the government reserve and from the wider European society in which they had been encapsulated. This was the world of the ideological reproduction of the Dhan-gadi men's cultural autonomy.

This identification with the bush also gained significance through the global encapsulation of the Dhan-gadi within a capitalist world. The recategorisation of social space occurred within the wider context of the transformation of the physical world as part of the domination by capitalist agriculture and pastoralism. The bush retained those aspects of a pre-existing 'totemic landscape'. Relations between human beings and the natural world are consubstantial and understood in terms of the personification of animate beings and inanimate objects which are endowed with a will, consciousness and efficacy analogous to humans. By contrast, the world of rural capitalism imposes a rational, symmetri-

---

1. One man recalled how when he was a young boy, 'We had those two fellas with us, they'd sing every night, every night, never miss a night. They'd be into it there. Sometimes they'd get a stick they would accompany with the singin' they would.'

cal ordering upon nature and a geometrical patterning across the landscape which signify property relations. In this world, human beings are dominant and the natural world subordinated to a means/ end relationship. The significance of the bush for Dhan-gadi men can be understood in terms of this radical transformation of their physical world. The work sites retained that continuity with the personalised pre-capitalist world. At the same time, such sites were an aspect of their domination, as the men were the principal agents of the transformation of that totemic landscape. The act of domination is associated with complicity in the destruction of the bush and thus the destruction of those essential objectifications of a distinctive cultural construction of self.

2.2. The Perpetuation of a Subsistence Ideology

The partial structural incorporation of the Dhan-gadi underpinned their participation in the local capitalist economy. Correspondingly, Dhan-gadi participation in the social relations of production must also be understood in terms of their partial subsumption. The dual role of worker/consumer, of labour exchanged for wages and wages exchanged for consumer goods, which characterises capitalist economies, is not simply a structural relationship. A capitalist economy, as Kahn (1981: 51) argues, is not 'a pure economy, an economy freed of its organic relation to culture and society'. It is also cultural and dependent on shared meanings and understandings. Such cultural categories not only define social relations, they also embody them.

Furthermore, the Dhan-gadi's world is also culturally ordered with understandings that give meaning to relationships and significance to objects and surroundings. According to Sahlins (1987), it is the 'contingent realisation' of these existing cultural understandings with the structural position that enables us to focus upon the 'unique actualisation' of such historical processes. At the level of consumption, a similarly complex interaction is apparent between the expectations of the Dhan-gadi and their participation in the European economy. From a superficial reading it would appear that the Dhan-gadi perception of employment was more instrumental and goal-oriented than that of a European. This is seen, for example, in statements such as, 'I had 25/- I cleared, I had to go to the Kempsey Show. I bought a shirt, sandshoes and a pair of trousers out of it and went to the show with it.' Such an instrumental approach to employment also appears to be confirmed by the many complaints by Europeans that in the past they had more Aborigines hanging around willing to work at show time than they had jobs to give them.

Yet, such a representation can only be sustained through an implied internalisation of instrumental rationality, albeit in a primitive or naive form, or, alternatively, as evidence of the universal aspect of instrumental rationality. Attributing an instrumental rationality to the Dhangadi, however, needs some qualification, as it provides a subtle yet pervasive way of reducing Aborigines to a psychological facsimile of European workers.[2] Such instrumental attitudes need to be separated out from the principle of utility, which is constitutive, and constitutive of, the forms of sociality within capitalist culture: that is, the quantification of the relations of exchange, i.e. personal worth reduced to exchange value. Furthermore, in capitalist culture instrumental rationality does not simply govern an understanding of the economic sphere, but is seen to be a contingent feature of all human activity (see Godelier 1972). It is the common sense of political economy and, as such, has achieved a universal and homogenising character. It is one thing to argue that the principle of utility was the force that transformed the social and physical world of the Dhan-gadi, but quite another to suggest it created a new moral universe.

Such contractual forms of economic interaction had neither substantially penetrated nor destroyed the patterns of sociality of the Dhangadi. By contrast, underpinning the sale of Aboriginal labour as a commodity of exchange is a subsistence ideology operating within a capitalist economy. The instrumental or goal-oriented perceptions of employment of Dhan-gadi men are an extension into a capitalist economy of a subsistence ideology geared to the securing of particular goods for their use value.

The perpetuation of a subsistence ideology was in part conditioned by the specificities of the incorporation of the Dhan-gadi into the local economy. As we have seen, the local economy relied on the Dhan-gadi to provision themselves independently for a substantial period of the year, especially in the spring/summer when their labour was not required. Therefore, participation may be seen to supplement traditional subsistence sources rather than to arise from dependency on returns from exchange relations with local employers. The general diet of the Dhan-gadi throughout this period retained a large amount of traditional foodstuffs. Wallaby (*bulgun*), pademelons (*mani*) and possums (*willai* and *wittai*) were regular sources of 'wild meat' at Bellbrook, while the wallaroo (*yindabai*) was also regularly eaten at Lower Creek. The other staple source of protein was from the river: mullet (*mundarr*), perch (*gubirr*) and catfish (*wiland*) were regularly eaten along with eel

---

2. The perception of the individual in terms of 'a bundle of preferences axiomatised by principles of self-interest and rationality' (Evens 1987) has been a prominent analytical approach in Aboriginal studies. The most recent has been Williams and Hunn (1982). In my own approach, I have taken the position of Mauss (1979) and Dumont (1972) that the notion of the individual is a distinctive feature of western thought. In this, it is argued that the constitution of personal identity, the notion of the individual, is not a pre-given entity.

(*barruwa*) and tortoise (*dhawarra*). These food items, gained by spontaneous appropriation from the immediate environment, provided the basis of the Dhan-gadi economy. The relations of exchange that predominated within the Dhan-gadi economy were associated with the production of use values, and these largely remained an unmediated process of direct appropriation from the environment.

The structure of the Dhan-gadi economy may be described as a 'mixed economy'. The engagement with Europeans in the mediated relations of exchange within the local economy was to secure such goods as flour, tea, sugar, tobacco and alcohol. Their use was described tautologically as 'when you had 'em'. It would seem evident that such items as flour, tea and sugar did become a regular part of the Dhan-gadi diet (see Chapter 4). For the most part, however, the satisfaction of the 'natural needs' of the Dhan-gadi was sustained through traditional food sources. It is possible to speculate that such European goods, carbohydrates and beverages, were categorically separated from 'natural' traditional foods and regarded as 'luxury' items procured in excess of 'needs'. 'Natural needs' were premised upon a continuity of culturally constituted priorities. (Indeed, it would be surprising if a radical shift in the composition of the diet occurred in an unproblematic way. This is more fully discussed in Chapter 4.) In this, there is a disjuncture evident in the worker/consumer relationship which is distinctively different from that manifested generally within the capitalist economy.

Within this mixed economy capitalist relations did not overwhelm existing understandings or totally disrupt pre-existing subsistence patterns. The limited penetration partially occurred as a result of giving Aborigines rations and the subsequent practice of issuing 'subs', i.e. extending credit to Aborigines prior to the job commencing. As one man described the practice, 'You'd get an order off the boss, you'd go over with that order, take that to the shop and then you pick out what you want then, flour, sugar, tea and baking powder. You go into the shop throw it on the counter, right. Just the bosses name on it that's all.' The men would then 'cut it out' on the job. The point is that money was not the medium of exchange in this relationship, rather what a job secured was access to certain goods.

In the situation where money was used as the medium of exchange, the general continuation of a subsistence ideology within the sphere of distribution of goods ensured that any intrinsic value attached to money was eroded. Distribution was based on relations of kinship and co-residence. As it was put to me, 'You'd come along and ask aunty or uncle do they want some of this *bulgun* (wallaby) here, or you'd share it up. You'd say, this is for there, this is for there, like that see. You'd only have enough to eat yourself. You didn't think about tomorrow.' Here, production is geared towards facilitating one's immediate needs. Furthermore, the distribution of such foods is constituted by, and constitutive of, the maintenance of patterns of sociality associated with the flow of such foodstuffs. The social relations of distribution remained dominated by kinship and personalised relationships.

The pattern of consumption associated with the subsistence ideology of the Dhan-gadi was maintained despite the local capitalist economy of the Macleay Valley being dominated by the production of exchange values (in which goods – commodities – are produced for their exchange value rather than for their use value). Friedman (1983: 32) argues that this quantification of exchange relations of the production process is associated with 'the breakdown of kinship relations to varying degrees and the establishment of new forms of *extra-kinship dependencies* mediated by bureaucratic abstractions, property and money'. Furthermore, personal relations, especially in the economic sphere, are converted into exchange relations. Contract work, however, enabled the Dhan-gadi to perpetuate their traditional kinship/personal relations, and the establishment of personal relations with employers formed a significant aspect of the pattern of Aboriginal employment. As one man put it, 'Different families, different places they worked. Some families may go to Towal Creek, some might go to Pee Dee, some might go to Burraga.' Embodied in the Dhan-gadi work pattern were a number of personal relations with European employers, which the Europeans usually took for Aboriginal loyalty. This emphasis on personal rather than on exchange relations within work groups and with European employers was a characteristic feature of the Dhan-gadi's involvement in the European economy.

The Dhan-gadi's incorporation into the local capitalist economy produced a complex web of interactions between the Dhan-gadi and the Europeans. The seeming instrumental rationality which characterised the economic nexus does, however, require some clarification to be useful. Unqualified, such understandings ultimately rely on a universal notion of instrumental rationality to sustain such characterisations, i.e. the pursuit of personal gain or advantage. In other words, the cultural categories of the dominant society are used as if they were analytical tools. An example of these different cultural expectations can be seen in an account by a European of the nuisance an Aboriginal man became in his later life. The man had been employed on a property over a number of decades to plough and tend the corn crops. The problem arose when he continued to turn up for work each year long after he had lost his usefulness or capacity to work, and he became a real source of annoyance because, although he spent most of his time there sleeping in the shade, he expected to be paid. For the man, the personal relationship formed the basis of the contract, whereas for the European the contractual arrangement was purely instrumental and not based on their long personal association.

The marginal role of the Dhan-gadi in the European economy produced a particular pattern of social interaction. The social forces which produced this marginalisation also enabled the Dhan-gadi to develop some degree of autonomy within which to reproduce the common-sense world of their own culture, understanding and social practices. The development of a mixed economy failed to engender a quantification of social relations amongst them; *direct interpersonal ties* predominated and not the quantification of such relations through the mediation of money. As the following illustrates, 'They'd buy food and they'd share the food with 'em. Mighten exactly give 'em the money but they'd share the food with 'em or say "come on over, we've got enough tucker here". Like that see.' Hence, money is not the medium of exchange *per se* but rather a means towards gaining access to goods within the European economy. The quantification of social relationships was not a marked feature of the economic relations of the Dhan-gadi. Thus, money was transformed into goods to facilitate the demands of reciprocity within the Dhan-gadi community. In effect, the quantification of exchange relations was restricted to the wider society. The functioning of this mixed economy was generated by capitalism but remained distinctly non-capitalist throughout this period.

Chapter 3

Encapsulation, Involution and the Reconstitution of Social Life

Culture contact, it can be argued, is synonymous with cultural growth. The incorporation of the Dhan-gadi into the European economy in-duced innovation and produced something new. The Dhan-gadi dem-onstrated a large degree of flexibility in acquiring new social and cultural forms, but this was not extended to other spheres of social life. The question of social change needs to be located within the broader context of social reproduction. The transforming power of culture contact upon the Dhan-gadi is quite clear. It is, however, also clear that Europeans were not subjected to such transforming power. The simple point is that such social changes were determined, not by participation in cultural exchange, but by the practice of imperialism.The one-way flow of change was in fact governed by the unequal power relations which existed between the two groups.

These unequal relations of domination cannot be understood simply in terms of the active deployment of coercive/repressive colonial power. Colonial control was not simply achieved by conquest through violence but also through legal, bureaucratic and democratic pro-cedures. Colonisation did not simply limit indigenous rights, as it had elsewhere, but denied their existence. Similarly, the legal processes did not curtail or restrict ownership of traditionally-held lands, but denied ownership completely. I am less concerned here with these legal processes, however, than I am with the indirect and pernicious effects of the extensive Europeanisation of the Dhan-gadi's social world that such processes enabled. The extensive nature of the dispossession effectively resulted in the increasing physical and social isolation of Aboriginal groups, which was an equally important aspect in breaking down and reshaping the social existence of the Dhan-gadi. An immedi-ate consequence for the Dhan-gadi and surrounding Aboriginal groups was that significant constraints were placed upon intra-group and inter-group relations. The physical and social isolation of such groups ultimately led to the disintegration of pre-existing social practices premised on inter-group relations. We are therefore looking not at the reproduction of the Dhan-gadi as an autonomous community (which in any case did not appear to have happened historically) but at the political creation of a reified community. As a result, Dhan-gadi ceremonial life and marriage relations underwent a process of involution. The historically-created community was increasingly forced to rely on its own social and human resources.

The most pervasive force on the decline of inter-group relations was the Europeanisation of the pre-existing physical, social and material world. The dramatic reshaping of the social landscape directly and indirectly affected the basic tenets of social existence. In the Macleay Valley, the pre-existing 'totemic landscape' was radically transformed into the rationally-ordered landscape that conformed to the economic imperatives of rural production. Similarly, as European settlement consolidated itself in the Macleay Valley, the movement of Aborigines outside the reserve was increasingly mediated through economic relations with Europeans. As we have seen, the occupation of land for any period of time outside reserves required the consent of European property owners. This was usually gained through employment. The most dramatic changes to the Dhan-gadi's social world during this period did not result from active political repression, but from the thoroughgoing usurpation of their physical world.

3.1. The Post-Frontier Context

In the 1840s, Hodgkinson states, there were 'six distinct tribes' situated along the banks of the Macleay River, each numbering between 60 and 80 adults. Belshaw (1978: 73) calculates that the inclusion of children in these figures would have brought the number of men, women and children in the valley up to between 660 and 840. The two tribes on the upper Macleay River with which this chapter is concerned, would have numbered between 160 and 180 adults. These figures would be higher if they included what Hodgkinson (1845: 222) refers to as the 'several others [tribes] near the sources of the river amongst the mountains'. Comparatively high populations have also been recorded for the Aboriginal tribes in the immediate vicinity of the Dhan-gadi. These social groups include the Gumbaingirr speakers to the north of the Dhangadi, the Anewan to the west, Birripai to the south and the Ngaku and Ngumbar speakers of the east (see Map 4). MacDougall (1900/1: 116) estimates that the pre-conquest population between the Bellinger and the Clarence Rivers (Gumbaingirr) was between 1,200 and 1,500 people. The evidence for the Aboriginal population on the northern tablelands is slight. Walker (1962: 2), citing MacDonald, suggests that the total population for this relatively harsh and difficult environment was

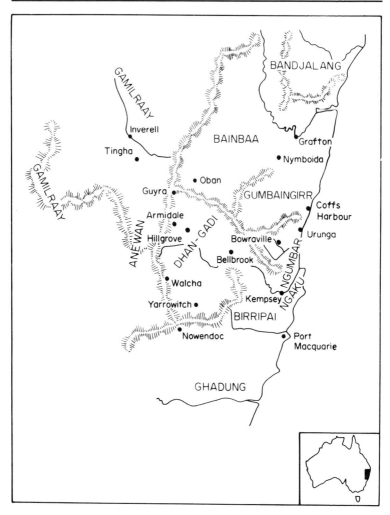

Map 4. Social and Linguistic Groups of the North Coast Region

around 500 to 600. This included the inland Gumbaingirr speakers, the Anewan, and the Bain Baa. No figures survive for the coastal and inland Birripai.[1]

The available figures of numbers in the post-contact period (1892)

1. There survives little evidence of the Birripai. The only evidence available comes from references by Curr (1886: 338) and Radcliffe-Brown (1929: 400) who describes them as 'the tribe on the Hastings River'. One exception is in a brief work by Enright (1932: 102), who elicited information from people whom he described as 'the four Aborigines living who

bear mute witness to the ravages that colonisation brought to the Aborigines of the region. The telegraph master in charge of Aborigines on Bellbrook put their numbers at about 50 men, women and children, which is a significant decrease from the figures recorded by Hodgkinson in the 1840s (see Chapter 1). Similar figures of massive population losses can be found for other groups in the immediate vicinity of the Dhan-gadi. The population of the Gumbaingirr, which had occupied the coastal belt between the Nambucca and Clarence Rivers had been reduced to 569 by 1891 (NSW Leg. Ass., V and P 1892: 1,117–18). This included the district south of the Clarence River to Nymboida (419), Bellingin and Fernmount (55) and, adjacent to the Dhan-gadi, Macksville and Bowraville (122). These three government districts made up roughly the original Gumbaingirr linguistic area. On the northern tablelands, adjacent to the Dhan-gadi, the statistical evidence reveals a similar drop in the population. Only 129 Aborigines still remained on the tablelands (ibid. p. 1,118). In short, the colonisation of the northern coastal region had a dramatic effect on the indigenous population. It was with these two adjacent groups, as I will show later, that the Dhan-gadi on the upper Macleay had most contact.[2]

Pre-existing inter-group relations were further undermined by government policy. In the post-conflict period, official government policy sought to centralise the remaining small groups of Aborigines on reserves throughout the north coast region. Reserves were established as part of a rudimentary policy seeking to control the remaining population through their segregation and concentration. The Aborigines Protection Board (APB) was created in 1883 to administer a comprehensive state-wide system of control (see Chapter 5). The concentration of Aborigines on reserves, as discrete communities, was seen as a necessary condition of such control. By 1892, Aboriginal groups were found scattered throughout the north coast region on a number of officially-allocated reserves (see Table 6).

These small reserves remained the only land formally set aside for Aborigines.[3] The extensiveness of European political and economic

---

spoke Birripai'. The language of the Birripai, according to Enright, 'differs little from Kattang (Ghadung), but the former I find was spoken by people who had class divisions (matrimoieties and sections) for marriage purposes, but the Kattang (Ghadung) had no such divisions' (ibid.).

2. My own informants confirmed that in earlier generations the Dhan-gadi had close relations with the Birripai and a number of the older generation were fluent speakers in Dhan-gadi and Birripai.

3. State control of the upper Macleay Dhan-gadi began with the creation of Nulla Nulla Reserve (later Bellbrook) in 1885. The first report stated that, 'On Nulla Nulla Creek ten able-bodied blacks with their families have settled, having built themselves comfortable quarters, and are clearing the Reserve (40 acres). Mr Toose, the telegraph master, looks after them. A great improvement in their condition.' (NSW Leg. Ass., V and P 1885, vol. 2: 606). By 1892, the following report of Aborigines on Bellbrook was recorded. It stated that they were on '65 acres, situated 44 miles from Kempsey. About 20 acres of [this was] open

Table 6. Aboriginal Reserves of the North Coast Region (1892)

Reserve	Area
Clarence River:	
1. Nymboida River	61 hectares
2. Orara River	46 hectares
3. Yamba	73 hectares
4. Grafton	61 hectares
5. Lawrence	34 hectares
6. Iluka	40 hectares
7. South Grafton	49 hectares
8. Grafton	80 hectares
9. Copmanhurst	65 hectares
Bellingin District:	
1. Island Bellingin Heads	101 hectares
Nambucca District:	
1. Brushy Island	28 hectares
2. Macksville	8 hectares
Macleay River District:	
1. Gladstone	5 hectares
2. Gladstone	1 hectare
3. Kinchela	11 hectares
4. Pelican Island	32 hectares
5. Fattorinni Islands	17 hectares
6. Shark Island	146 hectares
*7. Nulla Nulla	26 hectares
8. Sherwood	73 hectares
Armidale District:	
1. Walcha	130 hectares

* only reserve on upper Macleay River
Sources: NSW Leg. Ass., V and P 1892: 1,117–18

hegemony reduced the Dhan-gadi, along with other regional groups, to a *territorial minority* within the domains of their own traditionally-held lands. The almost total expropriation of the 3,308.95 square kilometres of land in the valley left only 498 hectares within nine government reserves by 1892 (see Table 6).

country, well grassed and suitable for vegetable and fruit trees, the remainder is rich scrub land suitable for maize, sugar cane and pumpkins. The fence enclosing the land was destroyed by bush fires, but material is being prepared by the Aborigines to refence it with a good two rail fence. About 10 acres has been cleared and more is being prepared for the coming crop – maize, pumpkins and potatoes. It is occupied by 5 Aborigines, who have two bark huts erected on it.' (ibid. 1891–92, vol. 7: 405).

3.2. The Decline of Inter-group Relations

There are insufficient data to analyse the changes that occurred in the late nineteenth century. I therefore propose to begin with the period between approximately 1910 and 1932 which, apart from coinciding with my Aboriginal informants' earliest recollections, was a time when power relations between the Aboriginal community and the state remained constant. It was also a time when the control of communities was maintained through the sporadic interventions of the local police (see Chapter 5).

The treatment of Aborigines as a homogeneous mass, in relation either to European society or to the pre-contact situation, sheds little light on the processes of social change and reproduction (cf. Rowley 1973; Broome 1982; Lippmann 1981). Because Aboriginal groups were differentiated, it is impossible to understand 'traditional Aborigines' in any specified region without reference to inter-group and intra-group structures. Likewise, it is also useful to differentiate between these two structural domains in analysing the transformations resulting from colonial domination. The perpetuation and modification of cultural forms grounded in inter-group activities were primarily determined within the social and political context of domination.

The articulation of three factors, (1) the disruptive effects of colonisation and depopulation, (2) the progressive confinement of Aboriginal residence onto government reserves and (3) the economic occupation of the social and material world outside the reserves, will be considered here in relation to the disintegration of inter-group relations. My focus shall be on the movement from exogamous to endogamous marriages and the decline of inter-group participation in initiation ceremonies held by the Dhan-gadi and other groups. I will be dealing with marriage relations and ceremonial life separately for heuristic purposes and because of the limitations of the available evidence. I do not thereby imply that they are separate realms of inter-group activity. Yengoyan (1970) and Sackett (1975/6), amongst others, make the marriage/ritual connections clear in relation to Western Desert Aborigines.[4] As Sackett (ibid. p. 44) succinctly states, 'Because of the rule of exogamy, marriages were arranged between groups – especially during ritual gatherings. The prescribed rule of marriage was to a *njuba* . . . who was ideally a daughter of the MB (mother's brother) or sister of the MBS/FSS

---

4. The works of Yengoyan (1970) and Sackett (1975/6) are particularly relevant as points of contrast. Both authors are concerned with changes in marriage relations as a result of the immobilisation of Aboriginal groups in the post-Second World War period. What is significantly different about their research is that they are working in areas where ritual life has remained a feature of the social life of the region. Similarly, they are dealing with relatively large communities, 350–450 in Ernabella (Yengoyan 1970: 72) and 355 in Wiluna (Sackett 1975/6: 47). The regions have not undergone dramatic transformation and, numerically, the Aboriginal populations are much larger than those of the Europeans.

(mother's brother's son/father's sister's son) who performed a man's initiations.' The maintenance of marriage arrangements and initiation ceremonies are closely interrelated. I stress the distinction, however, not because I wish to consider the nature of Dhan-gadi marriage patterns and ceremonies *per se*, but because I am interested in how their decline indicates a process of involution, which occurred as a result of the increasing isolation of this small group (its population was only 89 in 1900) on the upper Macleay River.

3.2(a) *The decline of 'right sort' marriages*

The only significant work carried out on these marriage and descent systems has been that of Mathews (1897; 1900/1). He concludes that for these New England and coastal tribes, 'the rules of marriage and descent are precisely the same as among the four sections of the Kamilaroi (Gamilraay)' (1897: 169).[5] Furthermore, Mathews (1900/1: 41) states that 'to each of the phratries (moieties) . . . there is an aggregate of totems attached, consisting of animals, plants, and inanimate objects, and descent is counted on the female side'. From this it would appear that the Dhan-gadi were divided into matri-moieties and clans.[6]

In terms of the matri-moieties, the mother-child pair of sections were in one moiety while the father belonged to a section in the other moiety. As people put it today, 'you got your marriage kind from your mother'. Section members were differentiated according to sex. In one matri-moiety, the sections were Garbungani/Gurangani and Marung-gani/Gargangani and in the other Wirunggani/Wanggangani and Wambunggani/Wirigangani (Mathews 1897: 169; 1900/1: 41; see also Appendix 1). Marriage was prescribed between sections as in Diagram A.

With regard to kinship categories associated with marriage, Mathews's information is inadequate. He simply states (1894: 25–6; 1897: 168) that a man marries the female children of an actual or classificatory father's

---

5. Prior to colonial occupation, matrilineal moieties, divided into four sections, were established throughout the major part of NSW. The system was common amongst various Aboriginal groups in north-western NSW, the major area that these matri-moieties covered being the vast inland area east of the Darling River and north of the Murray River where they were found amongst the Gamilraay in the north and the Wiradjeri in the south (Mathews 1894; 1897). While firmly entrenched to the west of the Great Dividing Range, the system would appear to have only penetrated to the coast in the three river valleys mentioned earlier. Elkin (1976: 208) speculates that this section system had spread from the Gamilraay on the western slopes of north-western NSW.

6. Mathews (1897: 169–70) states that, 'There is a group of totems common to Kurpoong and Marroong (Garbungani/Marunggani) – or as they are called on New England, Irpoong and Marroong – among which may be enumerated the native bear, flying-fox, plover, ground iguana, black opossum, emu, bee, native companion, yam, pelican, porcupine, perch. The Wirroong and Womboong (Wirunggani/Wambunggani) sections – called on New England Irroong and Imboong – have the following totems amongst others: kangaroo, dingo, jew lizard, turtle, carpet snake, crow, white cockatoo, platypus, eaglehawk, locust, death-adder.'

Diagram A. Matrilineal Moieties

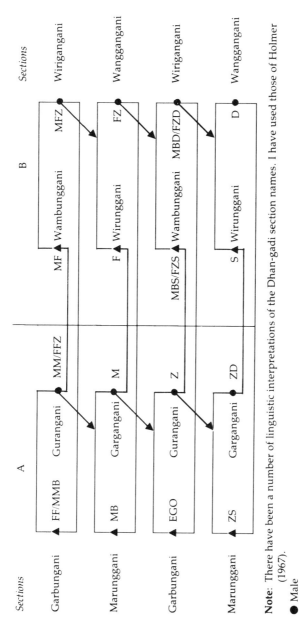

Sections	A				B		Sections
Garbungani	◀ FF/MMB	Gurangani	● MM/FFZ		MF	Wambunggani ◀	● MFZ	Wirigangani
Marunggani	◀ MB	Gargangani	● M		F	Wirunggani ◀	● FZ	Wanggangani
Garbungani	◀ EGO	Gurangani	● Z		MBS/FZS	Wambunggani ◀	● MBD/FZD	Wirigangani
Marunggani	◀ ZS	Gargangani	● ZD		S	Wirunggani ◀	● D	Wanggangani

Note: There have been a number of linguistic interpretations of the Dhan-gadi section names. I have used those of Holmer (1967).

● Male
▲ Female

sister or mother's brother. His perfunctory treatment of kinship terminology (1894: 25) was based on his belief that marriage was contracted
between groups. It was only in the later work of Radcliffe-Brown (1930)
that some attempt to clarify the relationship between kinship categories
and preferred marriage partners was made. He argues that the Gumbaingirr type of kinship system, which included the Dhan-gadi, Bain
Baa, Ngambar and Ngaku, was related to, but different from, the
Kariera system in which marriage rules are based on preferred cross-
cousin marriage, for example, mother's brother's daughter or father's
sister's daughter. As Radcliffe-Brown (1930: 52) states, 'In these (Gumbaingirr type groups) the classification of kindred is like that of the
Kariera type into two lines of descent. A man marries the daughter of a
man who is classified as "mother's brother", but he may not marry the
children of a near "mother's brother" or a near "father's sister"'. The
major difference was that marriage between 'near' mother's brother or
'near' father's sister was formally proscribed.

For my purposes here, the available evidence on kinship terminology
is too fragmentary to be pursued. My concern is with the matri-moiety/
section system where evidence exists to chart the changes in marriage
relations between generations. I would stress, however, that moiety
sections do not solely determine marriages (see Elkin 1933; Yengoyan
1970; and Sackett 1975/6). As I indicate, marriages are ultimately determined on the basis of kinship and genealogical considerations. The
correctness/incorrectness of section marriages pursued here is directed
towards an indication of something else, namely the movement towards
endogamous marriages. The evidence for this comes from two sources:
the biographical details recorded in Radcliffe-Brown's (1928/9) fieldnotes, including the names, section names, kin terms and totems of
Dhan-gadi men and women; and genealogical information from my
own research. These sources provide the basis for my consideration of
the rules of descent and right sort marriages which were still in
operation at the turn of the century.

The Dhan-gadi understanding of the origins of the Bellbrook community is traced through the knowledge of particular family histories
and their genealogical intricacies. This domestic history is traced back
by them to an original family or individual and his/her association with
Bellbrook in the post-frontier period (nineteenth century). The available genealogical evidence suggests a large degree of mobility for most
of the Aboriginal population in the area. It is said that people moved in
the area of Rollands Plain, Nowendoc, Walcha, Armidale and Bellbrook. Four of the major families today are descended from two
brothers, Lear and Unwin and their sister, Quinn (all fictitious names).
Each of the children (of the latter) had the same mother but a different
father. Quinn was born at Nowendoc, Lear at Hillgrove and Unwin at
Bellbrook. The marriage pattern for this generation followed a similarly

dispersed pattern: Quinn = △ Rich (Hillgrove) and then = △ Dean
(Wee Waa), while Unwin = ○ (Armidale) and Lear = ○ (Bellbrook).
Of the other main families, Thomas = ○ (Yarrowitch), Nile = ○ (unknown), and Ivy = ○ (Bellbrook). The other main family is traced to a
man, Wynn (Lachlan River) = ○ (Bellbrook). Some individuals also
moved out of Bellbrook, as was the case with a woman named Woods
= △ (Walcha) and with her brother who moved to Walcha as well
and Thomas (brother above) who lived in Urunga (see Map 4).

With regard to rules of descent and 'right sort' marriages, the information provided by Radcliffe-Brown shows that Quinn, Unwin and
Lear are recorded in terms of section names as siblings, Gargangani
and Marunggani respectively. Furthermore, the two husbands of
Quinn, Rich and Dean, are recorded as Wirunggani. (Dean's section
name is recorded as Appai, the Gamilraay equivalent of Wirunggani.)
The biographical details recorded by Radcliffe-Brown also provide the
evidence to map out the pattern of marriages in the following generation. Primarily, this is because the details recorded were of the children of Quinn's marriages who figured prominently in marriages
between families in Bellbrook.

The pattern of descent in terms of matri-moieties and marriages
between sections of different moieties would appear to have been
maintained. The children of Quinn's marriages to Rich and Dean that
are recorded follow the mother-child sections of one moiety. That is,
the mother was Gargangani and her children were Garbungani/
Gurangani (see Diagram A). Holmer (1967) also records one of the
daughters of Quinn's second marriage as Gurangani. The marriage
patterns of this second generation reveal a similar conformity. The two
male children of Quinn/Rich married two sisters from another Bellbrook family, the Wynns. Although the women's section name is not
recorded their brother's is, as Wambunggani. Therefore, as siblings,
they would have been Wiriganggani. Further corroborating evidence is
found in the next generation where two of the female children of one of
the Rich/Wynn marriages are recorded as having the section name
Wanggangani. Both in terms of descent and marriage the pattern
conforms with the functioning of matri-moieties and sections.

The careers of the children of the marriage between Quinn/Dean are
important as they reflect a wider conformity of marriage patterns in the
second generation. Quinn/Dean had seven children (two boys and five
girls). It is the women's marriages that are important here. Four of the
young women married men from Bellbrook, while the other sister
married a man from Kempsey. The men involved in the internal
marriages, Nile, Ebony, Ivy and Wynn, according to Radcliffe-Brown's
material, all belonged to the section Wambunggani. In the case of the
out-marriage, the man's section name was recorded as Wambunggani.
In terms of the genealogical evidence, the matrilineal aspects of the

section system is further reinforced by the fact that Nile and Ebony were half-brothers who had the same mother.

In this second generation the adjustment of social relations to meet the exigencies of the post-frontier context does not reflect a radical departure from pre-existing marriage patterns. What emerges, however, is a high percentage of in-marriages (60 per cent). Of the 30 people involved in marriages, 12 married out while 18 married within the community. This preponderant pattern of in-marriages, which continued in the third generation, effectively made the functioning of the matri-moiety system and section marriages unviable. In effect, there was a shift in emphasis away from section regulated marriages to an avoidance of 'close' marriages.

What occurred in the third generation was a scrupulous selection of eligible marriage partners within the community, regardless of section. Of the 52 people involved in marriages, 32 (62 per cent) married within the community, while 20 (38 per cent) married outside the community. With this continued pattern of in-marriages, it was important to avoid those 'wrong' marriages that were regarded as more heinous than others, for example close genealogically-related first cousins, or, what is called today, 'marrying like royalty'. The emphasis on avoiding 'close' marriages rather than 'right sort' marriages can be seen in Diagrams B (1) and B (2). Of the 11 marriages (two are repeated), presented in Diagrams B (1) and B (2), only one conforms to the correct section marriage. This, I would suggest, is a result of the narrowing of the choice of marriage partners which occurred in this generation.

'Wrong marriages' are not in themselves considered significant here, but the number of them is. In this regard, all marriages were not always 'right sort' marriages. In his fieldnotes, Elkin (1940) records the case of a Dhan-gadi man whose father had married 'wrong' (Marunggani married Gurangani instead of Wanggangani). As a result, the man was known as Marunggani (following mother's section), but was alternatively known as Wambunggani (the section he would have been if his father had married correctly). The section classification was simply realigned in the next generation to meet both possibilities.

In effect, Aborigines cannot be seen as social automatons rigidly adhering to immutable rules of conduct. There was always room for manoeuvre and flexibility in such rules of marriage. Nevertheless, as Hiatt (1965), Yengoyan (1970), Meggitt (1972) and Sackett (1975/6) report in other areas, there was also a high degree of conformity to such rules.

The pattern of marriages over three generations reveals a pattern of involution which ultimately made the pre-existing system impossible to sustain. The political factors inherited through colonial domination, i.e. the disruption of inter-group relations, depopulation and the increasing immobilisation and isolation of such groups, ensured that a tend-

Diagram B (1)* Changes in Pattern of Matrimoiety Marriages

Marung △ = ○ Wanggan   Garbun △ = ○ Wirigan   Wirung △ = ○ ×Armid.   Garbun △ = ○ ×Kemp.   Garbun △ = ○ Wirigan

		Wirung △				Wirung △ =				○ Wirigan

Wirigan ○ = ... Wirung △ =
Wirigan ○ = △ ×Kemp.   Wirung △ = ... ○ Gargan   Wirung △ = ...   ○ Wanggan
Wirigan ○ = △ ×Burra.   Wirung △ = ... ○ Gargan   Wirung △ ≠   Wanggan ○ = △×
Wirigan ○ = △ ×Armid.   Wirung △ = ...   Wanggan ○   Wanggan ○ = △×
Wambun △ = ... Wanggan ○   ○×
Wambun △ = ... Wanggan ○   △ +
Wambun △ = ○ ×Walcha   Wanggan ○ = △ ×Burra.   △ +
Wambun △ = ○ ×Armid.   △ +
Wambun △ ≠

Correct Section Marriages – Nil

= marriage
... marriage partners
≠ did not marry
+ marriage in
× marriage out
* The details of family structures presented here have been altered to protect the anonymity of the families involved.

Diagram B (2)* Changes in Pattern of Matrimoiety Marriages

×○ = △ Wirung   Guran ○ = △ Wambun   Guran ○ = △ Wambun   Wirigan ○ = △ ×Walcha   Wirigan ○ = △ Garbun

Garbun △ = ... ○ Gargan
Garbun △ = ... ○ Gargan   ○ Gargan
Garbun △ = ... ○ ×Bary.   △ ×Wood.
Guran   ○ = △ ×Kemp.   Marung △ = ...   △ Wanggan

							△ Wirung

Guran   ○ = ... △ Wirung
Guran   ○ = ... △ +
                                                           ○ +
                                                           ○ +
                                                           ○ ×

Correct Section marriages – One

ency towards involution was inevitable. The effects of these factors on the social life of the Dhan-gadi made the reproduction of marriage rules, premised on inter-group relations, increasingly difficult to sustain. The community had to rely more on its own human resources to facilitate marriages.

The situation on Bellbrook reserve was specifically related to the interplay of a number of social and political factors. In the case of the Aborigines in the far west of NSW described by Beckett (1965), the interplay of these same factors led to somewhat different consequences. As Beckett points out, the initial situation of the Aborigines at Carowra Tank reserve was similar to that of Bellbrook. The small group of Carowra Tank Aborigines was very much interrelated (descended from three sisters), but the isolation of this small group was broken as a result of state policies concentrating different groups onto government settlements. Aborigines from Hillston and then the Darling River peoples were resettled at Carowra Tank. Unlike the Dhan-gadi, the movement from exogamy to endogamy in this case occurred between different social groups within the bounded reserve community.[7]

3.2(b) *The end of the initiation ceremonies*

The significance of the initiation ceremonies on the north coast is that they continued long after ceremonial life had ended in other parts of NSW. Like the marriage rules, the initiation ceremonies underwent a process of involution with the disintegration of inter-group relations. Their decline was not the simple result of direct forms of political repression, which had occurred in other parts of NSW (see Fink 1955; Mathews 1977), but an indirect consequence of domination manifested through the Europeanisation of their social and material world. The effects of immobilisation upon small Aboriginal groups reduced ritual contact activity and the transmission of esoteric ritual knowledge between groups. Similarly, the radically-transformed physical and social landscape ensured that such ceremonies lost the context of their meaning. In their perpetuation, the Dhan-gadi attempted to sustain themselves as a separate entity in a social world in which Aboriginal identity was problematical.

---

7. Furthermore, as Beckett (1965: 20) points out, in later years these Aborigines married out as an effective means of avoiding close marriages. Of 119 marriages, some 89 (75 per cent) 'were contracted with a spouse who originated from a different locality'. This was very much the result of increased mobility which occurred in the post-Second World War period (ibid.). This pattern closely corresponds to the fourth generation at Bellbrook in the same period. This is reflected in both the percentage of out marriages and the diversity of their locations. Out of 59 people, only 17 (29 per cent) married within the community, while 42 (71 per cent) married out. The lower number of people recorded in this generation also reflects this increased mobility as families moved to Port Macquarie and to the major urban centres of Newcastle and Sydney. The pattern reflected a reversal of earlier ones.

Throughout Aboriginal Australia, the reproduction of ritual life provides the central tenet of existence and identity. The main ritual practices are carried out in the initiation ceremonies through which young men gain the secret/sacred knowledge of the 'truth' about mythology and cult heroes. Initiation ceremonies 'represent above all the revelation of the sacred . . . the whole body of the tribe's mythology and cultural traditions' (Eliade 1965: 3). They involve both revelatory and transcendental forms of knowledge which invest individuals not only with the 'truth', but also with the power to manage/manipulate mystical forces and objects. These ceremonies are important in the reproduction of social relations within and between social groups. It is through them that the initiate's relationships to other men, to women and to children, as well as to the world, are transformed. As one of them explained to me, 'Any boy, young boys, or even men that's old up to 70, 80 or 90 that hasn't been initiated is all kids to us.' In effect, not to be initiated was to be a *guruman*, the Dhan-gadi word for 'know nothing'. The difference was not simply in the possession of some higher form of understanding or truth, but in the experience, knowledge and ability to control mystical forces. This was what differentiated men and separated them from women and children who were excluded from initiation.

The initiation ceremonies of the Dhan-gadi were collectively known as the *Kiparra*. There were four differently ranked levels of initiation, the *Garunda, Wallungurr, Murrawon* and *Dilkirr*. The *Dilkirr* was an inaugural ceremony which required initiation at a full *Kiparra* before such young men were regarded as properly initiated. The full ceremonies, the *Garunda, Wallungurr* and *Murrawon*, were ranked respectively in a descending order of importance. The pattern of internal differentiation was expressed to me in terms of the differences between a *Wallungurr* and *Murrawon* man. The former, 'He's the elder, the elder of the lot of us and he's our boss. He's been put through the rule six times and that makes him a very high man. He's over me, over P, . . . He's got a brother in Bellbrook just the same [*Wallungurr*] as he is.' There was, however, no set sequence through which an initiate had to pass, for either a *Murrawon* or a *Wallungurr* were eligible to become *Garunda* (see also Lane (1978) on the Gumbaingirr people). For men to be regarded as 'cleva fellas', what Elkin (1977) calls 'Aboriginal men of high degree', there was an additional ceremony to pass through which involved seclusion and more individualised rites and training. Elkin (1977: 79–80) states that, among the Ghadung (to the immediate south), it was encumbent on the man to have passed through the highest stage of initiation before he could become a 'cleva fella'. It was through these men that mystical powers were manifested in the realm of everyday life, in their malevolent form as sorcery, or, more benevolently, to overcome the effects of mystical forces on other people (usually expressed in illness).

The unique survival well into this century of full ceremonial life among the Dhan-gadi and their northern neighbour, the Gumbaingirr, appears to be attributable to a number of different factors.[8] One of these was their relative economic autonomy. As I discuss in Chapter 2, the stability of pastoralism ensured Aboriginal employment in bush work and stock work as well as corn pulling and fencing. The establishment and continuity of such economic relations with local landholders throughout this period would appear to have been important with regard to government controls. This economic relationship between local Aborigines and landholders in the Macleay Valley guaranteed their relative autonomy from direct forms of government intervention. Where the economic nexus was broken, as occurred in other parts of the state, relocation and concentration with other Aboriginal groups frequently followed.

As Hardy (1976) points out, in western NSW the breakup of pastoral properties in the 1890s (along with incursions by freeholders) disrupted the pattern of economic relations that had developed between Aborigines and European landowners. Station 'blacks', as they were called, who formed an integral part of the squatter station economy, were sustained by the personal associations they enjoyed over several generations with particular station owners (Hardy 1976: 177). For these Aborigines the social and economic disruption of the 1890s brought an end to these relations and began their movement off the stations.

Displacement from the stations saw the emergence of camps 'on the Darling [River] a few miles above Pooncarie' and on the 'outskirts of Willcania and other towns until the Aborigines Protection Board (APB) set up reserves in 1910' (ibid. p. 185). What occurred was the displacement of semi-private forms of control of Aboriginal groups on pastoral properties to reserves administered directly by the state. This did not, however, happen on the upper Macleay where smallholder settlement was concentrated around Hickeys Creek (see Chapter 2). Here, pastoralism remained the dominant activity and provided the economic life that enabled the Dhan-gadi to remain relatively undisturbed. Although

---

8. The 'salvage' work of Mathews provides much of the evidence of the decline of ceremonial life in NSW in the late nineteenth century. As we have seen, ceremonial life for the Ghadung appears to have ceased after 1889. For those groups further south, where European settlement initially expanded, ceremonial life ended earlier. Amongst the Darkinjung, for example, Mathews and Everitt (1900) were unable to attend a ceremony but relied on the oral testimony of initiated men. In the 1890s, Mathews recorded the northern Gamilraay *Bora* initiation ceremonies. In 1891, 1894 and 1895, the *Bora* rituals attracted respectively 250, 203 and 150 persons to participate in the ceremonies (Elkin 1975: 138–40). Mathews also recorded the *Burbung* initiation ceremonies of the Wiradjuri, which were held in 1893 and again in 1897, when 200 people came from the central west of NSW to rituals held in the upper region of the Murrumbidgee and Lachlan Rivers (Elkin 1975: 136). These ceremonies were the last to be held by the two 'tribal' groupings that occupied the vast inland plains of NSW.

there were economic links with local pastoralists, Aborigines and Europeans continued to live separate lives.

Furthermore, the relocation on government settlements of Aboriginal groups in the far west was partially responsible for severing the connection between ritual life and sacred sites. They were moved from their 'own country' to 'strange lands' and concentrated with other groups (see Creamer 1977: 151; Mathews 1977: 72–9; Widders 1977: 93; and Hardy 1976: 192). Munn (1970) and Berndt (1976) show the direct social and cosmological relevance of the environment for Aboriginal groups. Munn, for example, discusses the sense of unity (consubstantiation) that exists between the Pitjandjara and Walbiri people's objectifications of self and the environment. That relationship is obviously rendered more tenuous by the move from their 'own country'.

The situation was made even worse by the consolidation of European settlement in NSW, for it meant that their social world was also being physically transformed. It was vital to the Dhan-gadi people's attempt to sustain themselves as a separate cultural entity that they should have access to the important ritual and religious sites and artefacts. But although they managed to maintain both their religious (albeit modified) links to the land and their structural niche within the European economy, because of their own economic role (bush work) in the Europeanisation of their world, there was an inherent paradox in their domination. Through bush work they had become complicit in the Europeanisation of their world. This is reflected in the contracting domain of influence of ceremonial life and the increasingly precarious perpetuation of a secret/sacred life in this transformed physical and social world. As Kelly (1979: 79), a Dhan-gadi man himself, points out, 'the initiators, still living, had gathered up the sacred artefacts from Petrio and Serpentine initiation sites (some 100 kilometres from Bellbrook) and relocated them in chosen sites around the mission'.

The major factor in enabling the Dhan-gadi to exercise and maintain a degree of cultural autonomy was the absence of APB-appointed managers, whose role it was to monitor and control social life on the reserves. As Mathews (1977) shows, managers appointed to reserves in the far west actively suppressed ceremonial life. Through such direct forms of state intervention, possibilities for increased ritual activity and the flow of esoteric knowledge, promoted by the concentration of groups, were actively repressed (cf. Yengoyan 1970; Sackett 1975/6). Unhindered by these direct and comprehensive forms of control, the Dhan-gadi were able to continue many of the cultural habits of daily life (to be discussed later). In the short term, Dhan-gadi ceremonial life could be adjusted to the pervasive European presence. The north coast in fact provided an isolated pocket where ceremonial life was continued under a unique set of structural conditions.

If such political factors constituted the external conditions for the perpetuation of ceremonial life, the maintenance of the inter-group structure of ritual activity provided the internal conditions. The evidence from Mathews, whose 'salvage' work in the late nineteenth century provides the major source of detailed information about such ceremonies, reveals the significance of the involvement of other groups in full initiation ceremonies. He repeatedly records that once it was decided to hold a ceremony, messengers were immediately sent to consult all the neighbouring 'tribes' about when and where it should be held and who should attend and participate. (See Mathews 1897a: 323–4 on the Ghadung; 1897b: 122 on the Anewan; 1897c: 29 on the Bandjalang; 1898: 55 on the Gumbaingirr; 1900/1: 35 on the Dhan-gadi and Howitt 1904: 515 on the Yuin). This is also reflected in the structure of the ceremonies themselves and in the elaborate procedures and protocol surrounding the arrival of different contingents. Mathews (1898: 57–8) describes how the Gumbaingirr received their ceremonial contingents:

> When a strange tribe reaches a point somewhat within an easy stage of the main camp they paint their bodies with colored clays in accordance with the style customary in their tribe, after which the journey forward is resumed, the men in the lead, with the women and children following. On the approach of the strangers, the men of the local mob, and also the men of previous contingents who have arrived at the main camp, stand outside the burbung circle with their spears and other weapons in their hands, and sway their bodies to and fro. The new arrivals then march on in single file, in a meandering line, each man carrying his weapons in his hands; they enter the ring and march round and round until they are all within it in a spiral fold. They now come to a stand and jump about, the headman calling out the names of camping grounds, water holes, shady trees, etc., in their country. After this they come out of the ring and each detachment of the hosts enter it in succession and act in a similar manner. For example, the contingent from Kempsey, who had arrived first, entered the ring and called out the names of remarkable places; next, the contingent from Armidale did likewise; then the contingent from Tabulam, and so on. Lastly, the men of the local Nymboi [sic] River mob enter the ring and act in the same way.

Following this, each contingent would then take up its quarters in relation to the close proximity to its own country. In effect, quite a clear and elaborate etiquette was followed which reflected the formalised incorporation into ritual life of inter-group participation.[9]

The protocols of reciprocal ritual interaction, which confirmed the legitimacy of full ceremonies, continued to be observed between the

---

9. In less detail Mathews (1900/1: 36) describes the same procedures for the Dhan-gadi: 'The men belonging to one tribe then commence to abuse those of the other tribes present for coming to carry off their sons. The men of each tribe take their turn in hurling invectives against the rest. After the free use of heated language for some time, the matter is allowed to drop.'

Dhan-gadi and the Gumbaingirr until the final ceremony held in the mid-1930s. As one man put it:

> One time ago, when one lot was going to have initiation they used to send to one camp, say to Bellbrook, one down to Nambucca, if we were having it at Yellow Rock, or if they was having it at Bellbrook or if they were having it at Nambucca they'd send one man to Yellow Rock, one man to Nambucca and maybe another further up to Grafton. Wherever there's people been initiated, the elder ones, our people, the elder ones used to send a messenger. They used to go an' tell 'em. But not in the way you'd think they'd go and tell 'em. They'd tell 'em in the night in different ways. I'm not going to tell you how but in different ways and that why our people knew why they were going to hold it and when . . . and they all go there and join to put the young fellas through the initiation to make 'em men.

The last full Gumbaingirr ceremony was held at Nambucca Heads in 1928. The Dhan-gadi held their last two ceremonies in 1932 and 1935. In the latter of these, which took place at Bellbrook, the messenger was sent to Bowraville only and a small contingent of Gumbaingirr men responded.

Nevertheless the vastly reduced scale of inter-group participation is apparent. In the nineteenth century contingents sometimes travelled considerable distances to attend ceremonies. White (1934: 223) recollects a ceremony in the 1860s on the Patrick Plains at Singleton some 300 kilometres away, where the Hunter Blacks (Worimi), the Macleay (Dhan-gadi) and Manning (Ghadung) tribes helped make up the numbers. At the Gumbaingirr ceremony, cited above, contingents came from Kempsey (Dhan-gadi), Armidale (Anewan), Tabulam (Bandjalang) and the Nymboida River (Bain Baa) (see Map 4). By contrast, by the 1930s only four communities (three Gumbaingirr and one Dhan-gadi) in a restricted area continued their participation in such ceremonies.

Also significant are the contrasting levels of comprehensiveness in the ceremonies of earlier periods. Both the Dhan-gadi and the Gumbaingirr ceremonies relied upon their own ritual and esoteric forms of knowledge. The pattern of deterioration occurred as European settlement extended along the eastern coastal belt and consolidated its control and use of the land. This is reflected in the sudden decline in the elaborate complexity of the *Kiparra* ceremony of the Ghadung to the south (see Map 4). The last full ceremony was held in 1889 (Mathews 1897a). In the following decade, the Ghadung increasingly relied on the *Dhalgai* ceremony, an abridged, inaugural ceremony of the same status as the *Dilkirr*, to perpetuate ceremonial life.[10] The importance of the

---

10. Mathews provides two examples of such ceremonies performed on the south east coast, i.e. the *Kudsha* or *Narramang* (Gundungurra and Darkinjung) (1900) and the *Dhalgai*

Dhalgai ceremony was that it did not require the attendence of neighbouring groups:

> The Dhalgai is used only when there is no time, or it is otherwise incon-
> venient, to hold the complete ceremony of the Keeparra. If a tribe has a novice
> who is old enough to be initiated, and it will be some time before another
> Keeparra will be held, it is sometimes thought desirable or politic to inaug-
> urate him into the rank of manhood. No prepared ground is required, nor is it
> necessary that the neighbouring tribes should be summoned, as is imperative
> in the case of the Keeparra, but each tribe initiate their own boys. (Mathews
> 1898: 338)

In short, the novices were admitted to the world of men and, like other
initiated men, they were bound by secrecy and could attend other
ceremonies. Despite this, however, ritual and mythological knowledge
remained at an elementary level.

The decline of inter-group participation in full ceremonies eventually
led to their replacement by less elaborate rituals:

> It is more than probable that the last Keeparra has been held by them [the
> Ghadung]; for as each year goes by their numbers dwindle and in January,
> 1899, they were not able to get a sufficient number of Aborigines together to
> enable them to celebrate the ceremony. Many of those I meet along the coast
> had never gone through the Keeparra, but had been merely initiated into the
> Dhalgai, a sister ceremony, much shorter however than the Keeparra and
> needing for its practice no assemblage of adjoining tribes nor any prepared
> ground; in fact it requires but half a dozen men who have passed through the
> Keeparra. (Enright 1899: 123)

In a less dramatic way, the initiation ceremonies of the Dhan-gadi and
the Gumbaingirr underwent a similar involution. The increasing isolation of the two groups led to a slower process of involution. The
decrease in the numbers of initiated men and tribal groupings brought
about a gradual impoverishment of ceremonial life. This can be seen in
the progressive change across generations of the initiation status of
Dhan-gadi men. Of the total men of the first two generations, eleven
were regarded as having the status of *Garunda*, of which four were
regarded as *garals* (cleva fellas). Of the rest, five were of *Murrawon*
status and three were *Wallungurr*. This was the last generation in which
men reached the status of *Garunda*. The *Garunda*, which was the most

---

(Ghadung) (1898). They performed a similar function and held a similar status to the *Dilkirr*
of the Dhan-gadi. As Mathews (1900/1: 275) suggests, these inaugural ceremonies were an
abridged version of the full ceremonies and introduced the young men into 'the privileges
of manhood' when it appeared that a considerable period of time would elapse before a full
ceremony would be held. The novice was then required to attend the next full ceremony to
receive further instruction to achieve full initiate status (ibid. p. 280).

complex level of initiation, required men to spend six months away from the community (see also Kelly 1979). 'Men of high degree' had to spend another year away. These *garals* had a central role in the performative and revelatory aspects of secret/sacred life which was closely tied to the reproduction of the *Kiparra* (see Elkin 1975; Howitt 1904; Mathews 1900/1).

The gradual decline in the complexity of ceremonial life is apparent in the next two generations. The men of these generations were either *Wallungurr* or *Murrawon*. The last *Wallungurr* was held in the early 1920s at Lower Creek. Nine men were initiated there. It was regarded as the last 'big' ceremony with an estimated 300 people from 'many parts of the coast' (Lane 1978: 233) in attendence. As well as Dhan-gadi and Gumbaingirr 'cleva fellas', Oban Joe and Joe Woods (the latter originally from Bellbrook) travelled considerable distances from Nymboida and Walcha respectively to attend. By the 1930s only the *Murrawon*, the most elementary form of full ceremony, was carried out. Eighteen men were initiated at the last two. The period away for both of these ceremonies was two to three months. Although some Dhan-gadi and Gumbaingirr were considered to be a 'bit cleva', not one was regarded as being a 'proper *garal*'. This reflected an end to a declining number of ceremony leaders. It was not so much that the ceremonies died but that the men with the knowledge to reproduce them had passed away.

Ceremonial life could not continue in the relative isolation that European authority imposed on Aborigines in the region. The integrated complexity of ceremonial life militated against it. The domination which Europeans exercised over the social world into which the Dhan-gadi were increasingly incorporated effectively transformed the social context in which ceremonial life had gained its meaning and significance. Furthermore, the consolidation of European settlement transformed the physical environment. The forms of domination were not only expressed in terms of overt political oppression but the power to possess and transform the pre-existing cultural significance of the landscape.

Chapter 4

Creative Bricolage and Cultural Domination

The changes brought about by colonial domination affected some areas more adversely than others. The establishment of loosely supervised Aboriginal enclaves did allow for the reproduction of intra-group cultural forms; and the creation of a segregated and isolated community at Bellbrook did enable the Dhan-gadi to sustain many of the cultural habits of their everyday existence. These routinised and regular activities of the domestic sphere of social life were neither immune to change, nor were the patterns of change chaotic. Changes in cooking, eating and sleeping arrangements were organised around a specifiable range of variations in the ordering of social space. The utilisation of new implements and raw materials to fashion new objects or to reconstitute old ones revealed a significant pattern of change. The use of such implements and materials, however, reflected their embeddedness within specific social relations.

The perpetuation and modification of intra-group, as well as inter-group, activities reflected the process of change and the parameters of such changes within the social and political context of domination. Whilst ceremonial life and pre-existing marital arrangements underwent pressures that led to their decline, other traditional forms of ordering and patterning social life were partly maintained because of the significance they had gained in the new order. This is because unconscious and unreflexive acts of everyday life may become conscious and conspicuous. The perpetuation of particular cultural forms by the Dhan-gadi were partly assertions of cultural autonomy and partly acts of resistance to encapsulation within the dominant culture. It was on the reserve that the Dhan-gadi maintained some degree of autonomy which was expressed in the spatial ordering of their social world and the cultural priorities and expectations of their social interactions.

In the pervasive sphere of mundane culture a creative process of bricolage (Levi-Strauss 1966) emerged, which reconstituted certain

74

forms of social and material existence. These customary domains, where identity is sought in cultural practices of the past, were able to emerge because of the absence of comprehensive political controls within the reserve. Their creative bricolage was a form of cultural synthesis, which embedded resistance to the dominating European world within everyday practices. Contrary to Rowley's (1974: 23), amongst others, assessment that 'as the frontier moved beyond a particular area, what was left was not conquered tribes but dispirited remnants', the evidence of the Dhan-gadi suggests otherwise.

4.1. The Reconstitution of Everyday Life

The policy of segregation on unsupervised reserves provided the basis for the perpetuation of many customary forms of cultural organisation and behaviour. Controls on the community included sporadic visits by the local policeman, who rode from Bellbrook village to give a cursory inspection of the reserve or to impose order on the Aboriginal community after an alleged misdemeanour or crime. The police station was also the place where the annual distribution of blankets and clothes to Aborigines and the weekly issue of rations to the aged and infirm occurred. Such practices conformed to a policy of separating and segregating Aborigines from the wider society rather than seeking to change the social content of Aboriginal relations on reserves. In this context, the Dhan-gadi were able to draw upon familiar patterns of social organisation in their response to a radically changed world.

As a result of the changes described earlier, in the early twentieth century the Dhan-gadi people of the upper Macleay lived in two main communities, but mixed freely with one another. These were at Bell-brook, which was the official reserve, and at Lower Creek (see Chapter 2), which consisted of a 'fringe camp' organised around the labour requirements of local European pastoralists. The siting of the reserve conformed to the APB's policy of situating Aborigines away from European settlements. It was located a couple of kilometres to the north-east, 'out of sight' of Bellbrook village and the main (Kempsey to Armidale) road which ran through it. Bellbrook village, which is about 80 kilometres from the main town (Kempsey), acted as a service centre for local European pastoralists and farmers. It had a general store, a butcher, a primary school (for European children only), a police station and two churches (Anglican and Roman Catholic). A guest house catered for travellers journeying between Kempsey and Armidale. The isolation of Bellbrook reserve from major concentrations of Europeans was reinforced by its physical separation from the small concentration of Europeans and European authority in the Bellbrook area.

The reserve, or *ngurra* (camp) as the Dhan-gadi initially referred to it, was officially registered in 1914; it covered 38.85 hectares.[1] The hills on its southern boundary obscured it from Bellbrook village. The boundaries to the north and east were marked by the meanderings of the Nulla Nulla Creek. Initially, the reserve covered both banks of the creek.[2] The north-eastern corner was occupied by an Aboriginal family, called Wynn, who had a farm there. The western boundary was close to the foot of steep hills and gullies. A property owner's house some distance from the northern boundary was the only evidence of a European presence. The predominant physical feature overlooking the reserve was Mount Anderson. Located a short distance to the north-east of the reserve, Mount Anderson, or *Baral Balai* as the Dhan-gadi call it, is a place of cosmological and social significance to the Dhan-gadi people and an important site for maintaining a sense of separate cultural identity. This was the site where the last initiation ceremonies were held (see also Creamer 1977; Kelly 1979).

On the reserve, the main area for social interaction was a large centrally-located flat, which was separated from the cemetery and from the hilly land of the southern boundary by a gully. A large 'black apple tree' (which has since died) provided shade and a meeting place. Until 1910, there were five wooden houses occupied by separate families, named Lear, Dean, Ivy, Nile and Unwin. These had been built by the people themselves from wood acquired from a local sawmill adjacent to the reserve. The roofs were of corrugated iron, and all but one had wooden floors. Each had an orange and/or lemon tree planted next to it (a common practice among rural Europeans), and one house had a large native fig tree as well. Four of the five houses belonged to men who cultivated maize farms. The four farms were situated on what was called the 'bottom land' along the edge of Nulla Nulla Creek, three along one side and another on the opposite *'uralgurra'* side. Each farm was approximately 1.2 hectares and grew maize for market and vegetables for personal use. A barn was erected on each farm for the storage and threshing of the pulled corn before it was sent to the city markets to be sold. Each family did its own ploughing and harvesting. Other men on the reserve sometimes helped during the harvest, but farming was mainly regarded as a family affair.

The majority of people on the reserve, however, were not involved in family farming but continued to 'ramble about'. These families gained temporary seasonal employment during the year and lived off the land (see Chapter 2). Most of the people on Bellbrook at this time lived in

---

1. The most common term for the reserve today is 'the mission', which appears to have superceded the use of *ngurra* in an earlier period. The use of the term *ngurra* is used today, along with the terms 'humpy' and 'gunyah' to describe traditional shelters. The latter were originally European terms.

2. This land is now owned by a local European. The last record of the land in Aboriginal hands was in its transfer from father to son through an application to the APB under conditions of 'permissive occupancy of reserve at Bellbrook' (SA: 4/7125).

traditional shelters (*ngurras*), which consisted either of substantial bark huts or of simpler 'bush camps', made up of bark and used by people as temporary shelters when they were on the move. The occupancy at Lower Creek was geared to employment on the European stations in the area, an activity which required some degree of mobility. Only one man, the main contractor, had a bark hut while the other families usually lived in 'bush camps'. The main camp was situated on Long Flat, a river flat which formed a high bank.

The persistance of these shelters indicates that little change had occurred as a result of colonial dispossession. Indeed, the manner of their initial incorporation into the European economy would seem to have perpetuated the use of such shelters. Previously (in 1827), Cunningham had written approvingly of such shelters, saying that 'the better order of things obtaining amongst Aboriginal people in this area [Port Stephens] and north, [is apparent] with all of them building comfortable huts of tea tree bark, capable of holding a number of persons' (cited by Coleman 1981: 6). The huts were made from available trees; the frame fashioned out of saplings and boughs; the floors were of dirt and the roof and the walls were made from the bark of the stringy bark tree. As one man described the process of curing the bark to me:

> Jest cut 'em round the bottom with the old axe, course you have to cut 'em round the bottom, and then cut 'em up the top, and then sorta cut 'em down the middle this way . . . and then jest get . . . the axe to right round the tree and strip it off and as soon as you strip it off it jest sorta automatically rolls up; and then you've gotta get 'em and lay 'em out flat and then the best thing to do is have the hot fire there and jest stand it up straight over the top of the fire there and they [the bark] get a bit soft and they come out. Well, when they come out you jest lay 'em flat.

When this has been completed, boughs and saplings were used to hold the bark down on the frame. Coleman's (1981) survey of early European sources shows that such huts were widely reported from Port Stephens to Morton Bay. They were solid constructions varying in length from eight to thirty feet and in height from five to eight feet. According to my informants, the large bark hut at Long Flat was fifteen feet long, ten feet wide and eight feet high. In the early decades of this century, most of the Dhan-gadi people lived in a *ngurra*.

The range of styles among the shelters at Bellbrook reserve and Long Flat reflected the formation of incipient divisions in the Dhan-gadi's material culture. The European style housing of the farmers embodied the requirements of a more sedentary existence and, to some extent, the needs of those who had taken up small-scale farming. This tendency should not be overstressed, as the demands on such farmers and their European counterparts required irregular rather than sustained inputs of labour into the seasonal cycle of maize. For the families that 'rambled about' shelter was generally of a more rudimentary kind, the 'bush camp' consisting merely of two forked limbs put into the ground and joined across the top with a pole. Along the pole on one side were ranged a number of sticks and bark, bushes, or tin, if it was available. The two ends were similarly closed in. These simple constructions were used when people were travelling, at work sites, or visiting.

Despite the perpetuation of such practices, the social context in which they had previously occurred had changed considerably. The world described by Hodgkinson (1845) and Rudder (1925) had been radically altered in the colonising process. The forces directing the continuing mobility of the Dhan-gadi had changed significantly. When a group were shifting camp in the nineteenth century, Rudder (1925: 10) describes how:

> Everyone would be astir early in the day, the bark gunyahs [see note 1] would be pulled down and all the good bark laid in heaps on the ground with weights packed on top to keep it flat. Canoes would be put under water until wanted or left in sand under shelter. Many things, however, were left for future use when food supplies had grown back sufficiently to entice that tribe back to the same camp again.

The regular pattern of subsistence was no longer the predominant organising principle of social mobility. Instead, the timing, scale and direction of mobility outside the official reserve was geared to European employment.

Such a change was less in the social than in the political context of the Dhan-gadi's social existence. The authority and control of their own social domain, or beat, no longer existed in this nexus of subsistence/ employment (see Chapter 2). Access to land outside the reserve was legitimated by the ability of Aborigines to provide useful labour for Europeans. As one woman put it, 'We just lived anywhere, camped anywhere, might do a bit of washin', ironin', whatever you could do for some and the men would do bush work and one thing and another like that, or corn pulling and then we'd shift on like that.' The basis for social mobility was now dependent on European employment rather than on independent, self-supporting forms of subsistence.

Nevertheless, the knowledge and skills associated with the Dhan-gadi's material culture, premised on mobility, remained a meaningful and integral part of the reproduction of their daily lives.

This transformation (through European usurpation) in the meaning of such practices is also reflected in the changing nature of the Dhan-gadi's material culture. By the 1920s the use of materials had undergone considerable change. As one woman stated succinctly, 'You'd start off with a bark hut then you got up ta hessian and tin humpies.'

This woman was outlining the changing pattern of her shelter in the early years of her marriage. The basic one-room design of the 'humpy' remained but the materials changed, probably because of the increased availability of new materials from the European economy. Maize production in the valley provided a supply of corn bags (which were pinned to the walls) and bark or tin was used on the roof. The tin came from four-gallon tins of kerosene fuel. For those who could get enough tin, both the walls and the roof were covered. 'Big four-gallon tins of kerosene, you know, well you'd jest open 'em down the middle like that, cut the tops open and bottoms and jest open 'em out.' The range of materials used in 'bark' huts had changed, been added to or replaced, and the repertoire of knowledge and skills had increased.

This also applied to the new objects fashioned primarily from materials acquired from European sources. Blankets, supplied by the government, and the *betick* were the only essentials for sleeping. The *betick* could be made from *gubby* (government) blankets or old corn bags sewn together as an outer cover and stuffed with corn husks or blades of grass. As one woman described the process:

> If you husk the corn, you got the husk for your own betick, your tick. You call it the mattai [corn], you know, when you're pulling it off, the thing that you're throwing away. That gets hard when the corn's ripe and you can tweeze that out and make yourself a pillow or a tick. It was good to lie on for people with a sore back, you know. It was nice and clean and you could chop the knobs off [the corn]. Anyone, you'd say, come on we'll make a betick today. They're husking over there. You'll go and get it, get a big bag full and go and get it for yourself.

The *betick* was fashioned by simple processes which transformed plentiful raw materials from the immediate environment.

The same can be said of the 'fat-light', which provided an additional source of light:

> This is a funny thing . . . You get a lid, you know, the lid of a screw top bottle, jar bottle. You'd put it there and then you'd get a piece of rag and you'd plait it and dip it in the fat . . . You hold up and down till the fat got into the cloth then you put it down there and you got a light.

Once again, in this innovation there is a combination of diverse new elements which reflect changes in the social environment. The tallow, or fat, came from rendering down the offal from cattle. The offal, like the other elements of the fat light, were acquired from European sources.

The technologies associated with the construction and provisioning of the domestic sphere retained a high degree of continuity. Technology remained simple rather than complex; materials remained uniform rather than diverse, and no elaborate division of labour existed. The construction of houses was carried out autonomously by individuals, either male or female, in the case of bush camps, whereas men tended to predominate in the construction of bark huts. Immediate and plentiful sources of raw materials were available for uninterrupted fabrication. It is important to note, however, that this situation was as much a reflection of prevailing social relations as of the technology and physical properties of the raw materials. Sahlins (1974: 10), who terms this 'the democracy of property', states that, 'Access to natural resources is typically direct – "free for anyone to take" – even as the possession of the necessary rules is general and the knowledge of the required skills common.' Those tangible objects usually classified as 'material culture' are never devoid of meaning and significance beyond their specific functional purpose, but reflect the wider relationship of their users.

By contrast, four of the five wooden houses on the reserve bore a rudimentary physical and social resemblance to European housing. The materials used – timber, corrugated-iron, nails, etc. – were not readily available and had to be purchased from outside sources. Implicit in this diversity is an elaborate division of labour whereby the autonomy of the individual producer and the unity of construction no longer exist. The interiors of the wooden houses were divided into two rooms. In its rudimentary separation of physical space, this design reflected a conformity with European housing and with the functional compartmentalisation of domestic space. The use of such space, however, remained the same as for the *ngurra*: the houses too were used essentially for storage and shelter.

Yet this process of creative bricolage is also problematical. On the one hand, almost exclusive use of European 'cast offs' as the raw materials of social life, as the basis for the reproduction of their own existence, suggests an increasing dependency and vulnerability to domination. The meaning of domination is embedded in the acts of increasing use of 'cast offs' or 'rubbish' of another culture. On the other hand, their very awareness of the Europeanisation of their social and material world turns the perpetuation of their own domestic cultural practices into acts of resistance. (This is discussed more fully below.) Both resistance and accommodation to the Europeanisation of their social world are, to a large extent, inseparable modalities of the same phenomenon.

This domination continued with the APB's intervention over housing in 1913. Six houses were built, thus replacing all but two of the wooden ones. The APB provided the materials, and a European carpenter carried out the construction. In conformity with European notions of town planning, the houses were arranged in a straight line across the middle of the flat. The residents of the reserve were not involved in either the planning or the construction. Nevertheless, one family did succeed in getting a house to replace their old wooden one near their farm. In 1914, the Australian Aborigine Mission (AAM) built a similar house on the southern end of the flat next to a school which had been built by the APB some time earlier. It was, however, vacated by the missionary shortly afterwards, and so it too provided accommodation for another family.

The seven 'little box places', remained the main alternative form of housing. Each consisted of two rooms – a kitchen (with a fireplace for cooking) and a bedroom. The design reflected a more pronounced physical separation of space into specialised and functional domains. As I mentioned earlier, in a rudimentary way these 'little box places' expressed particularly European forms of ordering domestic social space, i.e. the living space was assigned to the kitchen/dining room and the sleeping space to the bedroom. They were designed to cater for more privatised forms of reproducing the family unit within the house. The inclusion of the fireplace attempted to privatise cooking and eating patterns by removing them from public sites of collective consumption.

Encoded in such material forms is a set of culturally pervasive principles associated with fundamental patterns of social interaction within the dominant society. The wooden houses embody the patterns of social interaction found in the wider society, just as bark huts and bush camps represented those of the Dhan-gadi. The wooden houses and their internal ordering of space represent the 'correct' or 'civilised' way to live in terms of the dominant society. What emerged though was that the wooden houses were simply co-opted to fit Dhan-gadi patterns of social relations. The use of space within such houses remained largely undifferentiated. It continued to be related to storage and shelter. Similarly, the domestic sphere remained firmly located around the camp-fire outside, and cooking and eating retained their collective and public forms. It can be assumed that the Dhan-gadi were aware of the 'correct', 'civilised', way to live through their interactions with local Europeans and the presence of missionaries, but that they chose, both individually and collectively, to perpetuate their own cultural practices.

The introduction of the wooden houses did modify the spatial organisation of the community to some extent. Because of the location of the houses, the flat came to accommodate a primary cluster of the population. The six families housed there were all directly related through close kin ties of marriage. Furthermore, it was the norm for young married people to build a *ngurra* close to their parents. Another two clusters existed around the south-eastern corner farmhouse and the old mission house. This clustering showed that the spatial alignment continued to be constructed upon the personal ties of kinship affiliations.

Furthermore, the internal ordering of family relations reflected a social construction of public/private domains radically different from those embodied in 'the little box places'. The basic family unit of each *ngurra*, whether bark hut, bush camp or wooden house, consisted of a husband and wife and children. The parents, young children and young unmarried girls slept in the *ngurra*. As one woman put it:

> They [young women] weren't put out or anything. Like you wouldn't say 'well your grown up now you'd better get out . . . *There was no place to go. You had to stay there say if your mother and father and they had kids and your a young girl you'd get in behind them kids.* Made no difference. You couldn't hunt them away.

While there was no culturally-defined space for young women outside the *ngurra*, young boys slept outside from an early age. In terms of the norm, young boys and girls did not mix and were socially defined as separate entities within the community. This was the practice of sister avoidance. As it was stated, 'Say now, if you were seeing some boys down there swimming, girls wouldn't want to go down there. That's their place. Girls on their own. They keep to themselves like.'

Consistent with this practice was the presence of a camp in which the young men slept as a group. This was spatially separated from the rest of the community, some 200 to 300 metres from the southern end of the flat on the south-western boundary of the reserve. The young men would leave the main area after supper and not return until morning for breakfast. All that they needed for sleeping in this camp, or on work sites, was one blanket 'half over, half under and to sleep "guts on" to the fire'. Once the young men had been initiated and married they usually built their own *ngurra* within the main camp area. This ordering of social space effectively blurs any distinctive dichotomy between public/private domains in terms of sleeping arrangements. Indeed, the practice of sister avoidance is antithetical to the sibling familiarity associated with the social patterning of domestic space in the autonomous nuclear family.

The domestic domain is important because it is where patterns of cohabitation are expressed – it is the setting for daily activities. It is where people sleep; it is where they prepare and eat their food; and it is central to how they interact and express themselves and their values. The organisation and ordering of social space is not a random process but takes quite specific forms. As Mintz (1974: 139–40) states:

> . . . foods, arrangements for eating and sleeping, and all other technical and material details of ordinary life are not invented on the spot, borrowed uncritically, or developed only as needed by some casual hit-or-miss procedure. Tastes in food are acquired; tools are fashioned and employed according to socially learned and standardised practices; choice, taste, and preference became organised around specifiable ranges of acceptable varia-

tion. In fact, the universal characteristics of the social life of peoples are order and regularity, predictability of performance, and standardisation of behaviour. In other words, the organised social life of human communities is normally an end product, with variation, alteration, and change built into the system itself.

In the context of domination we are not simply dealing with changes that follow a specifiable range of variation. Such acts are no longer unconscious and unreflexive but conscious and conspicuous. The particular forms of cultural ordering adhered to in daily interactions also sustain a notion of the past in which a sense of separate identity is maintained. With the increasing Europeanisation of their social and material world such everyday practices gain an added significance.

4.2. The Social Significance of the Camp-Fire

Changes to mundane culture, in the area of food selection, preparation and eating, share similar features to those exhibited in the patterning of sleeping arrangements and other routinised and regular aspects of 'ordinary life'. The standardised habits associated with cooking and eating reflect a distinctive cultural ordering of the social space in which they are embedded. The diet of the Dhan-gadi, as discussed in the previous chapter, involved a synthesis of European and Dhan-gadi foods. Yet, when one looks at the method of preparation, it is also clear that such changes did not alter cooking in any significant way. The camp-fire remained the primary source of cooking. 'Cookin' in the ashes', as it is called, was not a simple process and there was a set of standardised procedures to be observed:

> Make a big fire, put bark and wood [on it] until the ashes come and build it up and then if you had big coals say about that big or a little bit bigger something like that you'd poke it all out see, then you'd have the ashes there, clean white ashes, then you'd poke it one side and whatever you wanted to put, you'd put it in the middle . . . even pumpkin and potato when we got that we'd put it in the ashes, we'd open out the ashes and lay 'em down there. You could go away and do what you want to do all day and by the time that ash is cold that food was cooked. Jest take the seed out [pumpkins] and lay 'em in there. You could put it on the tea tree, piece of tea tree stick. First, you know, limbs, little broom stick, lay it down and then put that on there, don't worry no more about it, got the ashes to cook it . . . Say instead of you thinkin' that it may get dirty, as the sayin', but you know that your puttin' it in the ashes, you jest lay that limb, little branches, down in the middle like that, lay it down and then you'd put that [ashes] on top and cover it all over . . . even if you had goanna, possum, anything, you could put that bit of oak stick or bit of tea tree.

While the cooking technique retained its standardised form, the scope of foods and taste preference had broadened.

The careful attention to detail in the preparation of food is also evident. Genovese (1975) points out that this expresses, implicitly, a pride in such culinary practices. As one woman put it to me, 'you jest don't chuck it on'. In effect, food preparation and eating are areas in which a conscious or heightened sensibility towards cultural boundaries and distinctiveness are more likely to be expressed than in other daily routines. As Genovese (ibid.) says, such culinary practices provide a vehicle whereby the 'natural' superiority to others in such matters is quietly expressed or assumed. Cooking, in this regard, is an idiom through which social groups express themselves.

For subordinated groups within a colonial context, culinary practices take on an ambiguous political role. At one level such practices become 'a politically safe way for downtrodden people' (ibid. p. 72) to remind themselves of their distinctive identity. However, in that food is a focal point around which the dominant society asserts its own superiority, regarding food as a distinctive aspect of a social group is somewhat problematic. In other words, the differences in foodstuffs and in techniques of preparing food provide a focus for ideological constructions about the superiority of the dominant society's own 'civilised' culinary practices as opposed to those of 'savages'. Statements such as, 'say instead of you thinkin' that it might get dirty, as is the saying', are more than assertions of careful preparation – they reflect how such activities have been rendered problematic. The European classification of Aboriginal culinary practices was 'eating dirty blackfella food'. Significantly the first manager on Bellbrook immediately took upon himself the task of 'correcting' such practices. He instructed the Dhan-gadi that cooking was to be done in camp ovens in the fireplaces *inside* the reserve houses.

As in other areas of mundane culture, the changes that were wrought took place as a process of creative bricolage. This was evident in the introduction of new cooking implements and materials. For example, mullet, perch, catfish and eel were traditionally cooked either 'in the ashes' or on a *baral*. The latter consisted of three forked sticks placed in a triangle around the fire onto which 'a lot of little sticks [were] put in a grill-like fashion across [the top] when the fire was made'. The fish was then placed on top of this structure and toasted. Changes introduced here were relatively minor and involved the materials rather than the method. People started using 'what they call grid iron; wire which was bent to form a griller to be placed on sticks, and in later years it was the shelves of "fridges" [discarded refrigerators]'. The involvement of men in fencing meant that bent wire was commonly available and could be promptly fashioned into a griller. Like other utensils discussed earlier, these new materials were appropriated and fashioned to meet pre-existing practices but were also mute testimony to the predominance of a new social and material environment which encapsulated the Dhan-gadi.

From this new environment, cooking methods also gained some additions. Many families acquired cast-iron camp ovens. These were hung above the fire and used to boil fish, wallaby and birds. The camp oven was also used for making yeast bread. As one woman stated:

> You'd make your fire, make the big fire, then you poke all the wood to one side, and then you put the dough into the oven, get the oven hot [first] and then you put the lid over one side to get hot and then you turn round and put the lid back on the oven again, then you pick up the coals and the bits of ashes and throw it on top of the oven lid.

Or, alternatively, the ingredients would be changed, so that 'instead of putting the dry yeast, you'd put the lemon yeast. Oh! raise it, you'd be very proud with your bread.' The changes also involved the introduction of new utensils, methods and skills, such as the 'little boiler and tin pannikin' and the introduction of tea. Yet the camp-fire remained; the new additions were merely assimilated into it.

The process of domination discussed here manifests itself in the community through the increased dependency brought about by the transformation of the wider social and material world. This loss of control reduced their access to the raw materials of their everyday existence. Within the community utensils or foodstuffs used in food preparation were indigenised through the perpetuation of cooking practices associated with the traditional camp-fire. This is best illustrated in the 'acquisition' of *damper*, which is made from a combination of flour, salt, baking powder and water. The high degree of selectivity, refinement and variation in the making of *damper* across a number of cooking techniques testifies to its significance:

> You'd make damper different ways, it seemed to taste different . . . fry it, grill it, cook it in the [camp] oven somethin' like that, tastes different altogether. You cook it one way all the time, you get sick of it see . . . You could put it in the fire, you could make your own grill, put it on that, long handle on it, stand right back here . . . [or] you could drag the coal out. They seem to have a different taste.

The widespread use of *damper* in its variety of forms reveals a great deal about changes in the diet. *Damper* had established itself as the predominant staple food in a relatively short period of time.

In itself, *damper* exemplifies the process of blending and synthesis. It is made exclusively from European derived ingredients, but is prepared with traditional cooking methods. The ingredients, particularly the flour, had replaced a plant called *conjevoi*, the roots of which were prepared for the same purpose. Rudder (1925: 13) describes the preparation of what he called one of 'the best foods of the natives'.

> . . . the old conjevoi in suitable soil also yielded a good crop of roots . . . to prepare them for food the blacks first roasted the roots on a fire, rubbed off the skin, and then pounded them into a soft mass with a stone. This was then put into a net and left in a running stream for two or three weeks, the purpose being to remove the poison that is in the fresh bulbs. When ready the mass was kneaded into the consistency of dough and then cooked in the ashes like damper. Of this food the Aborigines were very fond, but it was the gins (Aboriginal women) who dug up the roots and did all the preparation.

The use of native vegetables for the preparation of such foods was a lengthy process that required a high degree of familiarity and knowledge of the plant and its toxic properties. Flour, it would seem, provided an acceptable substitute, both in terms of taste and in the somewhat elaborate method of preparation:

> You'd go along and you'd find a suitable tree that's flat one side. The trees grow up flat like that. They cut it this way, they cut it that way and it'll come off . . . wash it down and mix your flour on top [of] that. That's your dish. Then you put it there one side, then you wait. Then you put your board down and you knead it up until you get it near ready and you keep kneading it; and when you think the ash is hot enough for it in it goes.

The use of flour required no changes in cooking techniques but simplified the process significantly.

Such an interpretation, however, all too readily regards the principle of utility as the agency of change – change reduced to a means/ends logic. Blainey's *Triumph of the Nomads* (1975) is an example of the inadequacy of such approaches. In his study of Aboriginal prehistory, produced from a synthesis of contemporary evidence from anthropologists and pre-historians, Blainey uses economic categories that reduce Aborigines to reflections of ourselves. Characterising Aborigines as pastoralists, or as cultivating the land with fire, or considering food in terms of diet, reduces complex social processes to a means/end relationship. Such interpretations are a triumph of the homogenising character of the principle of utility. The radical otherness of cultural/historical processes is reduced to the homogenous sameness of instrumental intentionality. In other words, our own cultural categories are used as analytical tools.

Such an interpretation fails to consider that we are dealing with a world understood through mythical thought, in which food and fire, amongst other elements, are believed to contain efficacy and constitutive properties (see Cassirer 1956). In this anthropomorphic world, food exists in a realm of heightened sensibility. Douglas (1984) illuminates this undivided world of efficacy in her consideration of foods (their preparation and eating) and of notions of bodily pollution. The latter are expressed in terms of specifically vulnerable points, the orifices of the body, through which substances traverse, either in-wardly or outwardly. The appropriation of European consumption goods is therefore fairly problematic, as it carries with it a threat to Aboriginal identity. The ingestion of such foods, culturally constructed as a constitutive aspect of social being, involves potential bodily pollu-tion. The significance of the camp-fire, then, is that it renders such goods less threatening. The camp-fire may be seen as transformative in that it mediates European goods and *indigenises* their consumption.

In the wider context, such changes in diet reflect changes in the women's gathering activities. My research revealed only one case of a yam (*gangin*) having been eaten and an exceedingly limited knowledge of wild vegetables. By contrast, *damper* and European vegetables such as pumpkins, potatoes, gramma melons and maize seemed to have been used regularly. It is in this context that the continuation of knowledge and skills associated with the cooking techniques of the camp-fire gain a new significance. The colonising process had de-stroyed much of the folk knowledge and many of the skills through which Aboriginal women had maintained control over and a sense of identity in their everyday world. The camp-fire, however, with the careful attention to detail in the cooking techniques associated with it, remains one of the few areas of social life in which folk knowledge has not been usurped and displaced.

The centrality of cooking and eating is similarly conditioned by its importance as a site for the reproduction of distinctive forms of social relationships. Such practices culturally ordered familial and group interaction and, therefore, cannot be fully explained solely in terms of habits associated with prevailing food and preparation techniques. Instead, the camp-fire maintained social relations premised on the absence of significant borderlines between public and private life. The open design of the *ngurra* and the lack of spatial differentiation within its walls provided only a limited sphere for the intimate aspects of private life. Culturally, the domestic sphere is not a closed territory of selective social interaction. The camp-fire acted as a bridge between private/public life. One woman described social interaction on the reserve as:

> Where-ever you might see a head of women's sitting over there or over there at that camp or somethin' like that and say "I'll go an' cook the billy there" and go over and cook it there. You'd sit down there, yarn away, lay down there, sleep away, or you might be cooking damper, if they ever wanted to, cook anything like that.

To the extent that we consider cooking space as domestic space, the 'domestic space' of each *ngurra* unit was open to the public gaze and was an important site for social intercourse.

By contrast, the fireplaces located within 'the little box places' were used in an auxiliary capacity when the weather was wet. The privatising nature of internal fireplaces violated such forms of familial and group interaction. A striking, if singular, example of the preference for cooking outside can be seen in the use of an iron stove bought by one of the Aboriginal farmers. Instead of installing it within the wooden house, it was set up outside. It can be assumed that this man was aware of the 'correct' place for a stove, yet, he chose to perpetuate practices consistent with a particular Dhan-gadi perception of the cultural ordering of social relations.

It is in eating at the camp-fire that the shared forms of consumption are maintained and reproduced:

> When they killed a bulgun [wallaby], they shared it all around. To each neighbour, like each gunyah, see, because he had no fridge to put it in, I'll give a leg over there, I might give an arm over there, I might give the tail over there, and then the liver and heart you'd give to somebody or you'd give 'em the head see. It doesn't matter about you thinkin' of the next meal, you didn't think about that. Then when you wanted another feed, away you'd go or somebody else would go out and get it.

Cooking and eating practices are a significant part of the public domain. The cultural emphasis on sharing is underpinned by moral obligations associated with kinship affiliations. Such patterns of food sharing are regulated by kinship, which differentiates different sets of individuals and determines certain obligations and privileges. They are based on the extension of moral analogues of immediate family relations to close kin outside domestic space. Amongst the Dhan-gadi, this was encoded in the distinction made by kin terms *meanda/galaku* and *nguka/balaw*. The term *meanda* (father) was applied to father's genealogical brothers while the kin-term *galaku* referred to father's 'distant' classificatory brothers. Similarly, the kin-term *nguka* (mother) was applied to mother's genealogical sisters, while *balaw* was applied to mother's 'distant' classificatory sisters.[3] These forms of kinship affiliation provided the cultural/moral bridge between domestic space and a wider sociality.

The social discrimination associated with sharing food appears to have been modified during this period and generalised reciprocity extended to a wider range of *community members*. Kinship affiliation seems to have undergone a process of change in which complex and specific rules were replaced by a more diffused and generalised system.

---

3. Radcliffe-Brown (1951: 44) differentiates the Gumbaingirr-type system from the Kariera system in that the latter has only a single term which was extended to all kinswomen classified as sister. For Radcliffe-Brown this distinction meant that in a Gumbaingirr-type system 'each man or boy had his own set of mothers-in-law'.

The large number of in-marriages, discussed earlier, seems to have been a contingent factor in this diffusion of generalised reciprocity, for it ensured that most families on the reserve were in some way related. Kinship affiliations were modified but still conformed to cultural notions of sharing. In this regard, the structural homology between the cultural practice of sharing and the camp-fire remained. The social significance of the camp-fire was that it continued to be a collective site for the reproduction of everyday expressions of sociality.

The post-conquest period saw a shift away from the kin/non-kin distinction and towards community affiliations which served a similar dichotomising function. The distinction was in keeping with the Europeanisation of the social and material world and the Dhan-gadi's encapsulation within it. The dichotomy circumscribed the Dhan-gadi community *vis-à-vis* the wider European population. Underpinning this division was a process of alienation which did not refer to the breakdown of social relations *within* the community but rather the loss of control over wider domains.

Chapter 5

The Evolution of State Control (1880–1940): Segregated Dirt or Assimilation?

Dhan-gadi life chances were restricted by the state's official policies towards Aborigines in NSW. Continuous oppression by the state had played a large part in shaping, if not fully determining, the relations of dependency which evolved in the Macleay Valley. Yet, the socio-cultural history of the Dhan-gadi was by no means static – it was merely rendered discontinuous by the changing deployments of state power.

Between 1880 and 1940 race relations in NSW were subjected to successive changes in legislation which increased the power of the state to intervene in Aboriginal communities. With the establishment, in 1880, of the inauspicious office of Protector of Aborigines, the NSW government invoked processes which reduced Aborigines to the status of colonial wards. The pivotal point in this process was the enactment of the Aborigines Protection Act (1909), which prefigured a change in the nature of control over Aboriginal communities in latter decades. Indeed, throughout the period a number of conflicting policies and practices existed side by side, while others remained inadequately applied. This shift in power relations entailed a movement from *legalistic custodianship*, where control is exercised from outside the community in a sporadic manner to facilitate repressive interventions, to a form of *bureaucratic custodianship*, where control is exercised from within the community in a systematic way to facilitate pedagogic interventions. Essentially, the period is one characterised by the increasing evolution towards more systematic forms of control, seeking as their end the creation of new forms of sociality amongst Aborigines.

The significance of the period is not only in the shifting relations between Aborigines and the state, but also in the correspondences between particular forms of state control and constructions of Aboriginality. The evolution of policy signalled a departure in content from the previous ideological constructions of Aborigines as a race. An interpretation of such processes must extend beyond the repressive and punitive forms of domination associated with state apparatuses to

pedagogic forms of cultural domination. By definition, colonial relations are relations of exploitation, domination and violence. Yet, the
dichotomy between the repressive (disciplining bodies) and the pedagogical (capturing minds) should be rejected (see Fanon 1976; Taussig
1984; Lattas 1986). The use of sheer force not only disciplines bodies,
but also creates meanings and shapes consciousness. The pedagogical
not only manipulates attitudes, but also habits, bodily movements and
gestures.

5.1. Legalistic Custodianship

(Circular re Aborigines. No. 693).
Police Department,
Inspector General's Office, Sydney,
3 July 1883.

> . . . The object in view is, as a matter of course, the amelioration of the
> condition of the aborigines [sic], and the distribution of the government
> bounty in such a manner as will prove most beneficial to them. In future the
> distribution of blankets will be under control of the Board, and any recom-
> mendations or suggestions in relation thereto will receive careful considera-
> tion. As regards further assistance food, clothing for the aged and sick, or
> helpless women and children, full information will be required in order that
> limited funds at the disposal of the Board may be expended with fairness and
> discrimination. Contracts for relations will be made upon the enclosed form.
> The able bodied should be encouraged to work, be given to understand that
> they will not be maintained in idleness. The police should exercise supervi-
> sion also over any boats, nets, or other implements or supplice provided for
> aborigines, to see they are not injured, neglected, or improperly used by
> private individuals. In the event of supplies of rations being authorised, it is
> hoped that the police will take an interest in seeing that the articles are of the
> stipulated quality, and not misappropriated in any way . . . The attention of
> the police should be at all times directed to the necessity for enforcing the law
> as regards the supply of spiritous liquors to the aboriginals, or against persons
> improperly lodging or wandering with them. Generally, the Board rely with
> confidence upon your co-operation and that of the police generally in the task
> they have undertaken, which is to provide for the reasonable wants of the
> aborigines and to protect the remnant of the race as far as possible from the
> injurious effects of contamination by vicious or thoughtless members of the
> community.

The Superintendent of Police,

I have, & c.,
Edward Mosbery

(NSW Leg. Ass., V and P 1883, vol. III: 943.)

The objectives set out in this extract (from a circular from the chairman of the newly-established Aborigines Protection Board (APB) to the Police Department) represented the first systematic and enduring intervention of the state into Aboriginal affairs in NSW. The APB had superceded the brief establishment of a Protector of Aborigines in 1880. The form of state intervention by the APB, and its predecessor, was limited to *legalistic custodianship*. That is, the essential role of the state was to 'protect the remnant of the race' and to provision in a limited way those Aborigines considered to be incapable of providing for themselves. The expanded administration of the Board was to fulfil the same function as the Protector of Aborigines, i.e. to 'ameliorate the conditions of the blacks and to exercise general guardianship over them'.[1] Such intervention was premised on the establishment of government reserves. In 1883 there were 25 reserves in NSW totalling 1,417 hectares and by 1903 this had risen to 145 reserves with a total area of 10,474 hectares (Duncan 1969: 255).

The policy was based on the segregation of the Aboriginal population within these reserves and on their self-sufficiency as communities. In 1882, Thornton, the Protector of Aborigines, felt that it would be 'wise and beneficial that reserves of suitable land . . . should be set apart for the use of the Aborigines, for purposes of forming homes, cultivation and production of grain, vegetables, fruit, etc., for their own consumption, this would prove a powerful means of domesticating, civilising and making them comfortable.' (NSW Leg. Ass., V and P 1882, vol. IV: 1,526.) Furthermore, aid was only to be given to Aborigines in their own districts as, 'they should be prevented from coming or staying in the metropolis' (ibid.). Through the application of such measures, it was expected that Aborigines could lead a sedentary and self-sufficient agricultural existence, adopting the type of production found in the local district.

The initial aims of the APB were to establish segregated and bounded communities throughout the state to 'protect' the Aborigines from the 'effects of contamination' from the wider society. The administration of the APB represented an initial tentative step by the state to remove Aborigines from the *de facto* and arbitrary control of individuals (pastoral property owners) and voluntary organisations in civil society (such as the churches and the Aborigines Protection Association) and to place them under the custodianship of the state.

The policy of segregation and immobilisation took two forms. One form of community self-sufficiency was sought through collective labour engaged in large-scale agricultural enterprises on reserves. Such enterprises were established on the banks of the Murray River at Coranderrk and Cumeroogunga (Massola 1972; Barwick 1972). On the

---

1. The APB was composed of four MPs, six private individuals and the Inspector General of Police, who was chairman.

MACLEAY RIVER VALLEY

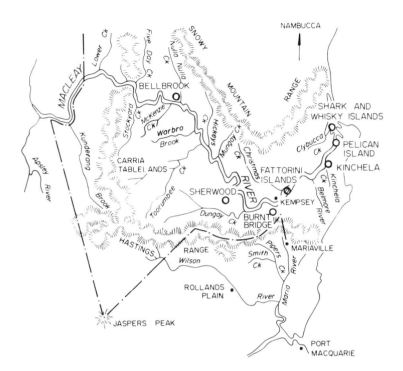

Map 5. The Major Aboriginal Reserves *Adapted from Neil (1972)*

mid-north coast Aboriginal men were encouraged to take up small-holdings on the reserves. Along with the majority of European small-holders, these men engaged in maize production. The proceeds from the sale of the crops were expected to support the man and his family. On the Macleay and in the two adjacent coastal districts some 16 reserves were set up ranging from 0.9 hectares to 205 hectares. Nine of these were established on the Macleay River. Depending on the size of the reserve, between one and three or four families would have land under cultivation (see Appendix II).

During this period the APB had little direct control over the Aborigines, for their supervision was exercised through the local police station. Applications to farm land on the reserves were made to the local police, who then forwarded the forms to the APB in Sydney for approval or rejection. The vast majority of these reserves (and hence farmers) were located on the lower Macleay River (see Map 5), with only one reserve being established on the upper Macleay (see Chapter

2). On these a number of men became individual smallholders, growing maize (as a cash crop) and vegetables. The development of these farms and their decline (discussed below) may be seen through the farming histories of two Aboriginal men who began farming in the same year as the APB was established. These two men, Jimmy Linwood and John Moseley, were given approval to begin farming on the Fattorinni Islands on the Macleay River in 1883 (SA 2/28349). The APB report of that year stated that there was no open country on the islands, they were poorly grassed and had been partly cleared and cropped with maize (ibid.). The report of 1889 reveals significant changes. '"Linwood" and "Moseley" with families (h.c.) [half castes] have been on the islands between 6–7 years and have had much uphill work clearing them and purchasing appliances. They have each three horses, 2 ploughs, 1 harrow. Last year's crop brought them out of debt within a pound or two. Linwood's realised £156.0s.8d and Moseley's £72.18s.2d.' (ibid.) Moseley's crop at this time was 2.8 hectares on a 4.9-hectare island and Linwood's was 5 hectares on an island of some 8 hectares (ibid.). Similar reports were recorded of the industriousness of other farmers on Pelican Island, Kinchela and other reserves (ibid.).[2]

Despite the success of a number of individuals in establishing themselves on small farms, the APB's overall policy was simply inadequate. The reserves were too small for Aborigines to pursue traditional practices and too small to provide anything but limited economic development. The smallest European-owned maize farm on the Macleay River was eight hectares, whereas only one farm, that of Jimmy Linwood, was as large as that. The size of the farms generally precluded self-sufficiency, while the size of the reserves restricted the number of eligible farmers. For example, by 1891 some 33 men, women and children were permanent residents on the Fattorinni Islands (17 hectares). Thus, one finds that both Moseley and Linwood sought work on local farms, as well as work as trackers for the local police.

During the 1890s the number of Aboriginal farmers in the mid-north coast region continued to grow with the establishment of a new reserve at Burnt Bridge (1893) (see Tables 1 and 2). In the flood of 1893,

2. The following APB report on Pelican Island was given in 1890: No. 251 — Pelican Island '9 August, 1890 — Situated 5 miles from Arakoon, 11 miles from Smithtown and 12 miles from Gladstone. Composed of rich alluvial soil, grass grows luxuriantly, very suitable for farms and will grow almost any crop. 25 acres swamp. Area fenced 20 acres, cleared 65 acres, cultivated 65 acres — maize. Occupied by
    George Drew (h.c.) about 15 acres as a farm
    Fred Drew (h.c.) about 16 acres as a farm
    Thomas Mark (h.c.) about 16 acres as a farm
    Ned Anderson (f.b.) about 9 acres as a farm
    Clarence Jimmi (f.b.) about 9 acres as a farm
The first three named have built themselves good houses, slabs with iron roof, the other two the usual Aboriginal houses. There are also huts, weatherboard with iron roofs built by Board for old and infirm Aborigines. Estimated value of improvements £626.' (SA 2/28349.)

Moseley's farm on Fattorinni Island was washed away (*MC*, February 1928). Moseley and his family moved to the reserve at Burnt Bridge. Once again, he 'felled, stumped and grassed the land at his own expense and labour' (ibid. July 1937). The area cleared included three 16-hectare paddocks, with the main farm, a large flat on Euroka Creek, fenced in. The other paddocks were for dairy cattle and bullocks. Moseley occupied the main farm, and two of his sons built houses on the other paddocks and had small farms. A number of other families, the Dungays, Mirandas, Richies and Davis', also had farms and ran cattle on Burnt Bridge around this period (see Map 6).

One significant feature of Burnt Bridge was that incipient economic cleavages were developing within the community. The men who had the farms saw their land as clearly demarcated from the Aboriginal reserve. In a map they sent to the Department of Public Instruction, the 'Reserve for Aborigines' is located on one side of Euroka Creek, while the farms are marked on the other side of the creek. As I shall show more clearly later, they believed that they did not live on reserve land. The other Aborigines who came to, or lived on, Burnt Bridge usually camped on the other side of the creek from the farms. Some men built their houses there. The relations that existed between Aborigines on Burnt Bridge also reflected a distinction. As one woman stated:

> [Grandfather] grew his own corn, pulled his own corn, had a barn. Grandfather used to kill his own bullocks those days they were allowed to do that. And the old fig tree, he'd launch it up into the fig tree, and everyone he used to feed, but it wasn't a mission but a lot of dark people used to live around here. They'd all feed up. He'd give meat out.

From such accounts of asymmetries arising out of 'use rights' over property and from the spatial separations referred to earlier, it would appear that economic cleavages were already developing at that stage.

Underpinning the development of these social cleavages was the belief amongst the farmers that they held title to the land as independent farmers. Moseley believed that the land had been given to him in recognition of his services to the state as a 'black tracker'. Other men considered the land a 'gift from Queen Victoria'. The state, however, viewed Aboriginal farming in terms of its scheme to keep Aboriginal activities segregated on the reserves. The development of Aboriginal self-sufficiency through farming was part of a strategy to minimise the need for state intervention and thereby to reduce the economic costs of running the reserves. For the APB the reserves fulfilled a dual role; that of providing protectorates for the so-called 'full-bloods' and land for farming. In effect, the reserves were treated as crown lands, set aside for use by the Aborigines but revokable at the discretion of the state.

This ascribing of a dual role to the reserves was consistent with the

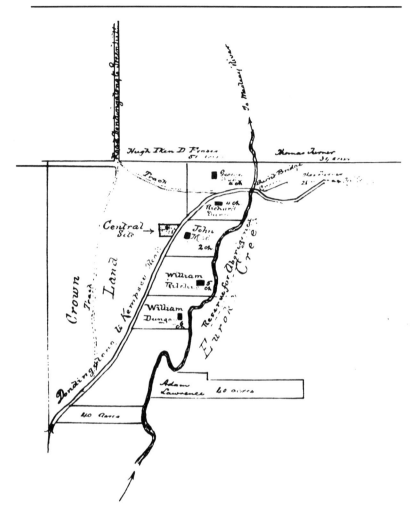

Map 6. Original Hand-drawn Sketch of Burnt Bridge Farms (1900)

prevailing commonsense view of Aborigines as a dying race. In accordance with APB policy, which was to 'ameliorate the conditions of blacks', the reserves were created as 'havens', as 'soothing pillows for a dying race', in which Aborigines could escape from the complexities and confusions of modern society. The apparently dwindling population was expected to pass away in the peace of segregated reserves under the protection of the local police. The NSW parliament of 1883 decided that there would be no need to increase the funding for Aborigines, for it was assumed that they were dying out (Rowley 1973:

10). The exclusion of 'full-bloods' from the 1900 census, under Section 127 of the Commonwealth Constitution, reflected the 'unstated consensus' that their exclusion 'would before too long be made a reality by the eventual demise of the "dying race"' (Smith 1980: 23).

The administration of Aborigines in NSW was distinctive in this period in that there was no explicit policy on half-castes. It was simply assumed that Aborigines 'should be brought into the settler economy' (Rowley 1973: 10). By contrast, the Victorian state government had passed the Aborigines Act (1886) which excluded all people of Aboriginal descent other than 'full bloods and half-castes over the age of 34 years' (Barwick 1972: 36). All other half-castes became 'legally white'. The differences in state policy were made apparent in the consequences for the Aborigines at Coranderrk. As Barwick (ibid. p. 37) states:

> By 1895 more than sixty half castes had been exiled from Coranderrk, and the dependent children of the eligible aged were sent away as they reached the age of fourteen. Many crossed the Murray River to settle at Maloga Mission or Cumeroogunga Station (where they had kinsmen and friends) as the New South Wales authorities still considered half castes eligible for residence and some aid.

In NSW the dual role of the reserves was further complicated by this non-separation of half-castes. It was assumed that full bloods would naturally die out and that half-castes and other lighter castes would just as naturally be absorbed.

5.2. The Construction of Aboriginality

In the late nineteenth century, colonial relations between Aborigines and Europeans were conceptualised in terms of race relations. The concept of race depicted relationships between Aborigines and Europeans as somehow governed by an inevitable natural causality. The violence of colonisation was subsumed under a law of nature and seen as a consequence of the contact of two races at different stages of progress, independent of its historical context. As Guillaumin (1980: 40) puts it, 'domination conceals itself behind the idea of difference'. In this respect, racial differences, imputed to be biological or cultural, are magnified and systematised into vehicles of domination. The construction of race is ideological as it provides the naturalistic camouflage that legitimates political and economic domination (ibid. p. 52). Race can be seen as the ideological means of legitimating and reproducing colonial relations.

The establishment of a legalistic custodianship of Aborigines through the APB ensured that the term Aborigines was no longer just a folk

category, but a legal category, which imposed limitations and facilitated European control. The representations of Aborigines as a race
constituted the ideology of state domination. Underpinning the intervention of the APB was a particular construction of Aboriginality in
which cultural and pseudo-genetic characteristics were magnified and
systematised into vehicles of domination.

As I mentioned earlier, Aboriginal reserves were set up on the
understanding that they would continue until the last remnants of the
indigenous population had passed away and the land set aside by the
state was no longer required. The APB's policy was, in many respects,
a response to the essential contradiction the surviving indigenous
population posed to the new state. The colonial process had reduced
the Aborigines to a residual minority, but they had not been elimi-
nated. The problem was expected to resolve itself naturally. The reserves, or 'soothing pillows for a dying race', had been created on the
understanding that Aborigines were incapable of transcending their
own biological limitations. The dominant society's appropriation of
Aboriginality was an abstraction which culturally and biologically froze
it to a particular historical moment. The ideological representations of
Aborigines had basically denied them a historical trajectory.

This increasingly secular and temporal view of Aborigines emerged
during the nineteenth century. The forms of knowledge that constructed them as a race 'frozen in time' reflect a shift from a spatial
(synchronic) ordering to a temporal-historical (linear evolutionary)
ordering of the world associated with the secularisation of knowledge
through an emerging scientific discourse. The contrast is with a Christian view of the world, associated with what Lovejoy (1936, cited
Friedman 1983) calls 'the great chain of being'. Friedman (p. 35) states
that in the great chain of being, 'every living creature is ranked in a
hierarchy stretching from the lowest creatures to God, their respective
positions being a function of their proximity to the deity'. What was
distinctive about 'the great chain of being' was that knowledge of the
social hierarchy of the world was constructed as being spatially organised. This particular view was evident in the early nineteenth century.
For example, Bannister (1830, cited Gunson 1974, vol. II: 358) states
that, 'The natives of New South Wales, although a kindly disposed
race, are probably further removed from civilisation than any other
people upon earth. They require, therefore, to be led with greater care
from their uncivilised state, and to be shielded from our ordinary
injustice [more] than any other barbarous people.'[3] This suggests a

3. The use of a spatial rather than temporal positioning of Aborigines in the social world
is also evident in the following quote by Rev Charles Wilton in 1828, 'It is the Providence of
GOD alone that makes him [Briton] to differ from the unlettered heathen – other savages,
and, amongst them, the proud Briton himself, have had written languages given to them;
and have gradually approximated a state of refinement, and; why should the Native of

unity of humankind linked to God through creation, which does not deny the Aborigines the prospect of 'civilisation' but simply asserts that they need more time to accomplish it given their distance from God. This view was upheld in Christian discourse about Aborigines throughout the century. For Parker, the assistant protector of Aborigines in Port Phillip in 1854, the Aborigine, along with the rest of humankind, 'stands forth as a CREATURE OF GOD, the off-spring of a common parent, the inheritor of a nature identical with his own, in its origin, its capacities, and its destination' (cited Reynolds 1974: 46). Yet, by the mid nineteenth century there was evidence of a more secular view of Aborigines based on a biological model. A circular published by the Aborigines Protection Association in NSW (cited Duncan 1969: 227a) reveals the emergence of a biological determinism in considering what has to be done with Aborigines:

> This race has been most sadly neglected hitherto, both by Government and Christian public. And, being impressed with a sense of their extreme physical wretchedness and moral degradation, as well as the justice of their claims upon us the Christian community we feel constrained to take such steps as will reach their case. *We would, in particular, call your attention to the up growing race of half-castes. Hundreds of children (some of them quite white), are at present running wild, in some cases perfectly nude. These unfortunate victims of the white man's sin should receive attention at our hands;* for them *especially*, homes must be established, into which they may be gathered, and where they may be taught the arts of civilised life, and receive instruction in the great principles of our common Christianity.

This focus on the half-caste reflects the intrusion of a more biologically-based perception of Aborigines, albeit still linked to a religious discourse expressed in terms of a moral concern for the white man's sin. Similarly, the focus on the moral and spiritual rejuvenation of the Aboriginal population still assumed that through an education in 'the arts of civilisation' and the 'great principles of our common Christianity' Aborigines were redeemable and, hence, part of the unity of humankind. And, of course, the half-castes were even better prospects for redemption.

With the emergence of secular and scientific forms of knowledge, however, the spatial antecedence of Europeans in the great chain of being was turned into a temporal and historical priority (Friedman 1983: 37). Spatial distance was transformed into temporal distance, and Aborigines ceased to be regarded as grown-up children (who could be educated to civilisation in the same way as European children) but

---

Australia be passed over — merely, because he may be inferior to other savage nations in intellectual powers, and because therefore a greater length of time would be necessary to accomplish his civilisation' (cited Gunson 1974, vol. II: 349).

contemporary ancestors. Aborigines as a race were located temporally, both culturally and genetically, within a fixed evolutionary hierarchy. They were frequently seen to be on the lowest scale of humanity, from which they could not escape. This depiction of Aborigines as a folk category can be seen in the following official account by a local historian ('The Sparrow' 1914: 125) of the Hastings District:

> An old friend of mine told me that years ago he was on a cedar expedition. In the away beyond, somewhere in the Hasting electorate, he missed his way, and was bushed for the night. During his peregrination, the next morning, he struck a black's camp. . . . Seated in a corner he saw a wizened up toothless old gin, of unparalleled ugliness. On the seeing him, her dim eyes sparkled like diamonds, and *springing up from her recumbent position, like a monkey*, before he could anticipate her intention, *she flung her boney arms round his neck, and her legs around his waist, slobbering on his face possum smelling tender epithets and caresses. Naturally disgusted* . . . he finally succeeded in freeing himself from her embraces . . . He gathered from her that she took him for her dead son, who had gone down in the dark valley 'Blackfellow' and had jumped up on the other side 'Whitefellow'.

Not only are the woman's actions described here as those of an animal (in that she springs 'like a monkey') but there is also a suggestion of incest in the way in which she wraps her legs around his (her son's) waist. Furthermore, confusing the stranger for her son suggests the absence of a defining characteristic of humanity: the lack of the facility for rational or critical reasoning. In this depiction moral degradation is clearly linked to biology.[4]

Yet another ideological representation of Aborigines as a doomed race was expressed in the notion of the 'full blood', which confused traditional culture (i.e. the comprehensive retention of customs, beliefs and rituals) with genetics. This blending of racial and cultural fidelity is

---

4. Markus (1974) and Stevens (1973) show that, throughout the later part of the nineteenth century, a major debate on the status of Aborigines was being conducted in the city and country press. The Aborigines were represented as both noble and ignoble savages, but whatever the perspective, it was accepted that they were doomed. Characterised as a noble savage, for example, the view was held that 'as a tame blackfella, he is despicable, [but that] as a savage he is a respectable member of his own class of society. When the Aborigine is in his natural wild state he works hard . . . The only chance for the native is to keep him apart from whites . . . Give the remaining natives a few detached areas of unoccupied land . . . whereon they can live unmolested: and let them die there as decent savages.' (*Bulletin* 1892, cited Markus 1974: 71–2). As an ignoble savage, by contrast, his degeneracy was seen as inherent: 'the blackfellow is not the noble savage he is depicted; . . . if he lacks one thing more than the other it is virtue; their songs, rites and ceremonies are utterly revolting and fiendish, but if you add a few white vices, and then ask the question as to the possibility of chastity among the women, the idea at once becomes preposterous. No less preposterous, therefore, is the idea of black women being outraged unless it is by stopping their supply of tobacco. As to the numerous murders being attributed to white men violating the moral laws of the tribe, I have already shown it to be impossible when such laws do not exist' (from a report (1899) by a pastoralist named Alfred Giles, cited Stevens 1973: 111).

most clearly expressed in the first two stanzas of Henry Kendall's (1966: 90) popular poem entitled *The Last of His Tribe* (first published in 1869):

> He crouches and buries his face on his knees;
> And hides in the dark of his hair,
> For he cannot look up at the storm smitten trees,
> And look at the loneliness there.
>
> The wallaroos grope through the tufts of the grass,
> And turn to their covers for fear;
> But he sits in the ashes and lets them pass
> Where the boomerangs sleep with the spear:
> With the nullah, the sling, and the spear.

This poem was a popular eulogy for the 'passing of the Aborigines' of NSW. The conflation of culture with genetics provided the dominant medium for expressing and explaining their plight. In the local Kempsey press, 'full blood' Aborigines were always referred to as a dying race. Statements, for example, ranged from the commonsense, 'We know that the full blood is fast disappearing from the coast' (*MC* September 1937); to the statistically supported, 'New South Wales is fast being depleted of its real natives. The annual report of the Board for the Protection of Aborigines . . . showed that there are now 1,081 full bloods' (*MA* January 1926); or in the form of eulogies, 'He was one of the last of the pure aborigines [sic] of long ago and his faithfulness and honesty will not soon be forgotten' (*MA* December 1920). In terms of this popular discourse, the only 'true' Aborigine of the region resided in the past.[5] While in some respects differing from the more animal-like depiction of Aborigines, the view that they were a 'doomed race' and the conflation of culture/genetics persisted.

Such views about the Aborigines also informed the state's sporadic official interventions into the communities on the Macleay River. As I mentioned earlier, the local police were in charge of administering and controlling the reserve communities, with interventions by the agents of the state generally confined to perceived threats to the wider society. The police tended to deal with threats to local order, affronts to morality or idleness and exercised their control through intermittent displays of force, which functioned to ensure conformity with European values or to deter

5. This same theme is also reflected in the work of anthropologist Radcliffe-Brown, who after research on the north coast of NSW, which included the Macleay Valley, stated (1929: 400) that, 'The scanty remnant of the original population is now gathered into reserves and camps, where nothing of original native life remains. In most of the camps the children and the younger men and women, of whom the majority have some white blood, do not know the native language. Information about former customs can therefore only be obtained from a very few old men of sixty or seventy who can remember what they were taught when they were young'.

and contain particular Aboriginal activities or behaviour. Coercion was thus used to ensure that the Aborigines engaged in or desisted from particular forms of behaviour.

Intervention into the social life of Aborigines was also sought by the APB where it was felt that conventional standards of European morality were absent. For example, one policeman stationed at Bellbrook regularly rode out to the Aboriginal reserve (some 2.5 kilometres) on Monday mornings to 'hunt' the men out to work. Similarly, in 1915, the unmarried status of Aborigines on Bellbrook became the subject of an APB report. An APB inspector called the 'attention of the Kempsey clergymen to the number of unmarried couples on the reserve' (ML 4/7124). As a result, a Seventh Day Adventist pastor went to the reserve and married the 'erring' couples. As one man recalled:

> My mother and father C.s., K.s., S.s., H.s. and all them. They just get married, Sunday. They'd just get married. He Pastor R. stayed in Kempsey . . . and he had a horse and buggy and drive up to Bellbrook and Wollomombi . . . They are more shamed, they don't want a mob. Black-fella terrible shame fella. Being shamed, you know, when you're doing things in the open and you don't want it that way. Pastor R. might go an' marry 'em on their own or in two's or three's.

As a means of inculcating the community with European norms, however, such sporadic interventions did little more than satisfy European sensibilities.

The use of force was applied in cases where Aboriginal practices came into conflict with the local European community. In this regard, the number of dogs kept by Aborigines on Bellbrook Reserve was a constant concern to local graziers. In the following episode a woman recalled the role of the police in the eradication of this problem:

> We used to have a lot of dogs. You know that they done to him [G.T.]. They were his only friend and he thought the world of them. D.D. [a local European] said they were killing his calves but they were never ever away from the old man and they were there with their guns. He brought the policeman with him. He started shooting the dogs. The dogs were running away and he was shooting them as they went.

The role of the local police was to maintain the interests of the wider community. The exercise of the law carried the force of prohibition through repression.

The expression of the power of the state was manifested in a highly personalised form. For Aborigines this power was primarily personified in the policeman. As one person put it:

> [if] that policeman was coming way over there you could jest see him there.

They'd all be wondering what happened, who did wrong and nobody did the wrong. But he'd [Aborigines] be standin' back, he won't face him, that the man you were always frightened of . . . *I ran away from policeman, don't fret, and I never did nothin' wrong* . . . Those days if you only jest saw him coming, out of sight you'd go . . . You'd be out of sight till he call for you. They had the fear of the policeman in 'em all the time.

What was seen as the indiscriminate and arbitrary exercise of power induced a form of terror in which being Aboriginal was seen as synonymous with moral culpability. The manner in which such forms of external control could be subverted is also revealed as adhering to strategies of avoidance, i.e. not being seen.

A characteristic of this personalised form of power was that it could be mediated by those who implemented control. In fact only one of the four policemen stationed at Bellbrook used his authority to 'hunt the men out to work'. Another, by contrast, would allow children to stay overnight in the local gaol rather than see them travel all the way back to the reserve, when they came to the village to see movies shown by Penns & Cummings Travelling Picture Show. He would give them a bowl of porridge, and they would 'cut off home' in the morning. Nevertheless, the 'real' policeman was seen very much as a figure of authority and hostility. As one man pointed out, the Dhan-gadi word for policeman is 'hard hand' (*yama ngalin*) (Widders 1979: 63) or *jama nagalanj* (Holmer 1967: 49).

Such forms of intervention had a number of distinguishing features and consequences. State power was executed in a personal and arbitrary manner at the discretion of the local policeman. Control was directed towards segregating Aborigines into specific areas rather than systematically dominating them within those communities. In that state control was imposed sporadically from outside the patterns of daily life, it could enforce and ensure only a veneer of conformity within specific social situations. The Aborigines thus had a large degree of autonomy and control over their everyday practices within the enclosed 'territory' of the reserve (see Chapter 6).

Patterns of intervention on Burnt Bridge varied depending on the circumstances but were consistent with the form of legalistic custodianship exercised by the state. The main conflict on Burnt Bridge was over the way in which the APB was attempting to control the reserve. When the north coast railway was being built (1913), smallholders were able to earn extra revenue cutting sleepers.[6] European smallholders involved

6. The construction of the railway line between Wauchope and Kempsey began in 1913 (Neil 1972: 80). For the young men of Burnt Bridge sleeper and girder-cutting became the main economic activity in the local economy. The Aboriginal men would go out together and camp for a fortnight and cut sleepers. The sleepers were taken to the railway station by truck, or if the terrain was too rough or muddy by bullock, where they were inspected and accepted or rejected. In the 1920s the price for each sleeper was 1/6d, while those rejected, if

in sleeper-cutting could cut them from their own land and thereby avoid the levy imposed on those who worked on state forestry plantations. The Aboriginal men assumed they had the same rights on the reserve. The APB, however, refused them the right to cut timber or to agist cattle on the reserve. The latter was commonly practiced by European landholders on their own property. The struggle for local control of the land farmers held on Burnt Bridge came to a head in 1910. In that year Davis (an Aboriginal farmer) agisted some bullocks belonging to a local European on the reserve. In response to Davis's action, the APB instructed the local police to warn Davis that 'If he offends again he will be put off the reserve and any money owing for agistment should be given to the Board' (SA 4/7119). As if to reinforce its control over Davis, the APB recorded his status as 'octoroon' (one-eighth Aboriginal blood) rather than 'half-caste', which is what it had been up to that point. The sudden change in Davis's biological status would appear to have been connected with the passing of the Aborigines Protection Act (1909) in which octoroons had the least right to be on government reserves.

The important point here is that state intervention in the form of *legalistic custodianship* was narrow and negative. Control was exercised in an essentially skeletal manner through the use of legal and punitive measures. While these sporadic interventions did discipline Aboriginal behaviour, they also shaped the meaning and understanding of their social world.

The other distinguishing feature about state intervention in the form of legalistic custodianship was the continuation of the link of Aborigines with private and philanthropic endeavours emanating from civil society. At this stage, the state had not assumed full control over the lives of Aborigines in NSW. In the Macleay Valley, as elsewhere, missionaries from the Australian Aborigine Missions (AAM) were placed in charge of the education and training of reserve Aborigines. The AAM had been established in 1891 and with the approval of the APB began appointing missionaries to reserves in 1894 (ML Q572 9901). Such private philanthropic enterprise provided the means whereby the state minimised its interventions.

Missionaries were concerned with the moral and spiritual rejuvenation of the Aborigines and perceived their role as that of spiritual custodians. Their success appears to have been limited. Although they

the men were fortunate, could be sold to farmers for fence posts for 6d. This pattern of work on the margins of the local economy replicated the pattern discussed earlier for the Dhan-gadi on the upper Macleay River. In this case, however, Aborigines and Europeans, many of whom were smallholders, were involved in sleeper-cutting. The distinction between Aboriginal and European labour is, as Morgan argues, a difference between 'free' and 'unfree' labour. '[If] white workers end up in these jobs too, the reason lies in the economic compulsion of free labour rather than the sort of coercion produced from the ideological and political mechanisms of racism.' (Morgan 1981: 29) found reasons to be pleased with progress in farming, they were, as a missionary on the lower Macleay stated, to see 'very little progress in the spiritual side of . . . [their] work'. On Burnt Bridge it was the same: 'We are pleased to note their increasing effort to improve their farms: but how we long to see more interest longing after the things of God' (ML Q572 9901: 1908). The moral highs and lows for the missionaries were punctuated by the cycle associated with corn production. The monthly reports are enthusiastic about the disciplined and productive behaviour of Aborigines in ploughing, planting and cultivating corn crops, but the 'moral backsliding' that occurred at harvest time was an annual source of disappointment. As one missionary described, 'It is once again corn pulling season, which brings many from other parts, who spend the money they earn on gambling and drink and cause much disturbance on Fattorinni Island, making it very hard for those who are trying to live respectable lives' (ML Q572 9901). Without the power to impose legislative sanctions (and to intervene forcibly), these voluntary organisations had very little real authority over the Aborigines. As one missionary put it, 'sometimes one feels tempted to take other steps besides gentle persuasions' (ML Q572 9901).

5.3. The Emergence of New Strategies of Intervention

The Aborigines Protection Act (1909) (1915 amendment) represented a major extension of control over Aborigines in NSW. Throughout the initial decades of control, the APB had felt increasingly constrained by the limited scope of its legal authority. Control had been largely invested in the police. In particular, the APB had for some time wanted to control the movement and activities of Aborigines. The only legislation to facilitate such control had been the Liquor Act (1867) and, in 1902, a section on Aboriginal segregation which had been included in the Vagrancy Act. It was not until 1909, however, that the Aborigines Protection Act provided the APB with the amount of control it required. The APB could now remove Aborigines living near towns and, in addition to its previous power to revoke reserves, was given direct control of the reserves and the power to relocate them.

The changes incorporated in the 1909 legislation not only represented the first fully formulated policy towards Aborigines in NSW, but also outlined a new strategy for intervention. Earlier policy had been 'to ameliorate the condition of blacks and to exercise general guardianship'. The Board was now empowered to 'exercise general *supervision* and care over *all matters* affecting Aborigines'. The mode of control on reserves was no longer to be haphazard and discontinuous, but constant and uninterrupted. Similarly, the emphasis in government policy was no longer to exile and hide from public view the 'remnants of a dying race'. The new legislation sought to alter the behaviour of Aborigines, to train and correct them, as individuals, to be useful members of the wider society. The agency of this surveillance and active intervention was to be the station managers and matrons, supported by other APB officers.[7] Centralised control was envisaged as another change which could be achieved through 'the vacating of small reserves with the view to settling aborigines [sic] on large areas under the control of managers' (SA 4/7117). The policy of the state was no longer concerned with notions of self-sufficiency and segregation, but with assimilation, at least for children and those classified as half-caste, quadroon or octoroon. Full bloods, it was still firmly believed, would somehow fade away and no longer pose a problem.

At the ideological level, there was a tentative shift in state policy away from an emphasis on an inherent, natural Aboriginal essence towards one in which the 'Aboriginal problem' was seen in terms of social/environmental factors. The intellectual basis was being laid for state power to take on increasingly pedagogic forms of control, for it was no longer assumed that the Aboriginal problem would resolve itself naturally. Instead it was thought that the colonial contradiction could be negated by implementing assimilationist policies through which Aborigines would become absorbed into the wider society. What was prefigured in the passing of the legislation was a more systematic form of intervention associated with *bureaucratic custodianship,* in which pedagogic and totalising forms of control were to be implemented.

The new policies brought major changes in the use of power, with strategies of intervention beginning to approximate those practised in a total institution (Goffman 1961) or carceral (Foucault 1977). Techniques for controlling and changing Aborigines applied, 'in-depth surveillance and control' as the primary means of 'normalising' individuals (ibid.). Such techniques, initially developed to discipline criminals in prisons, spread to other institutions such as asylums, schools, workplaces and barracks (ibid. pp. 210–11). Foucault's characterisation of the restructuring of the prison as an institution in terms of the techniques associated with the 'leper' and the 'plague victim' (ibid.p.198) captures in an analogous manner the transformation in policy toward Aborigines:

> The leper was caught up in a practice of rejection, of exile enclosure; he was left to his doom in a mass among which it was useless to differentiate; those caught up with the plague were caught up in a meticulous tactical partitioning in which individual differentiations were the constricting effects of a power that multiplied, articulated and sub-divided itself; the great confinement on the one hand; the correct training on the other. The leper and his separation;

7. An Aboriginal *station* was supervised by a resident manager, while Aboriginal *reserves* continued to have only sporadic external supervision as had been the case in the pre-1909 period.

the plague and its segmentations. The first is marked; the second analysed and distributed. The exile of the leper and the arrest of the plague do not bring with them the same political dream. The first is of the pure community; the second that of the disciplined society.

The transformation of the prisoner, or Aborigine, from irredeemable leper to redeemable plague victim was an 'intensification and ramification of power' (ibid.) which, in the case of the latter, was an aspect of colonial power.

The legislation prefigured a staggered progress towards the adoption of bureaucratic forms of discipline over the subject population. The policies associated with the bureaucratic custodianship of Aborigines did not gain complete ascendency until the reformulation of policy which occurred with the establishment of the Aborigines Welfare Board (AWB) in 1940. Throughout the period of APB control, the policy set out in the Aborigines Protection Act differed greatly from its practice. By 1914, only 14 manager-controlled stations had been established amongst some 170 reserves (Long 1970: 28), yet, if the disciplinary techniques were to proceed, enclosure and segregation were necessary. Only through segregation could the detailed management of the movements and activities of the subject group be monitored and corrected. Nevertheless, the manager's authority resided in a personalised and arbitrary power, much like that of the police except in that it was exercised from within rather than from outside the stations. In the exercise of control, however, legalistic forms of custodianship, which sought to deter and contain, mainly continued to be used instead of the more bureaucratic forms of custodianship, which sought to introduce pedagogic regimes for Aborigines or codified rules of conduct for managers. Similarly, the control of Aborigines continued to be shared between the state and the philanthropic AAM. In the Macleay Valley, missionaries remained on Bellbrook and Burnt Bridge reserves until they were replaced in the 1930s by government-appointed managers. Such diverse forms of control worked against the standardisation and codification of controls over Aborigines.

The legalistic control, invested in managers (and absent from missionary authority), did signify a change in the forms of control on government stations. The first manager in the Macleay Valley was appointed in 1915 to supervise the Aborigines on Pelican and Fattorinni Islands and on the nearby Kinchela reserve (SA 4/7214). The station was collectively referred to as the Lower Macleay. The control invested in the manager's regime under the new acts was immediately felt. In one incident on Pelican Island, Harry Mumbler, an Aboriginal farmer, took the manager to court for assaulting his son. Mumbler had married one of the original farmer's daughters and had taken over one of the farms. The court decided in Mumbler's favour. In retaliation:

The proceeds of his crop [were] practically confiscated, for the Board took £32 of it for rent, took his large crop of pumpkins for nothing, utilising Mumbler's boat to ferry them away, took £10.8s.0d for agistment of his two horses, for 2/- a head a week, took dentist fees incurred by others, and the price of timber to mend the Board's boat. (*MC*, July 1937)

Mumbler was also asked to sign an agreement prepared by the manager setting down the conditions for his continued residence on the island. He refused to sign and moved off the island to Greenhill (fringe camp). In effect, the new legislation empowered the manager to be the sole authority on a government station.

The farming of land by Aborigines came to a more or less abrupt end on the lower Macleay shortly after the appointment of the managers. Under the Aborigines Protection Act (1909) they were empowered to control Aboriginal income. The Act explicitly affirmed that the reserves had not been established to promote independent farming but to limit the use of government funding through the establishment of self-sufficiency on the reserves. In practice, this meant a self-sufficient budget for the APB not the farmers. When this was applied on the lower Macleay, the men who had been farming simply 'turned it in'. As one described it, 'The AP Board stepped in and wanted the money for the corn, for the sale of the corn. They got out of it then. My old fella was tellin' me that they said they couldn't handle it given 'em rations.' They simply refused to work the farms for rations. The attempts of the manager to gain greater control did not always work smoothly.

The farming on Fattorinni Island suffered a similar fate. Linwood had been joined by other farmers over the years. Prior to the managers' regime, a missionary report in 1908 (ML Q572 9901) stated that, 'We are rejoiced to see all the farmers pushing ahead with ploughing . . . Five of them too have nice little vegetable plots – potatoes, beans, cabbages, peas, pumpkins and melons being mostly favoured.' Despite the 'backsliding' that occurred during the corn-pulling time, when 'strangers' came and spent the money they had earned 'unwisely', the corn and vegetable harvests were an annual event on the island. The demise of Linwood was recorded in the local newspaper (*MC*, July 1937): 'James Linwood, of Fattorinni Island, an aboriginal [sic] who felled and cleared the land, lived there for 35 years, had cows and horses, grew corn and traded with storekeeper Magnus Thompson on the same footing as other settlers, was driven off by the Board to the bush and poverty.' Furthermore, when Linwood was awarded £10.0.0 by the courts after a car accident, it was collected by the manager, and Linwood never saw any of it (ibid.). The legal authority invested in the station managers provided the basis for the personalised, arbitrary power and total authority they exercised over the Aborigines on the stations. Under the managers' authority, the pattern of social existence that had developed on the islands ended. Moving to a 'bush' or 'fringe' camp became the only means of frustrating the exercise of such authority.

The considerable control the state legislation gave the APB over Aboriginal children effectively replicated the intentions of bureaucratic custodianship. Control of Aboriginal children had a major emphasis in the 1909 Act and in its 1915 amendment. Provision was made for the children of the state to be inculcated with European values and attitudes. The 1909 legislation enabled the APB to remove children without parental consent if a magistrate found that they had been 'neglected' (Read 1982: 5). While this policy equally applied to European children, the 1915 amendment removed the necessity for a magistrate's consent and gave the APB complete control (ibid. p. 6). This strategy reflected the more materialist focus of the legislation on social/environmental factors as the major obstacle associated with the Aboriginal 'problem', i.e. underpinning the movement towards bureaucratic custodianship of Aboriginal children was a materialist view which considered that individual development was acquired through experience and learning. Individuals were seen as the products of impressions received through learning and experience. The logic sustaining the major emphasis on children was that they were perceived to be far less likely to be contaminated by their social environment than adults.

This materialist view of the individual as the product of his or her environment upholds the pedagogic rationality of an institutionalisation that tries to control the social environment of the inmate. Pedagogic policies that seek to correct or retrain the inmate are based on a view of the individual as a social being that stands in direct contrast to the biological determinism attributed to Aboriginality. As we saw in the Victorian legislation, the incompatability of these ideas was partially overcome with the notion of the half-caste, i.e. one who also had European genes. However, the individual development of half-castes over the age of 34 years was considered to be irredeemably influenced by social environmental factors. Therefore, they were socially equated with the full blood. NSW did not develop an explicit theory of administration based on singling out half-castes and lighter-castes as *legally European*. Instead, the administration pursued a policy of institutionalisation.

The major thrust of the policy was to remove children from their Aboriginal environment. To facilitate this end, the practice of bureaucratic custodianship was directed towards children and adolescents rather than the Aboriginal population in general. At this stage, even the creation of the new stations was seen primarily as a means of training young Aborigines 'to take their places amongst the rest of the community' (Long 1970: 29). More specifically, an apprenticeship system was set up whereby young adolescent men and women could be removed from stations and reserves and bound over to Europeans to work for a period of three years. Boys' and girls' homes were established to take in and train children, and APB inspectors were appointed to remove any children they considered neglected or in moral danger in the stations or reserves. A 'home finder' was appointed to place girls in European homes. Between 1909 and 1916, 400 children were removed by the APB and, between 1916 and 1938, another 1,600 children were removed from various communities throughout the state (Read 1982: 9). The policy of institutionalising children was designed with the express purpose of establishing pedagogic control over their social environment.

The scale of this exercise can be understood in relation to the size of the Aboriginal population during this period. In 1910, the total Aboriginal population of NSW was only 6,957; and by 1938 had increased to 10,415 (cited Duncan, 1969: 352).[8] The removal of 2,000 children was a significant number. The policy of assimilating children, which was embodied in the legislation, attempted to solve the Aboriginal problem through cultural genocide. As Duncan (ibid. p. 296) records, the policy of cultural genocide extended beyond the retraining of children. It was extended to ensure that institutionalised children were sent to different regions of the state as a means of keeping Aboriginal youth apart.[9]

5.4. Dependency and Domestication

The relationship that emerged between Aborigines and the state (through the codification of government controls in the Aborigines Protection Act of 1909) can be most adequately understood in terms of

8. Smith (1980: 3) argues that the accuracy of such statistics should not be taken for granted, as they appear to have been influenced by prevailing administrative opinion of Aborigines. As he states, 'It is no exaggeration to say that the basic problem in Aboriginal population studies is to penetrate the mythology and ideology that surround the subject in order to discover what the real facts are; Australian native administration has been influenced by, and has also produced, a series of myths which have been promoted, accepted, and discarded as the needs of the majority society changed. Changes in official and other statistics have routinely followed the changes in the myths. For instance, when the Aborigines were held to be a dying race and no one was really interested, population figures showed a steady decline until the late 1930s; even minor technical adjustments to estimated numbers were hailed as evidence of the "black's tragic decline". Then, coincidentally, numbers began to increase as the new official policy of preservation and protection as a prelude to assimilation gained acceptance. It now appears distinctly possible that no overall decline occurred this century at all, and that official statistics merely reflected Government and community convictions that the Aborigines were destined, whether by destruction or absorption, to disappear from the face of the earth.'

9. 'An article, published in the *Sydney Morning Herald* on 29 October 1924, attacked the Protection Board's policy of sending Aboriginal girls from Cootamundra to the metropolitan area as nurse girls and servants; and keeping Aboriginal youths in rural areas to work on farms. The article pointed out that by keeping Aboriginal youths and girls apart it would expedite the passing of the Aboriginal race.' (Duncan 1969: 296)

dependency and domestication.[10] Previously, relative autonomy had been afforded Aborigines through legalistic custodianship, which provided the conditions under which farming could develop during the late nineteenth and early twentieth centuries. Dependency, by contrast, reflects the special relationship of control between government (in the form of an administrator) and Aboriginal communities. Increasingly, through the APB and more particularly its successor, the Aborigines Welfare Board (AWB), control was exercised over 'all matters affecting Aborigines', i.e. residence, food, clothing, education, employment and the control of children (see also Chapter 6). Aborigines lived in a *relationship of dependency* in which they were expected to exercise *no control* over the direction of their lives and in which there was no provision for them to be consulted or permitted to influence decisions made on their behalf. The ultimate authority rested with a government over which they had no control. In this, relations between Aborigines and the state extend beyond repressive and punitive forms of domination to those associated with relations of dependency.

Domestication, in this context, denotes a particular form of internal colonialism that seeks to dissolve the cultural distinctiveness of the indigenous population and to force its integration into the dominant society, while at the same time making a distinction between its political status and that of all other groups within the nation-state. The cultural integrity of the subjugated population is denied, and the political practices of the state are aimed at 'retraining' this population for *individual success* in the dominant society. No such form of administration was exercised over the lives of any other citizens of the state, apart from those judged criminal or insane; even the *children* of the criminal or insane were never subjected to such extensive controls. The severity of this regime of control reflected the colonial character of the administration.

This form of state authoritarianism sought to extinguish existing familial and communal ties as a pre-condition to granting equal rights

10. Domestication and dependency need to be distinguished from 'domestic dependency', which is used in the native American context (see Jorgensen 1974; Jorgensen et al. 1978). The term 'domestic dependency' was originally coined by Chief Justice Marshall in his consideration of the legal status of treaties between the Indian tribes and the United States government, in the case of the Cherokee nation vs. state of Georgia (1831). In his judgement, Marshall asserted that, 'it may be doubted whether those tribes which reside within the acknowledged boundaries of the United States, with strict accuracy, be nominated foreign nations. They may, more correctly, perhaps, be denominated domestic dependent nations'. In effect, the tribal groups were defined as existing within the sovereignty and dominion of the USA. Nevertheless, Marshall's judgement also affirmed that 'the Indians had always been considered as distinct, independent, political communities, retaining their original natural rights, as the undisputed possessors of the soil . . . The settled Doctrine of the Law of Nations is, that a weaker power does not surrender its independence, its rights to self government, by associating with a stronger (*sic*), and taking its protection' (cited McNickle 1973: 54–5). The term 'domestic dependency' was not associated with the denial of the cultural and political integrity of native American groups.

within the state. In the case of NSW this was to be achieved not simply by repression but through pedagogic intervention, which would establish Aboriginal equality. Such pedagogic interventions were designed to bring about the dismantling of Aboriginal identity and the breakup of communities. Initially, this was to be achieved through the resocialisation of children in special institutions or through their location with European families. As the Board report of 1921 states (cited Read 1982: 2), 'The continuation of this policy of disassociating the children from camp life must eventually solve the Aboriginal problem.' Such forms of bureaucratic custodianship were extended to include all Aborigines in later periods (see Chapter 6).

The particular logic behind such policies determined that while 'tribal' or group success was denied, individual success was possible, but only in terms of and within the dominant society. In this respect, there was a high degree of ambiguity associated with domestication and dependency. Government policies towards Aborigines embraced a broad range of repressive political practices, but these were ultimately directed towards facilitating incorporation into the wider society rather than towards continuing to bring about a formal separation between Aborigines and Europeans. Furthermore, the ambiguities associated with domestication and dependency ensured that a number of contradictory practices could exist alongside the APB's policies. Not only did the institutional forms of social control over Aborigines become more and more refined in the early part of the century, but they were also reinforced by various attempts by local government, other departments, or private organisations to erect formal barriers to exclude Aborigines from local European communities (see below).

Aborigines could never be sure of their position as their Aboriginality could either be invoked against them or totally ignored. They could be pushed or pulled in different directions depending on the attitudes of the local European population. The uncertainty of any given situation was described to me in the following way:

> You could tell like, you know, I don't know it seems funny, for you to get around, and up there [Bellbrook] you'd talk to anyone see and have a joke with 'em. Down here [Kempsey] didn't know who you were bumpin', you'd get knocked arse over head if you started talkin' to 'em and they didn't know who you was.

For the Aborigines in the area, towns were mapped out in terms of the level of harrassment. Kempsey and Bowraville were 'bad' towns, while Armidale and Port Macquarie were 'good' towns.

The enactment of legislation at the local district level and the active agitation of Europeans in some areas to segregate Aborigines from government-run institutions, such as schools and hospitals, ensured that state departments adopted policies different from those of the APB. As a result of the opposition of European parents to Aboriginal children attending the same schools, an Aboriginal school had been erected on Pelican Island in 1892 (SA 4/7108). In the previous year, Aboriginal children had been removed from the public school at Rollands Plain because of the 'objections raised by the parents of European children' (cited Duncan 1969: 237). In 1900, 20 Aboriginal children from the farms on Burnt Bridge were turned away from the local school at Euroka. The Burnt Bridge community responded by sending a letter outlining its situation. It stated, 'these children might receive instruction at the Euroka Public School but all who had presented themselves at the school were sent back to their homes' (SA 5/15182.1). As a result, they sought a teacher and a 'provisional school set on Government land reserved as an Aboriginal settlement' (ibid.). Their request was taken up by the APB, and a missionary teacher was appointed.

The formal policy of the Department of Public Instruction was that any complaint from a European parent was sufficient for all Aboriginal children to be removed. In the Macleay region, children were removed from all schools that had a significant Aboriginal population, namely Rollands Plain, Kempsey, Bowraville and Bellbrook.

The same pattern of exclusion and segregation was followed in Kempsey after the establishment of a new district hospital by the state government. The subsequent improvement of the hot water system in 1915 and the installation of electricity in 1917 brought about a significant increase in European patients treated there. Patient numbers rose from 258 in 1911 to 609 in 1917 (ML 362.1 M). At the same time, the doctors pressed the health authorities to have Aborigines removed to separate accommodation. In the Annual Report (1916) the reasons given for segregation stated that the 'average Aboriginal patient involves much more exacting work on the part of the nursing staff than the average white patient' and that the 'heat and humidity of the local climatic conditions make separate accommodation for the Aborigines extremely desirable' (ML 362.1 M). By 1917 the calls for the exclusion had grown more urgent. As the hospital Annual Report for that year (ML 362.1 M) states, 'The most acute problem of all, that of the separate accommodation for Aborigines, remains unsolved. It is nevertheless being vigorously attacked, and the interest of the district and of the Health Department is being gradually aroused.' This reflected the emergence of a scientific/medical discourse which defined the moral degradation of Aborigines in terms of ideas of biology. The discourse conflated infection with contagion and pollution and moved between notions of 'social-environmental' and 'natural' causality. A policy of segregation was proposed in the guise of a medical discourse which expressed the fear of the spread of contagious and infectious diseases, such as tuberculosis and venereal disease (see below). The source of such diseases, however, was related to racial typifications. The basis of Aboriginal illness was identified with the natural proclivity of Aborigines to engage in unhygienic, unsanitary practices and social vices. In keeping with secular scientific practices, the social environment of Aborigines was seen to be the continuing source of infection. At the same time, the existence of such infectious and contagious diseases was seen as evidence of the collective pollution and moral degradation of Aborigines.

The use of racial typifications increasingly determined medical practices towards Aborigines, which were the inverse of prevailing hospital procedures. Segregation treated Aborigines in terms of typifications which departed from the individualising strategies of patient care associated with monitoring, surveillance and hospitalisation as a means of controlling the social environment of the patient. The practice of exclusion through segregation was constitutive of the view that it was not simply an individual pathology that was being treated but a natural defect of Aborigines. This was quite clearly revealed in the distinctive procedures that were initiated in their treatment. As well as segregated accommodation, all cutlery, clothing, towels, etc. had the letters 'ABO' on them to prevent inadvertent use by Europeans.

Racial ideas of pollution, therefore, did not simply legitimate discriminatory relations, but also constituted them. By 1939 the discourse had become established as concrete fact. As one councillor seeking the complete removal of Aborigines from the hospital stated at a council meeting, 'He had it on good medical authority that at least 80 per cent of the Aborigines were infected with T.B. and in many cases with something worse' (*MC*, September 1939). The development of the discourse on pollution may be seen in the attitudes expressed towards the nurses caring for Aboriginal patients in 1916 and again in 1939. Whereas in 1916 the view expressed was that, 'nurses should receive special remuneration for handling Aboriginal cases' (ML 362.1 M), in 1939, 'it was not fair to have nurses attending Aboriginal patients at the same time as they had to attend patients in other wards' (*MC*, September 1939). Having established the possibility of contagion, the concern now was to organise schedules to deal with this medical reality.

Aborigines were systematically excluded from areas where hygiene was a high priority or where there was thought to be a chance of pollution. The ideology of pollution lay behind the widespread segmentation in employment patterns. As one Aboriginal man put it, 'they wouldn't let you milk [by hand], wouldn't get a blackfella to milk or in the butter factory, that was all whitefellas jobs'. For the Aboriginal farmers on Burnt Bridge, this exclusion also meant that they were excluded from dairy farming, an activity which most European smallholders participated in from around the beginning of the century (see Chapter 2). For Europeans, specialised corn production had been superceded by dairying in the early decades of the twentieth century. For Aborigines, however, 'you couldn't have a dairy farm, you have to have a licence or somethin' like that and then you wouldn't be granted that'. Indeed, one man on Burnt Bridge, Albert Moseley, did apply for a dairy farm licence, but his application was rejected. The ideology of the polluting potential of Aborigines as carriers of diseases unified a number of political practices of exclusion that were enacted or initiated at the local level.

In the colonial context, the analogies with the 'leper' and the 'plague victim' may be extended to suggest that the Aborigine was simultaneously both. As state government policy moved toward regarding Aborigines as plague victims, local council increasingly saw them as lepers. The racism associated with pollution was a major factor in these exclusions. The contradictions between local and state policies were not inconsistencies, but realisations of different political aims and ends. The ideology of pollution reflected the political contingencies of relations between Aborigines and Europeans at the local level. Notions of pollution institutionalised segregation in everyday interactions and formed the basis of a hierarchy of difference. At this stage state and local racial politics converged and the idea of pollution became consistent with the immediate political aims of an Aboriginal administration, which increasingly sought institutional enclosure for retraining.

The politics of segregation at a state level also focused on Aborigines as the source of contagion. Indeed, in 1936 a 'moral panic' over the possible spread of *gonococcal ophthalmia* to the European population led to the introduction of state legislation permitting the compulsory examination of 'any Aborigine or person apparently having an admixture of Aboriginal blood' (cited Rowley 1973: 59). The relationship between this event and the increase in Aboriginal segregation was made clear by the APB's parliamentary member, who stated that, 'The reason for the urgency of this measure . . . is because . . . the health of our *own* people is very seriously threatened at the present moment. Either we allow these people to roam far and wide and spread possible disease, or take them from the precincts of the villages and towns where all this wrongdoing happens' (ibid.). Such 'moral panics', expressed in terms of a medical discourse, were consistent with demands for more adequate controls over the social movement and the social environment of Aborigines. The increasing range of discriminatory legislation, enacted at different levels of government and department policy, worked together to increase the relations of control by and dependency upon the state.

5.5. Resistance to the 'Persecution Board'[11]

The Aboriginal population of the Macleay Valley was by no means passive to the changing patterns of domination engendered by the Aborigines Protection Act. As we have seen, the appointment of a manager to the lower Macleay reserves ended the pattern of farming that had developed there. Both Mumbler and Linwood responded by removing themselves from the station. This indirect form of resistance, whereby Aboriginal families moved from manager-controlled stations to set themselves up on reserves or 'fringe camps', appears to have been widespread. In response to this indirect form of resistance, the APB in 1922 specifically instructed managers to prevent such practices: the managers were expected to exercise their 'utmost endeavours' to 'dissuade' families attempting to evade the APB's control from leaving the stations and to ensure that 'younger children, and older ones, are not allowed to live a life of idleness' (SA 4/7126). In the Macleay Valley, the major unofficial camp, or 'fringe camp' as it was called, was at Greenhill. For those Aborigines who avoided, or were expelled from, the government station on the lower Macleay, Greenhill became an alternative place to live. It survived a number of attempts by the APB to have it removed.

The move to a fringe camp was for many Aborigines a difficult decision in that kinship and personal relationships continued to dominate social life. The movement from a station to a fringe camp was a movement from one's own kin-group to a non-kin group, in which the absence of personal relationships rendered interactions problematic. As one man described it:

> When you're born in a place it seems different to what other place is, see. You're not got your people like, you know, where ever black fella go they like to stick together and all that sort of game. Well, you that used to 'em up there that you not used to 'em down here. You more or less get away from 'em, you're glad to get away from 'em, go to work somewhere until you get used to 'em. Then they couldn't kick you out of the place then.

While expulsion from the station reduced the amount of control the managers could exercise over certain individuals, as a sanction it did give them more control over their own stations. This internal control was reinforced by the Aborigines' cultural practice of regarding expulsion, or at least the denial of residence amongst kin, as highly problematic.

At the same time, Aborigines also responded to the new government programme by trying to prevent the police or APB inspectors from

---

11. This is what the Aborigines commonly called the APB.

attempting to remove Aboriginal children to government institutions. State intervention in this sphere was sporadic and the seemingly random appropriation of children by APB inspectors, and the state police shifted the confrontation from the community to an individual family level. An exception to this occurred in 1912 when the residents of both Burnt Bridge and Rollands Plain sent petitions to the APB complaining about the Board's actions 'in taking away young children from the reserves' (APB minutes, SA 4/7120). Nevertheless, the response to such highly personal forms of state intervention into Aboriginal family life generated individual rather than collective strategies of resistance.

It seems as if families were often powerless to circumvent this form of state authoritarianism. A former inmate of Kinchela Boys Home explained how he had run away from the Boys Home three times to return to his family at nearby South West Rocks, and on each occasion an APB inspector and a state policeman had arrived to take him back to the Boys Home.[12] Nevertheless, there were exceptions as a number of small acts of great personal courage demonstrate. In two separate incidents on Burnt Bridge fathers resorted to threats of violence to protect their children from the APB's predations. On both occasions the APB's officers were threatened with guns. As one incident was recounted, 'Old D.C. . . . he had a mob out at Burnt Bridge, he had a fair mob of kids. This bloke [Board Officer] had 'em in a car or something to take 'em. He [Board officer] had 'em and he [D.C.] pulled a shot gun, "Let the kids go!", he said, "or I'll blow you over". He let 'em out'. On another occasion a similar exchange occurred between a particular Board officer, Donaldson, and a Burnt Bridge farmer: 'old Mr D. said to Donaldson, "I know what'll stop you". He was going away and Mr. Donaldson looked back like that and said "What?" He [D.] said, "A lump of lead". He never came back any more. He [D.] wasn't frightened at all' (see also Goodall 1982). These actions remained individual and spontaneous acts of defiance against immediate and personal expressions of the APB's power.

Perhaps the most deliberate symbolic defiance by a family (Murray) against the policy of cultural genocide, which was being perpetuated through the removal of children by the state, occurred at the Hasting River. In this confrontation with APB officers who had come to take the children away, the Murray's responded with a defiant symbolic

---

12. The APB had established a Boys Home at Kinchela on the Macleay River in 1925 (Long 1970: 29). It was this former inmate's grandfather who had cleared the land for farming in the 1880s. The following APB report was given on Kinchela reserve in 1894: No. 174 – Kinchela reserve '14th July, 1884: Land occupied by William Drew with his family for past 4 years. Drew has expended a considerable amount of labour and capital in clearing and cultivation. 10 acres of timber killed and scrub cut down. Barn, hut and fruit trees of various kinds, all the ground being under maize crop which itself is worth £250 to £300. Has housing and farming implements. Supports some aged residents, and other blacks occasionally camp with him' (SA 2/28349).

statement of cultural difference. As the incident was related, 'The father and the mother dressed in Aboriginal attire with boomerangs and spears and everything when they came to take their family'. Such actions were direct assertions of cultural integrity in a context where the main organising principle of state control and hegemonic domination was expressed in terms of the superiority of the values, customs and institutions of Europeans. The assertion of Aboriginal cultural identity in these actions reflected the transformation of what had been essentially unreflexive cultural habits into conscious, political statements of defiance. Such statements did not deter the APB inspectors; and in this instance they persisted with their efforts, and the children ultimately were removed to government institutions.

Given that these forms of intervention were exercised by agencies located outside the communities, collective resistance to such agencies was avoidance. As a Bellbrook woman pointed out, all children disappeared into the bush whenever the approach of APB inspectors or police was detected. *Wu bilisman* (policeman) would be passed around the reserve and the 'kids would scatter'.[13] As the woman stressed, all that would be detected by the time the state authorities arrived was 'a "thump-thump" noise like rabbits': they could be heard but not seen. The APB was forced to develop a counter-strategy which involved dawn raids. As one such raid at Bellbrook reserve was described,

> They [the children] got taken there from one of them box houses . . . the first house along where old T. used to stop, that house. I remember that well because H., young H.C. They came up to the first place on the other side, then they had to take 'em over past Uncle Athol [H.C.'s father] and the policeman pulled up there and he woke H. up and H. was almost in tears. He [the policeman] said 'Comin' over and show me where E. and J. are' . . . and they went over there and me and Grandma was making the fire in the morning and Grandma said 'Look there!', and when I looked around the policeman was coming with H. H. was walking behind the policeman. When he got up to the house, I watched. 'Oh,' I said, 'Nan, they're goin' up to E.'s place.' They knocked on the door. 'Who's that?' said old J. [the children's father]. He [the policeman] said, 'We're after E. and J.' Well, H. was on one door. If they'd come out that door H. reckoned he'da fell over and let them run away. But they [the parents] told 'em to go out and they took 'em. They walked off early in the morning, frosty morning too it was. Well, I tell ya, I nearly cried that mornin' when they went the two kids on a cold morning. No boots on or anything. They walked beside the police and H. behind them till they got over to his place and then he [the policeman] got on his horse and they walked along, all the way up to town, Bellbrook.

The possibilities of avoiding these exercises of external state control

13. *Bilisman* is the modified Dhan-gadi expression of the English word policeman (Widders 1979: 63; Holmer 1967: 29, Pt. II).

were undercut to a large extent by the increasing encapsulation of Aborigines into immobilised communities located in particular areas.

A major collective response was organised in the Macleay Valley as part of a state-wide political campaign by the Aborigines against the APB. The specific issue in question concerned the revocation of reserves as part of a policy to centralise APB control throughout the state. The revocation of reserve land had always been a significant feature of the APB's mandate, but in the Macleay Valley it increased dramatically in and around the 1920s. In 1919, two reserves (Sherwood, and Little Shark and Whisky Island) were revoked and in the following year Shark Island was revoked. The major reserves on the lower Macleay were revoked in 1925. Fattorinni Island and Pelican Island were revoked while Kinchela was converted into a Boys Home. The islands that farmers had transformed from bush and vines into valuable farm land in the 1880s were handed over to the Lands Department to be sold off. There were 192 applicants received by the local Land Board when the land was balloted off in the same year (*MA*, May 1925). The 44.25 acre island was purchased by a local farmer for £55 per acre (ibid.). Pelican Island attracted 61 applicants and sold for an undisclosed price (*MA*, October 1925).

A month prior to the sale of Pelican Island, both Linwood and John Moseley had addressed a meeting held by the Australian Aboriginal Progressive Association (AAPA) at the Kempsey Showground. The meeting had been organised to protest against the APB's policies. As the local newspaper report stated, the campaign had 'caught on wonderfully amongst coloured people . . . with the result that branches of the AAPA had sprung up in many districts where Aborigines still live' (*MA*, April 1925). Eleven branches had been set up in the first six months of operation (*MA*, August 1925). The Kempsey gathering proved to be no exception. Some 100 members joined the AAPA (ibid.). Linwood spoke against the APB; but he also, in an act asserting the primacy of his Aboriginal identity, addressed the public meeting in his own language. As the report (*MA*, April 1925) stated:

> Mr James Linwood, from Fattorinni Island, *spoke in Aboriginal language to the people urging them to join up and work together in the interests of their own race.* He referred to the unjust procedure of late years, when many of them, after years of occupancy of certain portions of land, and after clearing it and cultivating it had been set adrift to begin again in some unwanted portion of the country. (*MA*, April 1925).

Linwood's assertions of Aboriginal distinctiveness and the APB's unjust treatment of Aborigines were the major themes that sustained the growth of the AAPA. Indeed, the growth of this collective protest was such that the APB held discussions with the crown solicitor to 'ascertain what action if any could be taken' (SA 4/7125) to control the organisation.

The AAPA was probably the first attempt to form a pan-Aboriginal movement throughout NSW. The political ideology underlying the effort to bind together the various diverse Aboriginal groups in the state was rooted in the Aborigines' common experience of Anglo–Australian institutions. This ideology was spelled out at a conference in Kempsey and at meetings conspicuously held at the fringe camp at Greenhill. The conference held in the Good Templers Hall was attended by Aborigines from the local area and a 'number of representatives and delegates from the northern rivers' (*MC*, October 1925). Part of the speech by the organising secretary of the AAPA was a report of her recent tour of the state. As a newspaper report records:

> She said that it grieved her especially to find the same attitude of sullen resentment against the administrators of the department who had their affairs in hand, considering the enormous sum of money set aside by the Australian government for the development of these people, she was amazed to find this condition of mind amongst them. *The position in regard to selling their lands, which had always been considered as belonging to the Aboriginal people*, was a cause of deep, strong and resentful feeling. She found people huddled together in any old corner of the earth, housed in a most wretched fashion. They were asking for a small bit of land upon which to build their homes. *This question, and that referring to their broken homes, and the unsatisfactory method of dealing with their children, were matters absorbing all their thoughts.* (*MC*, October 1925)

The collective identity, which was being articulated to mobilise Aborigines to political action, clearly lay in the strong sense of a common past and of a common fate suffered at the hand of the APB.

The AAPA generally sought to end the APB's political oppression, but especially wanted to stop it selling reserve land and taking children. On the one hand, the movement was concerned to improve the Aborigines' material conditions, on the other to end political oppression both at the state and the local level. This is perhaps most clearly seen in the resolution passed unanimously by a meeting of some 200 people:

> As it is the proud boast of Australia that every person born beneath the Southern Cross is born free, irrespective of origin, race, colour, creed, religion or any other impediment, we, the representatives of the original people, in conference assembled, demand that we shall be accorded the same full rights and privileges of citizenship as are enjoyed by all other sections of the community. (*MC*, October 1925)

The political aims were thus expressed in the political idiom of the dominant society. By appealing to egalitarian principles, the AAPA was attempting to turn the logic of the dominant ideology against the state and to its own advantage. Such appeals for equal rights were, however, as much aimed at ending oppression as denying the wider definition of Aborigines as inferior and incompetent. The political struggle for equal access to the wider society's institutions and facilities also involved a cultural struggle to be regarded as human, to be treated as equals.

The AAPA's activities did not alter the APB's policy in any way. The agitation of the 1920s had failed. The reserves that had been created on the lower Macleay River ceased to exist. For those who were removed from Fattorinni Island and Pelican Island, a meagre three hectares of land was set aside at nearby South West Rocks.

It was not until the 1930s that the last reserves (Burnt Bridge and Bellbrook) were subjected to change. These changes were brought about by public and parliamentary criticisms of the APB's administration, which resulted in the establishment, in 1937, of a Parliamentary Select Committee of Inquiry (discussed fully in Chapter 6; see also Horner 1974; Goodall 1982). The criticisms that emerged were directed at the APB's failure to implement successfully the strategies of intervention associated with a thoroughgoing bureaucratic custodianship. The Committee of Inquiry's condemnation of the APB administration emphasised the negative aspects of manager control resulting from the retention of personalised forms of power associated with legalistic custodianship. Throughout the 1930s the APB had attempted to accommodate the bureaucratic strategies of enclosure for retraining by establishing more centralised, manager-controlled stations.[14] The reforms that emerged from the 1937 Inquiry involved the implementation of a more bureaucratically codified manager's role directed towards the pursuit of uniform rather than arbitrary practices. This was a shift towards more abstract and impersonal forms of bureaucratic power. At the same time, control of Aborigines was no longer to be exercised in a coercive manner from outside the community. Rather, the bureaucratic control was to take a pedagogical form and was to be applied in a standardised manner from within the communities.

This shift of emphasis in government policy resulted in major changes in the Macleay Valley. In the late 1930s, only two of the original nine reserves remained. In accordance with the policy of bureaucratic custodianship, reserves were to be phased out or turned into stations, i.e. with resident managers, where large numbers of Aborigines were to be concentrated. The APB decided that Bellbrook reserve was to be revoked and the people moved south to Forster (SA 4/7120). The move was prevented after strong protests from the

---

14. By 1938, the number of manager-controlled stations and homes had increased to 23, and another 13 reserves were staffed by APB officers (Duncan 1969: 322).

Aborigines and, perhaps more significantly, local Europeans who protested that they would be deprived of a work-force (see Chapter 2). Instead, the reserve was turned into a station.

The most significant change occurred at Burnt Bridge. The existing reserve was to be turned into a new model station with improved housing and service facilities. Forty new houses were to be built in an area away from 'old' Burnt Bridge at Euroka Creek. Most of the families were to be provided with a cottage situated on a small block, which the residents were to fence themselves with materials supplied by the APB (*MC*, June 1938). The APB aimed to turn the station into a facsimile of European housing within an institutional context. As it turned out, however, this 'new improved housing' consisted of the APB's standard issue to reserves, namely two rooms (bedroom and kitchen) with the addition of a back verandah. A communal ablutions block and laundry were provided, as well as an outside tap for each individual family's needs. The only facility provided inside the cottage was a fireplace for cooking. No electricity was supplied. Despite the absence of dormitories, the new station was much closer to a government institution than to the European standards of housing in the wider society.

The population of 'new' Burnt Bridge was to include Aborigines from another station, which the APB had closed down to comply with its policy of centralisation. The new Burnt Bridge included some 50 families from Urunga station who were moved down by truck, but there was insufficient housing. One woman stated that, 'we had half a tank we was livin' in; a half tank and a couple of bits of board to make two parts'. As the APB increased the population to conform to its policy of centralisation, it at the same time reduced the size of the former reserve from 205 to 40 hectares to comply with its wish for greater monitoring and surveillance of the population. This was to be carried out by the manager and matron (see Chapter 6).

The organisation of the 'new' Burnt Bridge objectified a more scientific approach to the Aboriginal 'problem'. The last vestiges of a religious paradigm, which had been inherited from an earlier period associated with spiritual and moral rejuvenation, were removed and replaced by a bureaucratic and scientific paradigm, in which gaining secular rights of citizenship within the state rather than spiritual moral salvation was to be the achievement of assimilation. Assimilation was to be the goal for the entire Aboriginal population, rather than for the children only. And this goal was to be achieved by supervising and monitoring activities, in other words by a form of pedagogic practice which allowed inappropriate behaviour to be corrected and rates of individual progress to be measured. The stations were established on principles associated with institutionalisation. It was through these totalising forms of segregation and control that Aborigines were to be assimilated.

The shift towards these more totalising forms of control ensured that 'old' Burnt Bridge became an anachronism with regard to the APB's policies. The revocation of most of the land of the former reserve was to include the Euroka Creek settlement. The long-time residents of Euroka Creek were to move to the new station. They refused to leave, and a confrontation ensued when the manager of the new station sent some men to remove the APB's property from 'old' Burnt Bridge. As one woman described the events:

The working men they arrived and went to the fence. And, of course, old P. [John Moseley's son] he was there and he hunted 'em see. Then they went back and told Jacobs [the manager] and Jacobs came up with the police see. Well then the police went in now through the fence, they all went under together. They never said anything to him [P.]. They went straight in now and got the things and when they got everything out like that they said 'We're gonna take these things'. So anyway old P. stood back for while and then he went down the road and tried to get Ph. [P.'s younger brother]. So they [manager/workers/police] went back down the town way to Burnt Bridge, to new Burnt Bridge, and they put all the things what they brought out of the school and toilets and things they took . . . and when they got down there they wasn't satisfied. They still went and got [more] police. Car load of them. There was more than . . . more than 7 in it and the inspector too. And up they come and when they got up of course the mission truck, as you call it, it came down. . . . They called out and asked him, 'Oh, Johnny, the Government wants the tank', 'Yea boss, take it, take it'. Poor old man, real helpless to himself and he couldn't talk very much. So anyway, they took the tank down and tipped it over, tipped the good water over. So he said [manager] 'We'll take this tank'. . . . When they were going, P. and Ph. came up behind 'em there and of course they started to whistle. Really what I thought they wanted Ph. to have a fight with 'em, but Ph. wasn't havin' any fight with 'em course there were too many for him. He [manager] drove off and then the police went home too.

Such actions reinforced the fact that the relative autonomy associated with reserve status had been extinguished. The rather tentative controls characteristic of the late nineteenth century were increasingly extended and systematised with a view to improving the efficacy of the state's policies. By the 1930s Aboriginal opposition could be more easily contained by a combination of law and force. The domination which was to emerge with bureaucratic custodianship denied all alternatives to state control as part of a policy of forced integration.

Moseley's response was to appeal against his eviction in a manner which assumed the perpetuation of personal forms of power and individual forms of mediation. He sent a letter to the local newspaper (*MC*, July 1937) to plead his case:

Dear Sir,

Will you please find a corner in your paper for me please. I would like you to print this brief report in your paper. The Board has interfered with me and my property. They have taken the tank from my house: I protested, and the Inspector of Police had come out with the police force and issued orders for the manager of the Aborigines which has a station about half a mile from me, to take the tank and anything he wanted. The manager broke down the fence, which was nailed and wired with barb wire, and went in and took the WCs from the school. These things are all my property, so I maintain some rights to these buildings. I made a protest to the Inspector of Police and was told I owned nothing, that the Board owned everything; that I owned not even the land which I had spent the best part of my life working and improving for the past forty-five years. I thought I had fulfilled the conditions of the homestead leases. If these lands, which I claim, are converted into an Aboriginal reserve, I know nothing about it. Now I ask is there any justice in that. If I had known these things long ago, while I had some strength left, I would have found residence elsewhere. Now it seems as if I have got to go and leave everything behind, my youth, my strength and nearly 50 years of hard labour. Oh Kempsey please help me. I have been a service to the state in my time. I served my state with honesty. The very thing I took pride in, the police force, two days ago made me feel as small as a slug under an elephant's foot. The state knows well of what service I refer to, when I was in the force as a black tracker, so I have no need to mention it here. I get a vote in the state and federal elections, so I appeal to the community for help.

John Moseley
Burnt Bridge
2 July 1937.

Such a personal appeal for moral justice stood in contrast to the impersonal legalistic and bureaucratic forms of control that characterised the new administration. In the absence of recognised legal title, Moseley and the other residents of 'old' Burnt Bridge were denied any entitlement to what they considered their land. This consolidation of bureaucratic forms of control was synonymous with pre-coded responses based on rules rather than personal mediations.

It is ironical that those Aborigines who were in fact 'assimilating' the most successfully – by way of industry, enterprise and smallholder farming – were in fact wiped out by state interventions seeking to *organise bureaucratically*, rather than to *encourage morally*, their assimilation.

Chapter 6

The New Order:
The Aborigines' Welfare Board

6.1. The Eclipse of the 'Persecution Board'

Assimilation of the Aborigines into the general community is the keynote of the Board's policy. When it is considered that 95 per cent of the so-called Aborigines of New South Wales are half and lighter castes, whose social fabric has been torn asunder by the onrush of western civilisation, and who if left alone would have neither the traditional background of the Aboriginal way of life nor the culture of the white man to stabilise or guide them, the need for this policy should be abundantly clear. The policy has a positive aim, to make the Aborigines responsible, active, intelligent citizens. The Aborigines Welfare Board realises the difficulties arising from a different mode of thinking, content of knowledge and emphasis on different values and ideals. It realises that the Aborigines inherit a different view of life, and that the value of our culture must be proved to them before it will be accepted. (AWB Report 1948: 3)

Such statements signified innovative shifts away from past administrative policies towards Aborigines in NSW. During this period, policies and political practices in Aboriginal administration were characterised by the emerging dominance of a liberal ideology. The granting by the state of equal rights for Aborigines was seen as an effective means of erasing the discriminations that were manifested when they were treated as a distinct social group. This was the ultimate aim of liberal political strategy.

In so far as Aborigines continued to be forced to surrender their cultural, social and political autonomy, however, the so-called solution simply continued racism in a different mode. The policy was based on an underlying racism which presupposed cultural instead of biological inferiority. It assumed that the values of western civilization were absolute and universal and that other cultural forms were obstacles to progress. The policy reflected the view that through systematic training at the local level Aborigines could be uplifted to take their place in a superior culture and society. Such totalising strategies aimed to break down any lingering cultural residues and to eradicate environmental disabilities or sources of inferiority through local intervention. Whereas earlier policies and ideologies stressed what Aborigines could not be, the new policy of assimilation stressed what they should and would become. This form of institutional racism should not, however, be condemned as an aberration, distortion or deviation from liberalism or scientific discourse, for it is in fact grounded in essential conceptions of knowledge located at the very core of liberalism and science. Institutionalised racism emerges from pervasive processes embedded in the wider society, i.e. from those universal and moral imperatives found so inseparably intertwined in liberal/scientific discourses.

The new policies in effect embodied the liberal critique of discrimination and segregation and the resolution of these practices through assimilation. In addition, by focusing on past errors, they were legitimated as positive and progressive. The policy of assimilation, which set out to deal with the Aboriginal problem in 1940, was grounded in a secular discourse. The residues of the more metaphysical view of the Aborigine as an irredeemable leper trapped in his own inherent imperfections were progressively removed. Policies designed to monitor and correct the redeemable plague victim gained ascendency during this new era of state control. A stress on the environment as the source of the problem underlay the escalation of pedagogic/sociological intervention by the state. The metaphysical biologism that had denied the possibility of such interventions was gradually transformed and ultimately displaced in the new policies. The restricted use of pedagogic practices to reclaim Aboriginal children (see Chapter 5) was now extended to include all of them through the expansion of government stations.

The forms of control exercised by the Aborigines Welfare Board (AWB), which superseded the Aborigines Protection Board (APB), closely approximated those of a total institution (Goffman 1961) or carceral (Foucault 1977).[1] Supervised stations, which became the major armature of administrative policy, centralised within one institution the functions of various institutions (for example, education, health and accommodation) found dispersed at different sites in the wider society.

The process of decision making was invested in the authority of the resident manager, and deference to and dependence on him became

1. As Hirst and Wooley (1982: 189–90) argue there are significant differences between Foucault's and Goffman's approaches to institutionalisation. 'Goffman considers that "total institutions" break down individual identity and reduce the person to an anonymous member of an enclosed collectivity. For Foucault, on the contrary, disciplinarity involves a definite form of "individuation". Individuals are actually constituted as such through isolation in discipline, surveillance separates and distinguishes those subjected to it, and the regime of government seeks to constitute forms of individuality, to confer attributes, powers and capacities.' I employ the approach of Foucault to analyse the institutional life of the Dhan-gadi.

regular aspects of the institutionalised life of the inhabitants of these newly-created reserves. By the late 1930s, the majority of Aborigines in the Macleay region lived on government stations. Prior to this they had lived on unsupervised reserves and 'fringe camps'. The AWB introduced a more comprehensive regime of control within the bounded communities at Bellbrook and Burnt Bridge. For these, the change in policy involved a significant break in the political and social relations of their existence.

The abolition of the APB in 1940 came as a result of growing public criticism from both Aboriginal and European groups. Organised public protests by Aboriginal organisations throughout the 1920s and 1930s had drawn attention to the Aborigines' dissatisfaction with the APB's control over their affairs (see Chapter 5). In 1937, the Legislative Assembly established a Select Committee to inquire into the administration of the APB.[2] The inclusion of an Aboriginal member from the Aborigines Progressive Association (APA) on the Select Committee may be seen as an indication of the effectiveness of Aboriginal agitation against the APB. For two decades, the APA and its predecessor, the AAPA, had been seeking the abolition of the APB as a fundamental precondition to full citizenship rights for Aborigines.

Contrary to one of the primary concerns of the APA, the proceedings of the Select Committee focused on the nature rather than the continuing existence of Aboriginal administration. The proceedings were reduced to what Duncan (1969) calls a witch hunt concerned with the personal misconduct and mismanagement of some of the Board's managers and the inefficiency of the general administration. Such criticisms of managers amounted to a critique of personal, arbitrary power. The recommendations, as we shall see below, were a demand that managers should be subject to centralised surveillance mechanisms and to rational, bureaucratic rules. The rejection of arbitrary, personal power rested on the bureaucratisation of power; the assertion of the rule of impersonal law rather than absolute, arbitrary power. The proceedings were concerned with establishing a more comprehensive custodianship of Aborigines by instituting more effective bureaucratic procedures. The criticisms of the APB's past performance were countered by the establishment of uniform and centralised bureaucratic intervention.

This bureaucratic critique of the previous regime provided the state with the means to pursue centralised lines of control in its policies towards Aborigines, while at the same time incorporating more and more Aborigines into its own power mechanisms. The misconduct of

2. The Select Committee met on 18 occasions between November 1937 and February 1938, although on five of these the meetings lapsed because they lacked a quorum. In June 1938, the chief secretary declined to reappoint the Select Committee and instead requested that the Public Service review the administration of the APB.

managers also provided the APA representative, Mr W. Ferguson, with grounds for concern. As he stated in his evidence:

> This meeting gives me the opportunity of placing before the public the conditions under which our people are living, and also to let you know the hardships and many injustices handed out to them by the so-called Protection Board. In presenting our case I will endeavour to put all my points as clear and concise as possible. I realise that we have all the best learned men and women in the world opposing our claim to freedom, for we have learned by past experience that the scholars and students will recommend that the race be preserved for scientific purposes. What a fallacy! What is there left to experiment with. . . . *To begin with, we are asking for the abolition of the Aborigines Protection Board.* You ask why should it be abolished? I say that it is not functioning in the best interest of the Aboriginal people. The Board appoints managers and protectors to help the people and look after their interests. But *the managers have so much power, their power is greater than any other public servant in Australia. I say that no public officer, no magistrate, or no other man, I do not believe the King of England, has power under British law to try a man or a number of men or women, find them guilty and sentence them without giving them a fair and open trial and without producing any evidence to convict* except in countries where there is no handy law to convict such as Papua New Guinea. (Parliament of NSW 1937: 53, 54)

Although, as Ferguson's evidence shows, the APA sought the abolition of the administration rather than its bureaucratic reform, the state's response in 'defending' Aborigines from the oppression of such arbitrary personal power was to bureaucratise state policies.

The final recommendations sought to elaborate and intensify institutional control. According to the Public Service Board (PSB) report (Parliament of NSW 1940: 12), 'the necessity for close supervision of all such Aborigines' was crucial in overcoming the Aboriginal problem. This reorganisation was to make AWB members more readily available to inspect stations and reserves and to provide more and better-qualified staff to control and monitor Aborigines more effectively on the stations. The policy would ensure that the AWB would be more successful than its predecessor (ibid. pp. 27–31). If the Aborigines were to be regarded as equal, pedagogic intervention was seen as essential. It was believed that this provided them with their only chance of becoming free, autonomous subjects.

Following the bureaucratic logic of the report, the establishment of a more efficient and effective chain of command was seen as an initial and inevitable step in the transformation of existing station residents into more disciplined and useful communities. It is my argument that the extension of state control and the use of what was called 'detailed administration' constituted a major change in the world of the Dhangadi. The changes in control did not simply represent an amplification in control for its own sake but a change in the aims of the administration. The principal recommendation of the PSB report had been 'to mould the administration as to ensure, as early as possible, the assimilation of these people into the social and economic life of the general community' (ibid. p. 12). The emphases on both closer surveillance of Aborigines and more developed techniques of obtaining biographical knowledge of the 'inmates' were in keeping with the practices of bureaucratic custodianship found throughout the wider society. It was the first time, however, that they were applied systematically to the Aboriginal population of NSW.

These new power techniques sought to train individuals and to socialise or resocialise deviants rather than to punish them. Patterns of social control were organised around systems of discipline rather than of punishment. Institutional control by the state was intended to be seen, not as a negative expression of repressive power that depersonalises and humiliates individuals, but as a positive pedagogic force that seeks not only to confine Aborigines, but also to remodel them as individuals, which is very much an act of power.[3] The AWB's new policy marked a major change in the way in which state power was applied to Aborigines.

In this we are not dealing with a benevolent, pedagogic apparatus of state power, nor are we simply dealing with power in its repressive instance, but with the gradual extension of power through mechanisms of discipline which produce trained individuals. As Foucault (1977: 138) so aptly puts it, such 'disciplines' constitute 'a policy of coercions that act upon the body, a calculated manipulation of its elements, its gestures, its behaviour. The human body was entering a machinery of power that explores it, breaks it down and rearranges it.' The body is conceptualised as a machine upon which the disciplines act to correct movements, gestures and attitudes in conformity with the principle of utility. As Foucault stresses, important to such control are comprehensive techniques of (1) surveillance, (2) obtaining and retaining knowledge and (3) ordering and partitioning the target of control. Enclosure provides the basis for ordering and regulating time and space. The accumulation of knowledge and the use of power act mutually to reinforce each other. Individuals are the objects of strategies of intervention and 'normalisation', which are the aim of the exercise of control, i.e. to internalise self-regulation within each individual.

The administrative guidelines for assimilation stipulated such practices and procedures. The PSB (1940: 17) was able to suggest 'no better policy than the present, viz., the aggregation on stations, under close supervision, of those Aborigines who are not yet fitted to be assimi-

3. I should stress that the word 'positive' is not used in a moral or ethical sense here but as an act of power. In contrast, Elkin (1936; 1944), Bell (1959; 1964) and Bleakley (1961) do employ 'positive' in its moral and ethical sense when considering the 'positive policy of assimilation'.

lated into the general community, with the provision of suitable train-ing schools'. A more 'detailed administration' was also recommended on the grounds that the report thought that the administration had been inadequate in the past and that improved methods and an in-crease in staff would inevitably bring better results (ibid. p. 29). To guarantee a consistent application of these new measures, an 'up-to-date code of instructions' was to be issued to managers and other staff to 'ensure uniformity of action' (ibid. p. 24).

The rational bureaucratic procedures associated with these new forms of power were particularly intrusive in that they facilitated the accumulation and use of much more knowledge about the station Aborigines. Monthly reports from managers were considered to pro-vide too little information about the station's inhabitants, and the monitoring of these Aborigines was to take a more sustained form in a weekly diary. As the PSB report (ibid.) concluded:

> It is the Public Service Board's view that at this stage, in order to deal adequately with the problem, there should be a complete record of all Abor-igines coming within the purview of the Act. *The Public Service Board cannot see how the problem can be dealt with otherwise than by close personal study of the individual and his problems and this is impossible without a comprehensive record of the individual.* This record does not exist in respect of adults and is not sufficiently comprehensive even in the case of children admitted to the institutions.

The individualised monitoring and surveillance serves to extend and reinforce the action of such positive power to transform individuals. Each individual is subjected to a 'normalising judgement' set by an administrative hierarchy. Each individual's 'performance' is differen-tiated and ranked according to his or her ability to conform to the set normative standards. The 'carrot', so to speak, was an exemption certificate, which absolved individual Aborigines from the discriminat-ory legislation of the APB Act. This created a means of individually measuring each Aborigine's rate of progress in terms of a European norm.

The application of such policies to the Aborigines of NSW was set out in amendments (1940, 1943) to the Aborigines Protection Act. For the Aborigines on government stations in the Macleay Valley the legisla-tion formalised the authority of the managers who had been appointed to Bellbrook (1932) and Burnt Bridge (1937). The most immediate consequence for the residents of these government stations was the invasion of personal and familial space. The administrative control of stations was codified in the *Manual of Instructions to Managers and Matrons of Aboriginal Stations and Other Field Officers* (1941), which was issued to all AWB staff as part of a policy of bureaucratic standardisa-tion. One of the main duties of the manager was to control access to the station. In practice, this meant that every person who entered the station had first and foremost to report to the manager and to give information on why they were there, who they were staying with and for how long. The manager decided if and under what conditions they could stay. In other words, the manager was able to regulate and scrutinise the residents' relations with their relatives and friends. In addition, the manager and matron had the right to enter houses on the station at any time. Such policies were in keeping with maintaining total control over the Aboriginal environment. Managers and matrons were expected, not simply to exercise control, but to create new forms of social identity amongst Aborigines through institutional practices.

This can be seen in the regulation (ibid. p. 3) requiring matrons to carry out twice-weekly house inspections:

> The women folk, with the knowledge that the inspection is to be made, can prepare their homes and have them bright and clean on that particular day. The inspection of homes should, therefore, be irregular, particularly in those cases where it is suspected that the occupants of any home are inclined to 'polish up' for the occasion. Residents should be given to understand . . . that when any visit is made by the matron it will be expected that the house will be clean and tidy.

The use of such techniques of control created a one-way relationship of visibility, in which the random nature of the surveillance in such a confined area rendered it continuous. In addition, the calculated use of such techniques ensured that the 'inmates' had limited scope to maintain any degree of autonomy, for even the most personal aspects of social life were open to the scrutiny and judgement of those in authority. As one woman put it, 'She was the matron. She'd go around want this done, want that done. Well I mean most of the women's knows, they knew how to clean their own . . . [if you] lived in a house with no water you can't keep it as much as you keep this [present house]. You think they'd know that. No, they want it spotless.' On Aboriginal stations the domestic sphere was never private space, but continually accessible to the judgement of those in charge. These invasions of domestic life provided information which was recorded and made available to the authorities. The appropriation of such knowledge is intended to increase the staff's power to intervene to 'correct' and control the inmates' behaviour, in other words, to govern the private sphere. This abolition of private space (through making it accessible to a specialised hierarchy) was essential to the task of totally controlling the institutional environment, which was considered necessary if the Aborigines were to change.

The pedagogic intervention was designed to impose a more effective regime of reform on the individuals, for monitoring and surveillance act to break down existing patterns of behaviour so that new ones can be constructed, i.e. the women had to attend to their housework as a *daily* routine. *The acquisition of a permanent and disciplined economy of habits for each individual was precisely what such forms of power sought to achieve.* The aim was to internalise individual self-government rather than to continue to maintain external forms of control.

The most explicit application of such disciplinary techniques was found in those institutions set up specifically for Aboriginal children (see Chapter 3). For the girls, according to a former inmate, the daily routine began at 5 a.m. The day began for the older girls with the regular scrubbing of the dormitory floors. It was each child's responsibility to clean six floorboards for the length of the dormitory. If on inspection the boards were found to be wet, the girl responsible would have to do the whole section again. As institutional life was strictly regulated, this meant missing breakfast. By the ordering of time and space into specific activities and actions through timetabled routines, individual movements were regulated, controlled and disciplined. Furthermore, each piece of equipment (hessian apron, scrubbing brush and bucket) was marked with the girl's initials so that those who misplaced, neglected or lost them could be punished. Punishment expressed the negative aspect of power; it was not the ultimate end. The pedagogic or positive aspect of power was to inculcate habits of work and the notion of responsibility for personal possessions. Avoiding such punitive interventions required the girls to police themselves.

The stress on self-regulation was an attempt to inculcate a regime of rational and calculating individual behaviour closely associated with cultural notions of possessive individualism within the wider society. In official policy, work had a pedagogic function associated with the acquisition of ordered conduct. For example, men unable to find work outside the stations were forced to work for the manager for three days 'to learn the value of work' before being given their rations. Such compulsory labour had a pedagogic function in that it was more concerned with the way in which work imposed regularity and order on the individual than with the actual product of the labour. This was also extended to consumption patterns, as seen in the widespread practice of managers withholding child endowment from mothers. The money was held in trust until a sufficient amount had accumulated. When the mother was eventually given the money, she was directed to buy something substantial with it, for example, building materials for a house or durable consumer items such as furniture. In such cases the managers were attempting to 'educate' Aborigines to save or use their money in a rational and calculating manner. The use of such pedagogic practices on the stations was, in effect, an attempt to restructure both the personal and the domestic spheres of Aboriginal existence.

The perpetuation of external constraints on (and physical segregation of) Aborigines in the state ceased to exist as an end in itself and became an indispensable part of the new pedagogic regime. Closer surveillance and control required segregation. As the PSB report (1940: 20) concluded, 'the restrictions imposed by the present law of the state are in the interests of Aborigines'. Similarly, instead of liberalising the repressive laws associated with the *Aborigines Protection Act*, such as the managers' wide-ranging powers and control over the movements of adults and children, the PSB recommended that 'greater use . . . [be made] of these powers' (ibid. p. 28). The same applied to state and Commonwealth discriminatory legislation against Aborigines, for instance exclusion from obtaining liquor, unemployment relief, pensions or maternity allowances and the direct payment in cash for child endowment (ibid. p. 20). Exemption from such discriminatory and repressive legislation could be achieved by individuals only through their ability to conform to the normative prerequisites of the state.[4]

Nevertheless, there was a fundamental change in official policy. Aborigines came to be regarded as 'redeemable' and, hence, assimilable through the systematic intervention of the state. Racist discourse became increasingly embedded in notions of environmental deprivation and attempts were made to 'civilise' Aborigines into a superior culture and society. Although the PSB felt that, 'their education had not yet reached the stage where the restrictions . . . [could] be lifted as a general policy, without harmful effects on the majority' (ibid.), state interventions now stressed the transformative potential of knowledge through education. They were being prepared for citizenship:

> It is obvious that in order to lead the aboriginal [sic] people to a proper understanding and appreciation of the mental processes involved in Australian civilisation and life an education system in its various forms and degrees must be established. This education must extend beyond the more formal primary school education and should involve technical, industrial, agricultural, secondary, and perhaps ultimately, professional education. (AWB report 1944: 3)

In this way the earlier ideology, in which race was thought to limit potential and which provided the government with the *raison d'être* for continuing to control the Aborigines, was thus replaced by another which stressed the development of potential through knowledge.

Within the rhetoric of the progressive potential of pedagogic intervention, the forms of control and manipulation are mystified and perceived as divorced from power relations. These forms of power are so commonplace within the wider society that they are regarded as neutral rather than political or cultural. And because disciplinary regimes

---

4. It was not until some 20 years later, in 1960/1, that a majority decision of the AWB repealed those sections of the Act which 'appeared to discriminate against Aborigines' (AWB report 1962: 5).

have been established throughout a broad range of institutions, such as schools, workplaces, hospitals and prisons, they have become dehistoricised or 'naturalised' as eternal, or necessary, forms of social existence. As Foucault (1982: 170) puts it:

> Discipline makes individuals; it is the specific technique of power that regards individuals both as objects and instruments of its exercise. It is not a triumphant power, which because of its own excess can pride itself on its own omnipotence; it is a modest suspicious power which functions as a calculated, but permanent economy. These are humble modalities, minor procedures, as compared with the majestic rituals or great apparatuses of the state. And it is precisely they that were gradually to invade the major forms, altering their mechanisms and imposing their procedures.

The PSB report provided the blueprint for the extension of such mechanisms of discipline to Aborigines.

The political underpinnings of this materialist intervention in Aboriginal administration lay in a liberal critique of previous policy based on a belief in the transformative potential of knowledge, which, in treating knowledge as an absolute category detached from power, failed to understand both power and knowledge. Contemporary commentators perceived assimilation as a progressive policy and pedagogic intervention as responsible and compassionate concern for the Aborigines of NSW. This positive policy of assimilation, as it was described, was continually contrasted with earlier negative policies (see Elkin 1944 and 1974; Bell 1959 and 1964; Bleakley 1961). As Bleakley (p. 218) states:

> The policy is to assist in the uplift of Aborigines, pure and mixed blood, to fit them for assimilation in the general community; by encouraging and helping these people to uplift themselves, and by winning the tolerance and forbearance of the white people. This laudable work is done by the superintendent of Aboriginal Welfare with a staff of welfare officers to inspect, instruct, guide and encourage their protégés: a female inspector of women and children; a trained nurse for mothers, babies and adolescent girls; and managers and teachers for the stations.

This rhetoric of 'progressive development' through specialisation, however, called for the multiplication of surveillance and monitoring techniques.

Such an unproblematic understanding of the progressive potential of 'knowledge' rests on a particularly narrow definition of power, witnessed, for example, in remarks such as, 'encouragement, rather than force, is the keynote of assimilation', or, 'force had not been employed . . . at any time in connection with assimilation policy' (Bell 1964: 61–2). Here, power is identified only in relation to its negative instance, in policies that repress and forbid, and domination only in the repressive state apparatuses, the judiciary, the police and the military.

The pedagogic forms of power underpinning an assimilationist policy are concealed not by intellectual laziness or bad faith, but by the commonsense, taken-for-granted nature of the educative process. Such forms of power were thus rendered invisible, and the premises and presuppositions upon which they were founded escaped attention. This major methodological and conceptual flaw shared the same uncritical and unquestioned presumptions underlying liberal support for assimilation; regardless of the historical origins of the social and political relations that developed within the dominant society, they were perceived as progressive, as universalisms.

6.2. Assimilation: The Construction of a New Discourse

Throughout the 1940s and 1950s the thinking of government officials, of those involved in evaluating policy in NSW and of Aboriginal studies in general was dominated by the idea that Aborigines were assimilable. Over the next two decades the assimilation policies initiated by the NSW government were gradually adopted by other states and by the federal government.[5] This shift towards assimilation reflected a growing concern about Aborigines' *secular rights* within the nation state and, in 1961, the federal government and all the states agreed upon a uniform set of aims and definitions. It was stated that, 'The policy of assimilation means that all Aborigines and part-Aborigines are expected to attain the *same* manner of living as other Australians and to live as members of a single Australian community enjoying the same rights and privileges, accepting the same responsibilities, observing the same customs and influenced by the same beliefs, as other Australians' (Native Welfare Conference, Commonwealth and State Authorities: Proceedings and Decisions 1961.) The sociological/materialist view, which held that the Aboriginal problem lay in the social environment and that Aborigines were assimilable, received very little support in the period between 1909 and 1940 when constructions of Aboriginality were mainly based on the scientific or biological model. Yet, when the NSW government first adopted an assimilation policy, the biological model was still dominant, and most people thought in terms of a progression through half-caste, quadroon and octoroon in which, to put it crudely, 'assimilation could be equated with the process of genetic change in the right direction' (Rowley 1973: 9). This was clearly spelt out in a report to a Conference of Heads of Protection Departments,

5. A number of Commonwealth government publications, which were produced as pamphlets, outline policy in this period: *Our Aborigines* (1957), *Assimilation of our Aborigines* (1958), *The Skills of our Aborigines* (1961), *One People* (1961), *Fringe Dwellers* (1964), *Further Steps in Assimilation* (1965) and *Aboriginal Advancement* (1967).

which 'considered that the solution of the problem of mixed bloods was absorption through miscegenation. For full bloods it would be of miscegenation for an undefined period' (NSW PSB report 1937).

The academic debate on the question of assimilation in the 1930s was conducted largely in terms of the Aborigines' biological (genetic) capacities or incapacities. Within this construction of knowledge, 'moral degradation' is measured against the capacity for cultural/genetic adaptability. Aborigines were noted for their inability to participate in a world built on secular, linear progress (i.e. evolution), in which colonial domination and dispossession were reduced to a scientific abstraction. As Elkin (1936: 470–1) put it:

> It may be that his [the Aborigine's] present adjustment [i.e. traditional society] has become part of his very nature – biological – and that he cannot become adapted to the environmental changes and so like the dinosaur in the face of a glacial epoch, he is doomed to extinction. . . . The present problem consists in the extent of the change and its far reaching nature, and the fact that it is sudden and external like a catastrophe of nature, a glacial advance, alluring as it is destructive.

From this materialist perspective, Elkin believed that the 'experience and learning' Aborigines derived from their living environment had become genetically inscribed.[6] Like the dinosaur, perhaps the most primordial evolutionist symbol of inadaptability, Aboriginal adaptation to the environment denied the possibility of change. It was this 'naturalness' of Aborigines, their fusion with nature, that characterised them as primordial beings.

The shift towards assimilation in these representations of Aborigines was also grounded in scientific knowledge derived from a biological model, with the problem of biological inadaptability being resolved by increasing the emphasis on the 'half-caste' or 'mixed blood'. As an ideology, this new construction of Aboriginality began to incorporate more of the features of a social rather than a biological scientific model, although both these elements remained evident throughout the assimilation period (1937 to 1968) and constituted a new ideology of domination. This was most clearly expressed in the AWB's 1948 policy statement. Here, state intervention was premised on two grounds, (a) 'that 95 per cent of the so-called Aborigines in New South Wales are half or light castes' and (b) the 'former social fabric had been torn

6. His main qualification seems to centre on the need for scientific proof. 'An examination of the problem of Aboriginal educability solely from a scientific point of view, should result in the working out of an important experiment designed to see whether the Aborigines, or rather a group of them, could be taken successfully through primary school and into high and technical school' (Elkin 1936: 499). Scientific knowledge and scientific method are seen to provide the basis for an understanding of the Aboriginal 'problem' and its possible resolution.

asunder by the onrush of Western civilisation' and left 'neither the traditional background of the Aboriginal way of life nor the culture of the white man to stabilise and guide them' (AWB report 1948: 3). These two aspects of Aboriginal existence were conjoined in various ways to suggest that Aboriginal contact with European society 'had progressed to such an extent that they must be absorbed into the general life of the white civilisation' (ibid. 1944: 3). The ideology of domination, based on the notion of the 'part Aborigine', ceased to stress difference and emphasised sameness as the basis for continuing domination.

This new ideology in effect simply teased out and extended the premises of the original racist discourse. Miscegenation provided the means of confirming the reality of the Aborigines' biological and cultural closeness to the dominant society. Many of the findings were presented to legitimate assimilation as the only logical choice and to allay any misapprehensions about it that may have been held within the dominant society. The development and confirmation of assimilation policies took two main forms, one biological and the other cultural/social. The Aboriginal administrators Neville (n.d.) and Bleakley (1961) and the anthropologist Tindale (1941) considered the 'half-caste problem' strictly a matter of race and saw biological and cultural matters as synonymous. The clearest expression of this is found in Tindale's (1941: 67) report, which was based on the research of the Harvard–Adelaide Universities Expedition (1938/9).

> A proportion of the mixed-bloods are making their way to the community and others would do so if given opportunities and assistance. A vigorous educational policy and training are wanted. Policies of isolation and segregation are palliatives; they do not reach the heart of the problem. *Complete mergence of the half-castes in the general community is possible without detriment to the white race.* Their Aboriginal blood is remotely the same as that of the majority of the white inhabitants of Australia, for the Australian Aboriginal is recognised as being a forerunner of the Caucasian race. In addition, the half-castes are increasingly of our own blood, *in places the majority of them already are more than half-white.* Two successive accessions of white blood lead to the mergence of the Aboriginal in the white community. There are no biological reasons for the rejection of people with a dilute strain of Australian Aboriginal blood. *A low percentage of Australian Aboriginal blood will not introduce any aberrant characteristics and there need be no fear of reversions to the dark Aboriginal type.*

The findings of the Harvard–Adelaide Universities Expedition were perhaps the first expression of the new orthodoxy in relation to Aborigines. Although their content questions the old discourse and develops and articulates a new one, the debate is located very much on the old terrain of biological determinism. In this, Tindale (ibid. p. 68), amongst others, also contends that full-bloods in settled districts would soon be extinct and, as such, the problem would solve itself.

Most discourse in the 1950s and 1960s emphasised the socio-cultural dimensions of the NSW Aborigines' 'plight'. The biological model was still evident in the retention of biological categories, such as 'part Aborigines', 'mixed bloods' and 'half-castes', but Le Gay Breton (1962), in his statistical analysis to quantify scientifically the absorption rate of mixed bloods, was the only person who retained a biological focus in analysis. Most of the research of this period confirms that the social fabric of these people had been torn asunder and concentrates on the separation of the Aborigines from their traditional culture. Fink (1957: 103) argues that the Aboriginal groups 'have undergone detribalisation' and, 'apart from a few vestiges of Aboriginal culture, one could not class this group as "Aboriginal" in the sense of having a living traditional culture of its own'. Similarly, Bell (1964: 64) states that, 'the part-Aborigines of New South Wales have no culture of their own to preserve. . . . The traditional social structure and culture had long since vanished. . . . There acculturation was a simple one-way process'. Aboriginality was assessed in relation to traditional culture and, implicitly and explicitly, it was assumed that detribalisation constituted a one-way process of cultural assimilation.

The regularity with which part-Aborigines were distanced from traditional culture was complemented by another systemic regularity which stressed their increasing closeness to European society. Bell (ibid. p. 68), for example, considers that part-Aborigines are 'to all intents and purposes assimilated'. He sees part-Aboriginal communities simply as socially and culturally deprived groups. As he puts it, 'What has to be recognised is that the integration of these groups differs in no way from the highly integrated groups of socially and economically depressed Europeans found in the slums of the city and in certain rural areas of New South Wales. In other words, these groups are just like poor whites' (ibid.). At the same time, the retaining of vestiges of traditional culture is viewed as pathological adaptation, especially by Elkin (1951), whose perception lies behind the division between 'intelligent parasitism' and 'intelligent appreciation'. Using this distinction he argues (ibid. p. 174) that Aborigines must be assisted to make an advance from 'external adaptation, making the best of the inevitable, to an inner understanding of the new way and the part they might play in it'. Otherwise, they would 'return to the mat' with its 'blend of native and European custom' which, *at best*, 'can lead to assimilation into the general cultural and economic life' (ibid. pp. 176–7). The general consensus was that assimilation was beneficial and inevitable, while links with the past were either a handicap or an unavoidable aspect of a transition phase.

From the late 1930s onwards, a new discourse on Aboriginality was being formulated, ordered and constructed. The appropriation of Aboriginal identity and its objectification in abstract scientific forms of knowledge meant that Aborigines were called upon to conform to other people's constructions of their identity as part of the process of domination. The very fact of domination establishes a hierarchy of knowledge in terms of the production, regulation and distribution of 'truth'. The new discourse reconstituted existing power relations and transformed the idea of assimilation into a self-evident aspect of European perception. Since the production of 'truth' is based on a *circular* relationship between knowledge and power (Foucault 1977a: 14), in that knowledge is not an absolute category detached from power, such knowledges not only reflect reality, but also constitute it. Dominance no longer concealed itself behind the idea of difference but in the idea of the achievement of sameness or equality. Assimilation, as an ideology of incorporation, reflected a major change in state policy which legitimated the growth of pedagogic intervention as a means of resolving the Aboriginal problem.

The dominant construction of Aboriginality in contemporary scientific research stressed, genetically and culturally, their assimilability into the dominant society. Such a construction was consistent with the move towards pedagogic strategies of control and absorption. This was reflected in a concern with the secular rights of Aborigines within the state, which the notion of race had effectively denied them (see Chapter 3). This new construction of Aboriginality minimised the 'innate differences' between Aborigines and Europeans as a means of asserting biological egalitarianism. As Dumont (1972: 305) suggests, it is upon the notion that 'all men are created equal' that citizenship is premised, and it is here that one 'discovers the close connection between egalitarianism and racism' in the modern state.

The apparent paradox of the state's exclusionary practices and an ideology of egalitarianism was overcome with the notion of race. The meaning of difference was constituted in a scientific view of the 'naturalness' of socio-human relations, which are genetically determined, immutably fixed by nature and unchangeable by state law. The emphasis on innate differences, which biological racism had pressed, had excluded Aborigines from the 'family of modern man'. They had been seen as incapable of participating equally within the modern state where biological egalitarianism was encoded in notions of judicial equality and universal franchise. The logical impasse this had posed for Aboriginal incorporation was overcome through the intersection of a scientific understanding which not only argued that Aboriginal 'culture' was a thing of the past but that their genetic inheritance was also weak.

6.3. The Emergence of a Culture of Resistance

The change of control wrought by the reclassification from reserves to supervised stations in the 1930s was not the only change for the Dhan-gadi. There was an increase in the amount of power and control the state exercised over them, as well as a serious decline in the institutional and other cultural practices that had neatly defined their cultural/political boundaries *vis-à-vis* the European community. In other words, there was a radical discontinuity at this point in the Dhan-gadi's social development. This discontinuity was not simply determined causally, but was overdetermined by the conjuncture of these two seemingly separate yet parallel developments, i.e. the specific conjuncture between the decline of conspicuous cultural practices and the imposition of managerial control. The adaptive strategies that had ensured the Dhan-gadi a relatively stable, distinctive and autonomous existence in relation to the European community in an earlier period were no longer sufficient (see Chapter 2). During the period of AWB control, new directions and different adaptive strategies were required and developed.

The conjuncture of events engendered quite a change in the life of the Dhan-gadi; in fact most of my older informants associate this period with change. The introduction of manager control marked a clear break with earlier patterns of social existence. Certain expressions were adopted to characterise how people saw this change – 'everythin' goin' out, nothin' comin' in', or, alternatively, 'whitefellas way comin' in'. There was now far more emphasis on the distinction between the 'black fellas way' and the 'white fellas way'.

This demarcation was most apparent in areas where cultural boundaries were explicitly expressed. In other words, there was an end to the initiation ceremonies, to the dancing and singing associated with such ceremonies and corroborees, and a decline in the use of the Dhan-gadi language. These profound changes, referred to as 'everythin' goin' out', particularly affected the initiation ceremonies which had been so important to Aboriginal life. 'Everybody whats on the station would have to be there. You can't go and say I'm not going and I'm gonna be here or there. You got to obey the Law see. [They'd say] "Come out and get over here".' Such ceremonies had been held regularly throughout the early part of this century. The young men of Bellbrook had been expected, as a matter of course, to go through at least one ceremony. Today, it is still known which men were put through the rule, at what ceremony, with whom and at what level they were initiated..Despite a rapidly changing and hostile world, the ceremonies retained the entirely unproblematic 'way of life' status encoded in the words 'you got to obey the Law see'.

Both the ceremony itself and its preparation provided a focus around which the community could express its social cohesion, as witnessed, for example, in the following exchange between an initiated man and his 'sister'.

[Man] When I was put through the rule, Kiparra, my sister here wouldn't eat the things I wouldn't eat, as if she went through too. She had a big part of the finishing of it when they are having the big ring; that's when she takes her part. She don't go in the bush, but I went out . . . I was put through.
[Woman] She'd [grandmother] be dancing there jumping and singing out.
[Man] She didn't dance for me while I was out in the bush; I'd get sick. She's taking her part by not eating anything she shouldn't eat. . . . You know you shouldn't eat porcupine, you shouldn't eat different fish unless the old people give it to you.
[Woman] You'd pick a bit [blow] and then you got it. You mustn't eat it but when he [old person] blow it he gives it to eat. Well you can eat them.

The sense of cohesion and cooperation engendered within the community during the course of these rituals was brought about through heightened social sensibilities. The temporal flow of the routines of everyday existence were suspended and demarcated from the profound activities of ceremonial life. In this respect, participation in ceremonial life was an existential reality and not simply a dispenser of doctrine.

In that the period of the AWB coincided with the first generation of uninitiated Dhan-gadi men, it marked a distinctive break between one generation and the next. It also marked the end of an important cultural practice by which the Dhan-gadi maintained themselves as an entity *vis-à-vis* their European neighbours. With the decline of these ceremonies, the Dhan-gadi lost one of their most powerful politico-cultural means of providing *explicit* membership criteria to the group. It now seemed as if it was 'all goin' white fellas way'.

The distinction between 'black fellas way' and 'white fellas way' was not confined to ceremonial life but was apparent also in other areas of conspicuous Aboriginal expression. It can be seen in the distinction they make between European and 'real' Aboriginal music and dancing, i.e. between European forms of dance and singing and those associated with the ceremonies and corroborees. As one woman recalled:

They really knew that they were singing about and if they had that boomerang or two sticks and hit it like that, you know, they'd keep time with that and they'd sing. Oh, they had real music them people and I don't think that there is anybody [left] that I can think of. Might have been over there [Bowraville] but none here on this Macleay.

The same applied to corroborees held at Bellbrook which were regarded as dancing in the _goorie_ way.[7] Many of the Dhan-gadi have vivid memories of the _gurginj gurginj_ (praying mantis) dance, in which, complete with a large mask and other dancers, the dancer acts out his particular 'story'. These corroborees were regarded as quite different from those that had been performed at shows for Europeans. (A number of men from Bellbrook had performed pseudo-corroborees at agricultural shows in the Macleay River region, the last occasion being in 1938 for the 150-year celebrations in Kempsey of European 'settlement' of Australia.) As my informant on this latter-day version put it, 'Oh, I don't know what you'd call it, it wasn't really the old timers song, I think it was only made up one, song, but it was there with the beat'.

Although the distinction between 'black fellas way' and 'white fellas way' was applied to Dhan-gadi versus European dancing and singing, European dancing and singing were by no means rejected. In fact the Dhan-gadi had been holding European dances for many years. The men had learnt to play the violin, the accordion, the concertina, the gum leaf and the bones or spoons and these musicians accompanied the dances that were held on the river flat by the light of a big fire. Similarly, a number of men were called to sing their set pieces during the evening. Aboriginal and European dancing styles coexisted side by side, but what made the 1930s a watershed was the end of Aboriginal singing and dancing as distinctive and significant cultural practices.

The expressions of discontinuity here form part of a process by which the Dhan-gadi present an image of themselves which they themselves have produced, but which none the less necessitates coming to grips with both their past and their present situation. Although this involves ordering the past from the present, it is not merely an imaginary projection into the past. I take issue with Reay's (1949: 101) remark that, 'without hope for a different future they look backwards to a Golden Age which is believed to have existed in living memory'. Such an approach is derived from a deprivation theory sustained by ahistorical, psychological reductionism. It suggests that the content of such recollections is illusory. To dismiss such recollections as historically irrelevant, however, effectively denies the reality of the people's own experience. This rejection of the authenticity of the knowledge of Aborigines' own experience is an act of power which, in that they are reduced to passive objects of knowledge, reproduces their domination.

If such a historical ordering is 'illusory', it is because of what has been left out rather than what has been included. But even given such omissions the historical renderings of the past still contain a definite sense of what is meaningful and significant and an awareness of the

---

7. The Dhan-gadi use the term to _goorie_ to refer to themselves and other Aborigines, rather than the European word Aborigine. _Goorie_ or _koorie_ have wide currency amongst Aborigines along the eastern coastal region of NSW.

social conditions under which they lived. As we saw earlier, they were conscious of change and, as I shall discuss below, were knowledgeable about the processes that oppressed them. The different ways in which the periods of APB and AWB control were perceived clearly reflected changes in the modalities of state power imposed upon them. In terms of what was meaningful and significant, a great deal of emphasis was placed on the cultural aspects of social life in the earlier APB period, but on social change and domination during the AWB period.

In the earlier period the Dhan-gadi had been able to maintain a significant degree of cultural autonomy, primarily because the rudimentary forms of control, which had been exercised through the local police and APB officers, were in the form of sporadic interventions on the reserves (see Chapter 5). The pervasive controls exercised through managers and matrons in residence on the stations were, however, significantly different. In this new era, Dhan-gadi culture no longer produced the doctrines, cultural practices and artefacts that used to be handed down to each succeeding generation through formal institutions, for the overarching institutional forms that subsumed the Dhan-gadi were now those of the dominant culture. They could no longer continue to develop their own independently determined form of culture and consciousness. Instead, most of the cultural forms, practices, values, attitudes and feelings generated over this period assumed the character of concrete forms of resistance against the coercive structuring of the wider society. We are dealing with a 'profane' culture (see Willis 1978) developed through concrete forms of struggle. Such cultural forms are, in part, a response to the specific context of cultural/institutional subordination: they are attempts to subvert the most immediate and oppressive aspects of that domination. These conditions of existence profoundly shaped (rather than determined) Dhan-gadi culture by providing the agenda with which that culture had to deal.[8]

This culture of resistance also involved the remaking of a cultural distance from European society, which had been lost with the disappearance of the more conspicuous boundary markers of a distinctive Dhan-gadi social identity. Here, the formation of behavioural and symbolic ordering enabled the Dhan-gadi to confront and invest with meaning the transformed conditions of their social existence. Opposition to European domination for them was grounded in attempts to subvert total subordination by creating 'free space' where some degree of autonomy could be exercised within the stations.

Dhan-gadi meanings, knowledge and experience were developed in

8. The genesis of such cultural forms has been dealt with and developed largely through the work of a number of cultural Marxists (see Thompson 1977 and 1982; Genovese 1974 and 1975; Sider 1980; Willis 1978 and 1978a; Willis and Corrigan 1983; and Hall and Jefferson (eds) 1977).

two major ways: (a) in the accompanying struggle against the most immediate forms of their oppression in institutions, and (b) as a rejection of the wider aspect of racial/cultural secondariness associated with such institutionalisation. The AWB period was characterised by one informant as, 'Just like buying bullocks up at Bellbrook and bringing them down to Burnt Bridge, packing them into one paddock. After a few weeks there is no grass. That's the way it was!' This statement links the two major aspects of institutionalisation, namely the feelings and emotions associated with a sudden loss of personal autonomy and control (which accompanied the change from reserve to supervised station) and the interpretation of institutionalisation as an expression of collective racial/cultural secondariness (associated in the analogy with being treated like a mob of cattle, as less than human). (This latter aspect is discussed more fully later in the book.)

Cultural resistance was at one level structured by the struggle against the most immediate forms of control, experienced as a set of physical and social constraints and liabilities. It was not the AWB members themselves who were the focus of attention, but their representatives on the stations, i.e. the managers and matrons responsible for implementing AWB policy. Managers and matrons were supposed to uplift and encourage Aborigines through instruction and guidance, but their presence was continually referred to as a denial of such possibilities. As one man stated, 'stead of the Board thinkin' if anyone want to get on in life, let him go. No, they want to put him down a step instead of letting him go up a step!'

The manager had complete control over running the station. He was the person who decided who could and who could not take up residence; he controlled the distribution of rations; he could recommend people for exemption passes, and he could expel people from the station. As one woman put it, 'you couldn't do much in them days . . . you just had to grin and bear it sort of thing'. Stations Aborigines were given no opportunity to make decisions about or to control matters that affected them directly.

On the station Aborigines were expected to be submissive and suppliant to the manager's and the matron's authority. This hierarchical structure of command was concretised by a number of gestures and actions. Verbal acts of deference were expected. The manager and matron always had to be addressed formally, and some managers even insisted on being called 'master'. Similarly, no matter how trivial or menial, all the manager's decisions were expected to be obeyed. This provided them with a great deal of scope for making humiliating demands on the Aboriginal 'inmates'. Adult men were frequently used as 'messenger boys' by the manager or matron, and one man indignantly recalls how a matron expected the men who cut wood for her to clean up all the wood chips as well. Such petty tyrannies could be legitimated by staff on the pedagogic grounds that they inculcated men with values of discipline and orderliness. In an earlier period, men had had the option of simply withdrawing their labour from employers as a face-saving device, but such self-protective measures were no longer available to those who wished to remain on the station.

It is hardly surprising, then, that the characters and capacities of the managers and matrons received close scrutiny from the 'inmates'. As one person stated, 'You only got to do one wrong, see, the whitefella, and its goin' round the mission straight away. Broadcast what sort of fella he is.' Such staff/inmate interactions are characteristic of institutional relationships. A system of intelligence and covert communication networks are essential if the responses or actions of those in authority are to be predicted and avoided. Rather than comply with institutional authority, they produced covert, collective information to place limits on the manager's control. This also generated an oppositional sense of identity.

Similarly, Aborigines deliberately concealed information about themselves and their social relationships to those in authority.[9] This was especially frustrating for the managers given the AWB's emphasis on 'detailed administration' through the gathering of biographical information. As one woman stated, 'I can remember a manager sayin' to me that you can go to any of them and you know they know about it, but they'd say they don't know.' The denial of knowledge was doubly pointed, for not only did it mean that the Aborigines refused to give information that could be used against them, but, in a more immediate sense, at the interpersonal level, it also meant that they engaged in acts of tacit defiance of authority or insolence. Such resistance sought to limit the power of state officials who exercised seemingly unlimited control over their social relations and personal lives.

These phenomena are more complex than the usual power relations associated with institutionalisation. The gathering of reconnaissance information was not restricted to the Europeans in charge of the station but also extended to anyone with whom they might interact in the wider society. A knowledge of the dominant society was vital if the Dhan-gadi were to limit their own vulnerability to control. In these matters the main index of success is in how much the different communities know about each other. Here the Aborigines consistently had more information about the European community than visa versa. European information about the Aborigines was usually very rudimentary,

9. Hausfeld (1963: 50), a former AWB manager, discusses the problems he faced in an Aboriginal community on the north coast. He states that he was deliberately given false and misleading information and claims that, 'at Woodenbong a whole body of material was secret in the sense that it was kept from the outsider . . . the non-Aborigines'. This included traditional secret/sacred knowledge, as well as more secular forms of information and knowledge.

often containing pejorative stereotypes which passed as information. The Aborigines, by contrast, could usually supply detailed information about the personal proclivities, social and economic status and careers of the Europeans with whom they interacted. For them, the possession of knowledge about Europeans and, conversely, the limiting of knowledge about themselves served a strategic and, hence, political function. Limiting information was synonymous with limiting the capacity of Europeans to control and dominate their lives.

Similarly, reconnaissance is also used to ensure the success of other forms of opposition to the station manager's control. This can be seen in terms of creating 'free space' where people find scope to engage in a specifically unauthorised activity or range of activities. Goffman's (1961: 189) concept of 'secondary adjustments' is useful in this respect. He defines these adaptations as, 'any habitual arrangement by which a member of an organisation employs unauthorised means, or obtains unauthorised ends, or both, thus getting around the organisation's assumptions as to what he should do and hence what he should be'. The two major areas in which Aborigines have resorted to 'secondary adjustments' that have been widely recorded in the literature (Reay 1945; Fink 1957; Calley 1957; Beckett 1964) are illegal drinking and gambling. And these 'vices' have remained prevalent despite the 'strenuous efforts of the police and the local officers of the Board' (see also AWB reports 1944 and 1945). The creation of 'free space' on the stations for such activities was, at one level, an attempt to subvert the manager's authority and, at another level, an effort to deny what Aborigines should be according to the explicit charter of assimilation that local authorities of the AWB were expected to carry out.

Although Goffman's notion of 'secondary adjustments' may cover a range of attitudes and responses to institutional control, it nevertheless tends to obscure crucial differences that occur in the wider social context (cf. Rowley 1973). In Goffman's use of the concept, 'secondary adjustments' are made up of the many legitimate aspects of 'everyday life' that are denied in an institutional context. Yet, in the case of station Aborigines, both the institution and the wider society imposed the same kinds of restrictions and, therefore, called for a similar set of 'secondary adjustments'. The methods of surveillance and control used on the stations were in fact exaggerated prototypes of the less comprehensive forms of control found in the wider society.

The retention of the repressive and discriminatory legislation of the 1943 amendment of the Aborigines Protection Act during most of the AWB's period of control accentuated the need for secondary adjustments in all sectors of social existence, for the legislative authority of the Act encompassed both the stations and the wider society. The 'fringe camps' were one attempt to create 'free space' away from institutional control and to defy the local authorities, for the legislation decreed that Aborigines could be forced back to stations and their houses knocked down without any need to proceed through the courts (Rowley 1973: 272). Similarly, through finding employment in the local economy the Aborigines acquired an institutionalised form of secondary adjustment. By securing temporary forms of contract work, they could 'be their own bosses' and thus minimise European control outside as well as inside the 'total institution'.

The notion of 'secondary adjustments' is particularly relevant in the wider context of Aboriginal drinking, for, being illegal, drinking alcohol was a complicated and essentially clandestine process. One informant recalled how, to obtain 'grog', it was necessary for someone who could 'pass' for a 'whitefella' to get it or, more frequently, to secure 'sly grog' illicitly at the back door of some local hotel, while everybody else waited out of sight. The procurers of the 'sly grog' then had to proceed back to the station in the most inconspicuous manner to avoid detection. This journey was, however, made considerably easier by the local railway line being built through high ground and providing cover until they reached the 'free space' on the station. Such practices can usefully be regarded both as 'secondary adjustments' to institutional life and oppositional practices to everyday life.

The meaning of such practices, therefore, goes far beyond a response to the domination of institutional authorities. This point has been made by a number of studies (Reay 1945: 300–1; Fink 1957: 103; Beckett 1964: 40). Reay, however, sees such activities as pathological adaptations to European domination, whereas Beckett regards them as measures to secure a degree of Aboriginal autonomy. In many respects, drinking and gambling were direct acts of defiance against the AWB's policy of assimilation, for they were clearly inversions of bourgeois notions of social respectability (sobriety, industry and self-discipline), which the AWB purported to value.

> Alcohol: The vice of drinking still persists to a degree amongst a certain section of the Aborigines, and money, which at present time is able to be earned in large amounts, is often misapplied, causing misery to the families and trouble to the administration . . . [and]
> Gambling: Gambling amongst Aborigines is prevalent throughout the whole state. While it must be regarded as a vice that should be discouraged, it must be remembered that gambling amongst Aborigines lacks the economic and social consequences which it frequently has amongst white people. It does, however, tend to become an obsession and an obstacle to the development of more useful forms of activity. It is a retreat for the Aborigine from the hard facts of the white man's world, a means of putting in time, and doing something emotionally exciting in a purposeless life (AWB report 1945: 11).

Nevertheless, excess indulgence and wastefulness acted as effective statements of opposition to those European values the AWB sought to cultivate.

The considerable emphasis on suppressing gambling and drinking is related to something more fundamental in the dominant society's culture. *Collective* activities, such as gambling and drinking, act as a counterbalance to relationships based on individual rights and property. Assimilation essentially sought to achieve a general line of social 'development' based on the individualisation of the collective: that is, people consume as isolated individuals/nuclear families and accumulate goods (things) as *personal* property. The individual asserts himself as a separate entity by affirming his rights to personal possessions over and above the rights of the group. This perception of 'bad' behaviour (drinking and gambling) and 'good' behaviour (saving and work discipline) was informed by a focus on the individual. By contrast, Aboriginal drinking and gambling remained collective group activities based on the exigencies of establishing 'free space'. Such collective activities, in a sense, reproduced the cultural emphasis of sharing. In the context of assimilation, where the dispersal of sites that might produce a sense of collective identity was an essential part of the policy, their persistence was very much a political act and remained so through to the 1960s.

In a more immediate sense, however, illegal drinking was a way of rejecting one of the most discriminatory laws applied to Aborigines. As Reay (1945: 103) records, 'being drunk expresses the Aborigines' contempt for a law which they consider unnecessary and ineffective'. She points out that drinking and imprisonment carried a certain social prestige because they signified that such men were capable of securing what was legally forbidden (ibid.). Beckett (1964: 40) states that, 'often drunken Aborigines made no effort to keep out of the way [of police], and certainly they were not deterred by fines, prison sentences, and beatings allegedly inflicted on them'. He describes such activity as, 'a continued cycle of defiance, arrest and renewed defiance' against a bitterly resented discriminatory law (ibid.). The Europeans' easy access to alcohol acted as a constant reminder to the Aborigines of their inferior status. What is perhaps cruelly paradoxical is that this defiance through drunkenness expressed assertions of equality with Europeans: political assertions of their humanness.

The genesis of social existence in this context is determined by dialectical relations of conflict. The historical conditions established for the development of such 'contested cultures' ensures that they are constituted in many respects as a culture of resistance. The culture of resistance develops in opposition to structures of domination. These acts are not necessarily expressed in terms of overt political consciousness or overtly political acts, but constitute a structural opposition as a 'way of life'. In the cases of drinking and gambling, for example, such resistance to European authority and values is not consciously associated with every act of drinking and gambling nor the status associated with imprisonment. Yet, quite clearly, they are ritualistic acts of opposition which are expressed in this case as a way of living rather than as overt political actions.

Nevertheless, there is no question that a heavy price was paid for these acts of resistance, both socially and physically, especially among those who became addicted to methylated spirits. One woman recalled the consequences for her close family and relatives:

> I don't know whether I should say it, but ah, they [local property owners] were only paying them 5/– a week and methylated spirits. A couple of bottles of methylated spirits they were paying them. A lot of them died. A's three brothers died because of that, my brother died. We had an adopted brother and when he was 15 he died. . . . Metho killed a lot of our people. My brothers and cousins, some of them were younger than me.

These acts of personal annihilation represented the dark underside of Aboriginal drinking. This extreme and dramatic example serves to show the 'brittle dichotomy' (Genovese 1975: 78) between resistance and accommodation. Ambiguity underlines the dialectical process whereby resistance cannot be readily divorced from accommodation but is organically connected to it (ibid). To ignore the 'antagonistic unity' that exists between resistance/defiance, on the one hand, and resignation/powerlessness, on the other, is to underestimate the enormous pressures which are brought to bear to render the cultural and social identity of Aborigines problematical. To focus on such activities only in terms of resistance and defiance is to avoid the problem of hegemonic domination.

The ambiguity embodied in collective, spontaneous and immediate acts of opposition, summarised by Fink (1957: 103) as 'gambling, drinking to excess, wasting money, and neglecting homes and personal appearance' also reflects a resignation to those very structures of domination. The anti-social behaviour involved in these inversions of bourgeois values ensured that the Aborigines were contained by such values. In effect, acts of resistance were incapable of transforming the most immediate effects of their oppression. Yet, as defensive strategies, there is a clear refusal to submit to European domination. The defensive strategies did provide the basis for a distinctive group identity, described by Fink (ibid. p. 118) as a 'self-conscious sub-society' and by Reay (1949: 117) as 'the strongest integrative force', namely 'common membership in a rejected minority'. Similarly, their actions were quite a clear rebuttal of assimilation policies, which sought nothing less than an admittance of cultural inferiority. Nevertheless, the defensive strategies could not change such relationships; they could simply contain them and be contained within them.

6.4. The Struggle for Social Meaning

The immediate effects of the assimilation policy on the Dhan-gadi were to intensify their experience of racism and to heighten their awareness of inequality and discrimination. In the past, racism and inequality had been experienced on an intermittent, more or less random basis, but with the establishment of manager-controlled stations, such inequalities were institutionalised and came to be experienced as an unavoidable part of everyday life. The managers and matrons ensured that daily encounters expressed deference and dependence and that the institutional techniques of control contained in government policy served to increase rather than decrease European domination of the Aboriginal communities in the Macleay Valley.

Government policy not only imposed considerable physical and social constraints, but was also a pervasive factor affecting a consciousness of the Aboriginal socio-cultural identity. Aboriginal hostility to institutional control was more than a statement against an instrument of state oppression; it was a protest against the low esteem and status accorded to Aborigines by the wider society. The Aborigines interpreted institutional oppression very much in terms of racial oppression. There was a radical disjuncture between the meanings and values embedded in government policy and those of the Dhan-gadi. Dhangadi meanings and values were constituted in their own forms of knowledge and derived from their own different sets of experiences with the dominant society.

Nevertheless, the knowledge and meanings of experience were not simply constituted within a particular cultural logic, but also as subversive 'readings' and symbolic violations of the social order imposed upon them. As Sider (1980: 26) argues:

> Counter-hegemonic cultural forms often use an arsenal of symbols which are borrowed from the existing hegemony (and inverted, mocked, etc.) in order to express experiences and claims different from the élite's; the use of these symbols implies limits and constraints to the thoroughness of the opposition. These constraints can, however, be partly breached; first, by the fact [that] counter-hegemonic strategies can expose the contradictions within the existing hegemony, and second, by creating an experience of opposition. Counter-hegemonic strategies, like other forms of culture, do not just emerge out of people's thoughts and individual experiences, but out of their mutual understanding of their social relations.

The intensification of institutionalisation in effect provided the raw materials for the ordering of a domain of meanings which continually reinforced their group distinctiveness. Yet, expressions of subordinate group identity are also ambiguous as an oppositional culture. In this instance, group distinctiveness was generated in a social context in which Aborigines experienced themselves in terms of a response to the agenda set down by the dominant society. The central tenet of hegemonic domination was the denial of the integrity of a separate Aboriginal identity. The hegemonic aspects of control sought to render Aboriginal identity problematic as a precondition for their acceptance of the 'superiority' of the norms and values of the dominant society.

The Macleay Valley stations reproduced the sense of secondariness and subordination that the Dhan-gadi had been accustomed to in their dealings with the wider society. The stations institutionalised, in a more intense and systematic way, those features of low status and disrespect accorded them in the wider society. Many practices that were common within these institutions were regarded as racial slights. For example, the Aborigines saw the subordinating practice of assembling for rations, as well as the quality of the rations themselves, as a sign of their collective disrepute. As one woman observed, 'Different stores would put in for it [supply the ration]. The cheapest thing he could find. I can remember that K. had the shop in Bellbrook. I can see them measuring the tea out and the sugar, brown sugar, all that sort of thing. They'd have white sugar, but this was the ration supply.' The items supplied were interpreted as symbols of disrespect: the 'black' tea was 'like dust' and regarded as 'the sweepings off the floor'; inferior brown (raw) sugar instead of white (refined) sugar which the Europeans would buy; and inferior meat that was 'mostly bones'. What is equally significant is that the assertions also contain a moral critique of the dominant society: that is, they expose a contradiction residing within the dominant society's claim to a superior set of human values, customs and laws and thereby challenge such a claim. The inattentiveness to qualitative equality in the critical sphere of food exchange, especially in a community where reciprocal sharing of food has been (and remains) a cultural norm, provided a particularly negative evaluation of the 'superior' values of the dominant society.

Similarly, the manager's conduct and relations with the people on the station were seen as important indices of how the wider society perceived Aborigines. The manager's control over all aspects of station life was symbolic of the notions of inferiority and incompetence which sustained European paternalism. If racial inferiority was implicit in such paternalistic control, it was often made quite explicit in the treatment of them by some managers. As Fink (1955: 27) points out, the AWB's recruitment policies did enable, unintentionally, a number of 'maladjusted individuals, drunkards or people who hated blacks' to be employed.[10] The number of these people in the ranks of the AWB and their constant rotation ensured that station Aborigines would never

---

10. This lack of expertise was compounded by the numerous tasks staff were expected to fulfil. Their duties included the facilitating of raised standards in housing, homemaking,

know when they would get a 'bad boss' who would make life intolerable for them. On Bellbrook, one manager even patrolled the station dressed in a white suit and a pith helmet. These managers and matrons exemplified, through their actions, what were felt to be appropriate ways of dealing with Aborigines as inferior and subordinate people. 'They was *real* bullies they was [to] men's, women's and kid's. When they found out they were bosses over the people, they treated them like dogs'. Although an extreme example, the attitudes embodied in such remarks reflected the essential patterning of their interactions with Europeans. Yet, what is also indicated by and inscribed into such comments is the Aboriginal understanding of the contradiction between the values of the managers/matrons and their pedogogic role of 'uplifting' and 'educating' Aborigines. In effect, their role as representatives and dispensers of 'superior' cultural values was being questioned: that such men and women, who treated people 'like dogs', should be put in charge of their lives was also a statement about the values of the dominant society.

In this context, the manager's credentials and competence in running the station were also subject to scrutiny:

> They [AWB] don't care who he is, if he's from overseas and never seen a blackfella before, he get the job and yet he come to run the true Australian. Well, look at Mr. L., he come from overseas. He didn't know anything. He was down at Laper [La Perouse Aboriginal station] there, well what did they do in Laper. Then he came up to try and rule us in Burnt Bridge.

Scrutiny, here, carries with it a double meaning. On the one hand, the appointment of these men reflected the inferior status and lack of care accorded them by the wider society, while on the other, the rejection of the manager's credentials and abilities denied him the legitimate authority in the eyes of the community to govern their affairs.

Refuting the manager's authority in this manner was especially provocative in an institutional context in which the manager needed to limit and discredit the inmates' initiatives to sustain his own authority (see Goffman 1961: 154). As one man put it, 'you couldn't tell 'em anything. If you knew too much they'd send you'. This staff/inmate conflict effectively meant that if the Aborigines were to be remoulded

---

hygiene and education. In addition, they were responsible for the general control and orderly behaviour of the 'inmates'; the specific suppression of gambling and drinking; the allocation of employment for Aborigines on the station; the weekly and, on some stations, twice weekly issue of rations; and the furnishing of comprehensive weekly and monthly reports. In effect, stations were grossly understaffed and staff poorly equipped to do their job. In institutional terms, they were highly inefficient and incompetently run. Underlying this was the specific context in which the principles of bureaucratic custodianship were applied. It was not individuals removed from familial to institutional contexts to be retrained, but individuals within familial surroundings that the AWB sought to retrain.

by the assimilation policy, it was in the manager's interests, in establishing his 'credentials' and authority, to impose his own particular ideas about how this was to be done. Hence:

> Whatever work we did for this manager to make [things] up to date. Get another one and he'd change it all around and do it his way. In that way I reckon they was no good. Instead of building it up to follow on the right way, they'd pull it down. See Bellbrook we had our fences in front of the house and had a garden right around. The next fella come and pull it down.

Or, to show another example, 'We had a banking account. We called it Bellbrook Progress Association. We had to get people to sign to get any money out. That's alright. We had so much money in the bank. Well, when some other manager come, he wouldn't go on with that. . . . One fella do, the other fella come and change it.'[11] The people on the stations could expect constant changes, for the practices and policies of one manager invariably bore no resemblance to those of the next. During the period of AWB control (1932–1968) Bellbrook was said to have had no less than 20 managers. Although such changes were integral to the establishment of the manager's authority and control over institutional life, paradoxically, in rejecting the work projects of the previous manager, each successive manager relativised and subverted his own authority.

The Dhan-gadi's understanding of their own secondary status and subordination was firmly grounded in the constant changes which took place in the social world of the station – a station in which they had no formal control. The uncertainty generated by such exercises of authority and control, the undermining and debilitating effects on Aboriginal initiative built into the various manager's practices and the relations of dependency also expose a fundamental contradiction in such policy. As one man emphasised, 'They wouldn't let you tell 'em anything. If I did anything and went and told 'em, I'd be wrong. As we saying 'takin' notice of a blackfella.' The maintenance of the manager's authority and control through the denial of any Aboriginal expertise effectively sustained dependence at an individual and collective level. As we saw earlier, the Dhan-gadi interpreted such practices as attempts to 'put him down a step instead of letting him go up a step!'.

What was paradoxical about this form of institutionalisation was that the 'discrediting' was not internalised as individual incompetence, but as a collective rejection in terms of 'takin' notice of a blackfella'. Instead

---

11. The Progress Association would appear to have been formed in the late 1950s and early 1960s. 'The total amount derived from the joint agricultural project launched by the Bellbrook Progress Association and Mr K.W. Waters, from the sale of corn, was £105. After £4 5s 6d had been paid to Mr Waters for labour, the use of his tractor and the corn, a balance of £60 14s 6d was left to be credited to the Bellbrook Progress Association Account.' (*Dawn* 1959: 19.)

of inculcating notions of possessive individualism, such practices sustained a collective identity based on an experience of opposition, and this led them to interpret institutional oppression as racial oppression. The intensification of institutionalisation generated a collective identity with which to oppose the dominating society. This is not meant to imply that there was no collective identity in the years before the 1930s, but rather that it became more significant in the context of pedagogic interventions and institutionalisation.

A manifest contradiction clearly exists when a programme of state intervention stimulates a sense of collective identity among the Dhangadi when it is explicitly designed to achieve the reverse, i.e. to individuate the Aborigines as a precondition for their assimilation. That such a situation should have arisen should not, however, obscure the brittle dichotomy that existed between resistance and accommodation, for, although difficult to categorise, both moments can conceivably result from the same phenomena. The sense of opposition, on the one hand, and the unintended paradoxes in administrative policy, on the other, do not necessarily deny the struggle for meaning that the Dhan-gadi people experienced in their relations with such structures of domination. In terms of Aboriginal policy, the total institution was a cultural apparatus with which to implement a cultural programme of homogenisation to eradicate the 'otherness' of Aboriginality. The policy was seeking to achieve cultural hegemony over the Aborigines in preparation for their incorporation into the dominant society. Hegemonic forms of control attempt to render identity problematic by turning unconscious, unreflexive acts into problematic, conscious and conspicious ones.

Hegemonic domination had complex consequences. This complexity is reflected in the changes to the pervasive cultural expression of 'shame' or the practice of 'shaming'. As one man put it, 'You know, blackfella terrible shamed fella. You know when you are doing things in the open and you don't want it that way.' The word shame has a wide currency amongst Aborigines and is used in a number of contexts, usually jokingly, to comment on some social *faux pas*, 'flashness' or cheekiness. The regulatory aspect of 'shaming' has a distinctive cultural/structural basis associated with small, non-stratified and essentially closed communities with homogeneous rules of conduct (Heller 1980: 216). As Heller (ibid. pp. 217–20) points out, shame regulation is associated with *acting differently* and *being different* and is based on transgressions of the codes, rules and rituals of conduct of a collective communal authority. It is paradoxical that the separation and social homogeneity engendered by institutionalisation provided the conditions under which such collective community mechanisms of social control were perpetuated among the Aborigines. As we saw earlier, it was self-regulation by *internal authority* (each individual's conscience) that institutional practices sought to achieve through the application of mechanisms of discipline. By contrast, shaming as a mechanism of social control is characterised by regulation through *external authority*, which is manifested in an egalitarian and communal form of surveillance. Whilst the form of such egalitarian mechanisms remained constant, the content of shaming practices took on more complex and ambiguous meanings associated with their specific social and political context.

In the context of institutional life, shaming took on an oppositional role in that it was used to subvert attempts to appropriate European 'ways of life' amongst community members. As Fink (1955: 37) working with Aborigines in NSW describes it, 'shaming' operated as a form of internal social constraint on community members. She depicts it as an ahistorical phenomenon which was very much a part of Aboriginal socialisation in that individuals try 'to conform and accept the group's standards as much as possible to avoid being laughed at'. She sees shaming as a form of leveller whereby people in the group who appear to 'out do others' or to 'show off' are prevented from 'doing better' (ibid.). Fink misses the point, however, that 'doing better' implied the appropriation of a more European life-style. On Bellbrook, for example, this levelling process affected a man who, with the manager's permission, attempted to build up a herd of cattle. It was opposed and subverted by other people on the station. Similarly, another woman complained to me that she and her husband had set up a kiosk on the station which, once again, was subverted. These individuals had not exactly supported assimilation, but in supporting an idea had conformed to European standards, and this was seen as a rejection of Aboriginal identity. In this respect, 'shaming' functioned to direct hostility to those who attempted to approximate European values.

The notion of 'shame' also, however, embodied in its usage a seemingly contradictory aspect because it could also be applied to 'old blackfella ways'. 'Shame' in this context was the concrete form to which hegemony aspired. It had become part of the process of cultural domination. Such instances usually involved conspicuous aspects of Aboriginality, such as public use of the language (speaking the lingo), eating bush tucker or dancing in the '*goorie* way'. One man told me that when the managers effectively put a stop to cooking on an open fire, many people were already 'too shamed' to cook that way. Another man forbade his family to eat bush tucker, for example, wallaby, possum, pademelon or echidna. In this case the necessity of bush tucker as a supplement to European sources of food was restricted to eating 'white meat', bush turkey, fowls and pigeon. Similar accounts were given of young people who felt embarrassed to see older people 'spinning the leg', as dancing in the *goorie* way was commonly referred to. In this respect, then, racism and paternalism had the distinctive hegemonic effect of undermining the Dhan-gadi's sense of worth. Certain aspects of Aboriginal identity were turned into reified objects – objects which existed outside them and which were set against them like some alien and hostile force.

The most damaging aspect of this form of domination was the way it suppressed the Dhan-gadi language. Language is, after all, a very important cultural marker (see Reay 1949: 90–1) and, except for the frequent use of its vocabulary, the Dhan-gadi language has been virtually lost. Its decline over the past couple of generations was explained in the following terms:

> . . . all them older fellas, the way their talking, more joking, in the language, none of them talk dirty or anything, more enjoy it if they speak in the language, they can't talk English. They could talk English a bit, but I mean more their own. . . . Old granny C. she tell us what to do in the language that's how we picked it up. You understand it, that's how we know what to do. Spoke to them [parents] only in the home outside they spoke English. They shy, don't like to talk it.

'Speaking in the language' had become a covert exercise. In this regard shame is not a sanction against showing off, but a means of avoiding attracting the kind of attention that would lay one open to criticism or ridicule. This form of internal group control, whereby the capacity to remain inconspicuous becomes a virtue, is also a manifestation of the wider mechanisms of European control and dominance.

European contempt and prejudice were such that 'doin' things in the open' was always likely to invite European hostility and public embarrassment through ridicule. The most significant aspect of shaming is that it is a public form of social coercion. In this it may be differentiated from the concept of guilt as a social process of coercion. The inculcation of guilt to bring behaviour into line with what is considered normal is an individual and internalised process seeking to attain self-regulation. As Heller (1980: 221) puts it, 'Internal authority is *autonomy*. To obey nothing but our conscience means that we are the authors of our *actions* and or our character'. By contrast, shame/shaming inhibits and represses but is regulated by an external referent. Whereas guilt is manifested by deviance from an internalised set of norms, shame in this context is constituted in a tension between a set of habitual acts and values, which were originally valued but which had now been rendered polluting. In this sense, shame/shaming, as a social process, had gained added meaning by becoming a social feature of a pariah group and of the modes of its external domination.

Chapter 7

The Deregulation of a Colonial Being: the Aboriginal as Universal Being

7.1. The Politics of Assimilation

Relations between Aborigines and the state underwent a significant transformation in the 1950s and 1960s. This period was characterised by the progressive deregulation of Aborigines as colonial beings. The politics of exclusion was gradually replaced by the politics of inclusion. These changes were part of a broad societal critique of discrimination and exclusion, which redirected policy away from institutionalisation and towards assimilation into the wider society. By the 1960s assimilation was universally accepted throughout Australia (see Chapter 6). Broad-based public support was most emphatically revealed in the results of the 1967 Commonwealth government referendum. Under section 127 of the Commonwealth Constitution (1900) full blood Aborigines had been excluded from the census on the grounds that they were not citizens (see Chapter 5). The referendum was a 'submission to the electors of a proposed law to alter the Constitution so as to omit certain words relating to the People of the Aboriginal race', which meant 'should we count them in the Census as citizens or not?' (Widders 1977: 97). A staggering 89 per cent of the voters were in favour of their incorporation (Altman and Nieuwenhuysen 1979: 188). Its political significance was blown up into a rejection of exclusionary practices against Aborigines perpetuated at the level of the state and local government. This technical change in the census signalled a major political reform.

The movement towards equal rights by the state in the years before 1967 made apparent the conflicting political aims of the NSW and Commonwealth governments on the one hand and local councils on the other. As I suggest in Chapter 5, the policies of exclusion and segregation at the local community level had been complemented and reinforced by the Board's control on government settlements. In the 1950s and 1960s, however, this complementarity was dissolved as the

157

state increasingly sought to assimilate the Aborigines, while local councils attempted to maintain their exclusion. Indeed, as Widders (1977: 97) points out, the voting pattern in the 1967 referendum revealed that, 'the greater proportion of Aborigines resident in an electorate, the lower the vote recorded in favour of the proposal'. The majority of voters in the Kempsey electorate opposed the constitutional changes of the referendum. Since a majority of Aborigines lived in rural areas, the split that was apparent in the voting patterns was between urban and rural voters. What this reflected was the local European rejection of equality. It was in this context that throughout the 1960s a struggle was developed by Aborigines and progressive Europeans against local discriminatory legislation.

The politics of assimilation was carried out at the level of the local community. Throughout the 1960s, a number of committees and organisations were formed by local Europeans, usually with AWB support, to promote Aboriginal assimilation into the local communities. The struggle for equality in Kempsey was spearheaded and controlled by liberal Europeans who formed the Macleay District Welfare Committee (MDWC). The MDWC's constitution stated that, 'The aim of the Committee shall be the assimilation of all people of Aboriginal blood into the Australian community on the basis of complete equality with the other members. The Committee will investigate educational, employment, health, housing, and social problems in the Macleay district and assist where possible.' The composition of the committee was initially entirely European, being made up of representatives from local church and community groups, for example, Apex,[1] the Rotary Club, and the Country Women's Association (CWA), as well as representatives from the local council and AWB managers. The aims and the structure of the MDWC were very close to those of the AWB[2] and reflected a form of voluntary philanthropic support for Aboriginal equality. The MDWC was formed in 1957, but it was not until 1959 that it was moved 'that an Aboriginal member or two be on the committee'. Similarly, although Aborigines were elected by the predominantly European membership, it was not until 1965 that they were office bearers and then only in nominal positions of vice-president or assistant-secretary. Throughout the life of the MDWC its aims and direction remained firmly in European hands.

The main concern of the MDWC was to break down discrimination at the local level. The opposition to its aims was widespread, vocal and

---

1. A voluntary community organisation for males aged between 22 and 40.
2. The following statement appeared in the AWB Report (1960: 8) 'It is gratifying to the Board that the several associations throughout the State, formed with the object of promoting the welfare of Aborigines and assisting in their assimilation, continued to function with vigour and in close collaboration with the Board. . . . At present there are ten such district organisations in existence, these being located at Armidale, Coffs Harbour, Condobolin, Coonamble, Kempsey, Maclean, Moree, Tamworth and Griffith.'

entrenched. There was especially strong local resistance to housing Aborigines in Kempsey and, whenever the MDWC tried to find houses for them in the town, it was met with opposition, usually from rate-payers' associations, which would lobby local council and state parliament, the AWB and the MDWC with petitions, letters and delegations of protest. The pressure applied was so great that not only was a selection panel appointed to choose the most suitable candidate for housing, but in 1958, the MDWC considered it necessary to invite two representatives from the South Kempsey Ratepayer's Association to be present at the selection.

In the MDWC's first years, pressures from the local European community were considerable and went way beyond organising local ratepayers' associations. In 1960, when a Christian youth group from Sydney built a house for a second family, the work site and construction were vandalised. The gains for Aborigines were insignificant, as only two screened and selected families were located in the town. Similarly, plans for rehousing Aborigines in the town in 1967 were circumvented because 'unfortunately none of the nine blocks located could be bought by the AWB' (MDWC Annual Report 1967). By contrast, the MDWC was successfully able to support the building of 14 houses outside the town, at Greenhill in 1967.

This attempt to perpetuate exclusionary practices demonstrates the unequal, but mutual, manner in which racism affects social relations. The opposition by Europeans is a manifestation of the tensions that arise when mutual dependency is threatened. Racial discrimination is not a one-way process that only imposes limitations and constraints on the dominated group; it is also a constitutive part of the dominant group's consciousness and identity. At the local level, the patterns of segmentation provided concrete forms of hegemonic unity in which the European community expressed its own sense of superiority. Aboriginal housing within the town threatened the categorisation of social space on which such hegemony was partially sustained. This is evident in that it was the ratepayers' associations that were at the forefront of the opposition, which was expressed in terms of an instrumental logic associated with a perceived decline in property values for individual home owners. The proposed re-categorisation of social space, not only violated the identity of the group, but also that of the individual, as this was bound up in objectifications of self in relation to property. Where no such re-categorisation of social space was required, as in Greenhill, no such opposition occurred.

The conflict between the NSW government and the local council flared up over the question of Aboriginal access to the local swimming pool. Ever since the swimming pool had been opened in 1949, a local council by-law had, on the grounds of hygiene, banned Aborigines from using it. The admission of Aboriginal children to state schools in

1952, however, produced a major anomaly in the functioning of the ban. The egalitarian ethos associated with state schooling ensured that Aboriginal children attended the pool on school excursions, but they were not entitled to access outside school hours. The MDWC was more successful in changing this, as its annual report (MDWC Minutes 1965) records:

> Last year we asked the municipal council to reconsider its ban preventing Aboriginal children from using the Baths. Council refused to alter its policy. We asked, 'What are the grounds for refusal, if they are medical, what is the source of council information?' As a result of this letter council asked Government medical officers to make a report. It is common knowledge now that as a result of the medical officer's report, council lifted the ban on the Baths. We are pleased that we have a council which is broad minded enough to face facts and not simply resist change.

In effect, the MDWC turned the council's own practices of legitimation against them. In any case, such discriminatory practices were becoming increasingly difficult to sustain in areas in which discriminatory legislation was being systematically revoked, for example separate schooling (1952), social security restrictions on unemployment benefits, maternity allowances, family allowances and sickness benefits (1957), government pensions (1959) and the repeal of special legal provisions relating to vagrancy, consorting and the ban on drinking alcohol (1963). Discriminatory by-laws affecting Aboriginal populations in particular local areas became increasingly anomalous in this changing social and legal environment.[3]

This increasing divergence accentuated the different political objectives that exclusionary practices held for the local and the state administrations (see Chapter 3). For the former, segregation was an end in itself; for the latter, it was a route to assimilation. The local response by Europeans may be characterised as one of political accommodation to, rather than social acceptance of, Aboriginal equality. This was evident in the attempt by Aboriginal women in Burnt Bridge and Greenhill to join the local CWA. Some CWA women also belonged to the MDWC, yet acceptance of Aboriginal equality by some members was not enough to ensure Aboriginal participation in the association. The women of Burnt Bridge and Greenhill had to form their own branches,

---

3. This was a period in which political action by Aborigines and Aboriginal groups returned to the public political platform. The Aborigines Progress Association re-formed in 1963 over the question of the AWB's wholesale selling off of reserve/station lands (Rowley 1973: 83). Similarly, in the spirit of the civil rights marches in the southern states of the USA, Aborigines and university students organised a 'freedom ride' and travelled throughout the rural areas of NSW to fight the discriminatory practices which still continued in the country towns. The confrontations between local Europeans and the 'freedom riders' received widespread media coverage (see Perkins 1975, Chapter 8).

but their affiliation to the CWA was in name only, since the facilities provided by the Kempsey CWA for mothers and babies in the town area were only available to European women. An Aboriginal member of the MDWC (Minutes 1961) spoke of how, 'It was felt by Aboriginal mothers that it would not be diplomatic to use these, as at the time of forming the Burnt Bridge/Greenhill CWA, some feeling had been expressed by members of the Kempsey Branch on this matter. Mr. C. and Mr. W. will investigate the possibilities of mothers being able to use the Red Cross rooms.' At the level of interpersonal relations, notions of purity and pollution continued to maintain the physical separation and exclusion of Aborigines.

The MDWC's struggle for equal rights made only a limited impact on the racial attitudes of the local European community. Its assault on entrenched exclusionary practices rendered a number of taken-for-granted racist practices conspicuous and problematical. The MDWC effectively challenged the hegemonic unity which had sustained practices within the region, but the Aborigines were still treated as a distinctive sub-group.

The MDWC also acted as a vehicle for protest after a small Aboriginal child, who had been rushed from Kempsey hospital to Sydney, had subsequently died. The routine dismissal of the death as a case of malnutrition, which located the 'problem' in the Aboriginal community rather than with the medical authorities, sparked off a major protest. With the MDWC as an outlet, Aborigines were able to use the incident to criticise the differential treatment they routinely received at the local hospital. A number of allegations emerged at meetings held between the MDWC and local Aborigines from Greenhill, Bellbrook and Burnt Bridge. As the first meeting (MDWC Minutes, Sept. 1964) reported:

> A discussion was held on the deaths of pre-school Aboriginal children. There seems to be no information about reasons for deaths. An example was given of one child who was quite well in hospital and apparently for no reason got gradually worse and was rushed to Sydney and died. *Most of these children seem to have been in hospital for weeks before their deaths and yet most reasons for death are given as worms and malnutrition.*

After this beginning, the criticisms became more general, and a number of questions were raised about Aborigines having received unsatisfactory and pointedly different treatment from that given to other patients. A letter was sent to the Hospital Board:

> Asking it whether it is true *that medical files on Aborigines, on their being discharged, are most infrequently again consulted, even on readmission within a short time,* as we heard. What is standing procedure? If they are not being consulted, could a system be introduced to prevent such valuable information not being used? Several cases were quoted of children being discharged before

they were properly recovered, and quickly going back in. Mr. S. and Mr. H.
moved in the letter to the Hospital Board, that a request be made that in future
no discharges of Aborigines, adults or children, be made, unless a doctor's
certificate is issued. No verbal discharges . . . Mr. S. and Mr. C. stated that
the following should be added: We are not satisfied with reasons given for the
deaths. There is insufficient details, a disparity between Hansard's report and
evidence parents of the children have given. We are not satisfied that parental
neglect is the cause as has been said. An inquiry should be carried out at the
highest medical level. (MDWC Minutes, Oct. 1964)

The allegations asserted that the individualising strategies common to
medical interventions, i.e. the gathering of specific biographical information from the patient, had been routinely laid aside and replaced
with differential treatment which reduced Aboriginal patients to
anonymous racial typifications.

The most important feature about the Kempsey equal rights' movement was that it was based on challenging a number of social practices
within the local community by which Aborigines were being accorded
inferior status. Its struggle for equality, by definition, aimed to place
Aborigines on an equal footing with Europeans. It was a political
struggle in which Aborigines joined progressive Europeans to demand
an egalitarian opening up of the dominant society to incorporate those
Aborigines who could assimilate the norms and values of the dominant
society. The conflict between Aborigines and Europeans took place on
the dominant society's terrain and within the framework of a liberal
critique of inequality. The MDWC's policies and aims reflected at the
local community level what had emerged as a predominantly urban-
based critique of policies of discrimination and segregation. The
MDWC's strategies effectively broke up or rendered problematic the
hegemonic unity of a racial discourse which had constituted and
systematically ordered a range of practices within the local community.

At the same time, the struggle for egalitarian access to the wider
society corresponded to the state's programme of cultural homogenisation via assimilation. Overt expressions of Aboriginal distinctiveness
in relation to political equality were excluded from the public political
arena, for, as we have seen, they had become a social liability in the
assimilation process. The movement towards equal rights was
grounded in an opposition to the inferior status accorded Aborigines as
part of their exclusion from the wider society. It reproduced an inverted
form of racism which considered Aborigines in terms of their similarities to the wider society rather than the particularities of Aboriginal
existence or their cultural imperatives. What emerged out of these
struggles was a new form of hegemonic domination which endorsed
the breakup of communities and their incorporation, as individual
families, into the dominant society.

Gramsci's (1982: 57–8, 161, 275) concept of hegemony, developed to account for the active role of ideology and politics in the class struggle, is important in understanding the process of Aboriginal incorporation. At one level it is associated with the systematisation and elaboration of concepts of Aboriginality as the means by which the dominant society has attempted to impose its own ideology and to construct the world in its own image. Such dominance, however, implies the ability of a class or group to determine the context, or establish the parameters, of ideological and political struggle. The *relative* stability of hegemonic dominance lies not simply in its *pre-givenness* but rather the ability to control the framework within which antagonistic relations can be negotiated. The politics of opposition to local racist practices, to a large extent, reflected the breakdown of the hegemonic unity which had established the parameters of the racial discourse. However, the struggle for equal rights reflected the extension of new forms of domination. The rationality of these new structures was expressed in terms of Aboriginal assimilation.

7.2. The Deterritorialisation and Scientisation of State Control

The reformulation of bureaucratic forms of intervention regulating the lives of Aborigines within the state occurred through the establishment by the NSW government of a Joint Parliamentary Committee on Aboriginal Welfare (1967) to review such policies. The recommendations of this committee signalled a new deployment of state power with regard to Aborigines. The Joint Parliamentary Report (1967:17) formally proposed an end to policies of segregation in Aboriginal administration, recommending that (a) 'the Aborigines Welfare Board (AWB) be abolished'; and (b) 'a Director of Aboriginal Affairs, responsible to the Minister of Child Welfare and Social Welfare, be appointed'. The director was to be responsible for all aspects of welfare and was to liaise with the specialised departments (Child and Social Welfare, the Housing Commission, Education and Health) which had taken over these general responsibilities from the former AWB. In addition to this, an Aboriginal Advisory Council made up of six Aborigines, elected by Aborigines, was set up (ibid.).

The abolition of confinement on supervised settlements brought an end to segregation and, as I have shown, was part of the emergent broader critique of discrimination and segregation. The earlier findings of the Joint Parliamentary Committee (1937) and the later PSB report (Parliament of NSW 1940: 17) had found that 'no better policy' existed for Aborigines than their 'aggregation on stations, under close supervision' (see Chapter 6). By contrast, the 1967 report (p. 19) concluded:

The Committee believes that the congregation of Aboriginals on reserves is one of the main factors retarding them from becoming full members of the community. When any group of people live in isolation they tend to fix their own standards which very often are quite different from the rest of the community. This is particularly so in the case of Aborigines.

In effect, the findings of the committee were a critique of past processes of normalisation rather than of the policy of assimilation *per se*.

The decline of supervised stations was seen not as a vindication of their success in assimilating the state's Aborigines, but as a failure to achieve those aims, i.e. to retrain Aborigines for their assimilation into the wider society. The new policies were aimed at increasing the efficiency of state policy by removing the impediments to assimilation which had been generated by institutionalisation. The major criticisms of previous policy were in two areas. One of the main rejections was the policy of segregation. The major criticism of the total institution, in this regard, was that in practice it *reinforced* rather than *broke up* the Aborigines' sense of collective identity. The committee was satisfied that institutionalisation had been successful in eradicating most of the influence of 'Aboriginal culture' on the 'inhabitants of reserves' (ibid). However, as we have seen above, it concluded that the social conditions produced on reserves were responsible for the perpetuation of differences between Aborigines and the wider population. This was due to 'the fact that people on reserves live in virtual isolation from the rest of the community' (ibid.). It was the congregation of Aborigines into segregated communities that provided the major impediment to their assimilation.

The other related criticism of segregation was that the social environment of the total institution tended to undermine Aboriginal 'progress'. In effect, the same concern with the social environment of Aborigines that had been used to remove them from 'fringe camps' and unsupervised reserves to institutionalised 'stations' was now applied to the institutions themselves. This was specifically expressed in concern about the inadequate standards of Aboriginal education. The Joint Parliamentary Committee (NSW Parliament 1967: 8) reaffirmed the argument presented previously by the PSB report (1940) that education was the foundation on which Aborigines would 'achieve social and economic equality with the rest of the community'. The committee found, however, that 'Aboriginal children generally had a poor vocabulary and were slow readers' (ibid.). It was thought that the main reason for their poor progress was 'that many Aboriginal children came from sub-standard, overcrowded homes, lacking a cultural environment' (ibid.).

The same stress on environmental factors that had underpinned earlier bureaucratic interventions was reiterated. Paradoxically, it was this materialist approach that had ideologically supported the institutionalisation of Aborigines. This was because institutionalisation rested on the assumption that Aborigines as a race were redeemable because the responsibility for their 'backwardness' lay in their social and cultural environment. In the 1930s the total control of that environment through manager-supervised institutions was recommended so that Aborigines could be retrained and inculcated with the superior values of the dominant society. In the 1967 recommendations, however, it was the total institution that was seen as the major source of environmental deprivation. Segregation had been proven 'insufficiently corrective' and provided the basis for one of the main criticisms of earlier policy.

Another major criticism took the form of an internal critique of institutional procedures, in which it was asserted that the rudimentary nature of these procedures and inadequate staffing had contributed to the failure of these institutions to retrain Aborigines. The bureaucratic rationality that sustained these criticisms of the AWB differed from that levelled against the earlier Aborigines Protection Board (APB) in the 1930's, where the major concern had been over the use of arbitrary, personal power by the managers (see Chapter 5). The aims set out in the PSB report (1940) were to 'democratise' such absolute power through a process of bureaucratic rationalisation. This was an attempt to implement a policy of uniform control based on what Weber (1947: 125) calls 'legal authority', i.e. authority legitimated in a body of normative rules which establish obedience to an impersonal order rather than to an individual. Authority is embedded in a hierarchy rather than associated with individuals and, as he puts it, 'each lower office is under the control and supervision of a higher one' (ibid.).[4] In other words, the aims of the PSB report (1940) were to bureaucratise the chain of command to make it accountable to higher authority and to create uniformity and consistency in Aboriginal administration.

The decline of the total institution as the primary instrument of such administration was an extension of this bureaucratic model. Whereas the PSB report (1940) expressed the need for a uniform chain of command, the Joint Parliamentary Committee (1967) stressed the need

---

4. O'Neil (1986: 45) argues that there is some complementarity between the approaches of Weber on bureaucracy and Foucault on the definitive features of the disciplinary society. 'Weber's discussion of bureaucracy is largely framed in terms of the legal and rational accounting requirements of political and economic organisation which in turn give legal domination its administrative rationality and adequacy. The formal–analytic features of the Weberian concept of bureaucracy are to be found as constitutive practices of the army, church, university, hospital and political party – not to mention the very organisation of the relevant discovering sciences. Although Foucault . . . does not study the bureaucratic process in the Weberian mode, his studies of the hospital and school go beyond Weber in grounding the legal-rational accounting process in techniques for the administration of corporeal, attitudinal and behavioural discipline. Foucault thereby complements Weber's formal–rational concept of bureaucracy and legal domination with a *physiology of bureaucracy and power* which is the definitive feature of the disciplinary society.' (Original emphasis.)

for the kind of efficiency and consistency found in the specialisation of the tasks or functions of administration. It was the general nature of the total institution that was being criticised in that it reproduced, within one apparatus, those functions usually performed by a number of different specialist institutions, for example policing, education and housing.

The total institution, in this case, was found wanting because it lacked a specific domain of competence. Similarly, its staff was found to be performing a number of overlapping functions which should have been performed as part of a specialised division of labour. In this respect, senior AWB officials situated 'in their own departments could not devote sufficient time to Board matters' (ibid. p. 16). The inadequacy of the specialised training of staff and station managers presented the major problem. According to the report (1968: 16), the qualifications and training of the staff of the AWB 'left much to be desired'. In reply, the AWB acknowledged 'considerable difficulty' in finding 'suitably qualified' staff (ibid.).[5] It had secured only 'one officer with an arts degree who had majored in psychology and sociology', which had raised the total number of fully-qualified staff members to three (ibid.). These staff recommendations reflected a general movement towards rational specialisation. In short, specialised functions required specialised credentials which were assessed in terms of educational criteria. What emerges is a scientific ideology to legitimate the bureaucratic management of Aborigines.

The stress on professional, formal qualifications not only undermined previously valued personal knowledge or experience of Aborigines, but also reflected the general shift away from treating them as a specific group within the general community. The logic associated with the *formal egalitarianism* of equal rights asserted the entitlement of all citizens to such rights. The removal of particularistic discriminatory legislation was accompanied by the removal of all particularistic practices associated with Aborigines as a distinctive group. In staff recruitment, the use of universal criteria, for example rational, impersonal forms of knowledge, was premised on the same logic of providing expertise and a service which could deal with and be available to all members of society regardless of status or history.

The institutionalisation of Aborigines did not fulfil the criteria for this new emphasis on formal egalitarianism. The non-specialisation of functions and the lack of formal qualifications was due to the *qualitative*

5. In 1966, the AWB was reorganised into ten welfare areas, each with its own Area Welfare Officer (AWO). The minimum qualification for AWOs was 'a diploma of social sciences or equivalent qualification' (AWB Report 1966: 4). This reorganisation indicated a general shift towards more qualified staff during the period of AWB control. The stress on formal qualifications reflected the movement away from an emphasis on personal knowledge or experience with Aborigines (or, less specifically, 'natives' in other colonies) which had been an earlier practice (see Beckett 1958).

and *particularistic* concerns of institutionalisation, i.e. the administration of Aborigines as a distinctive group. The submission of the Department of Child and Social Welfare reflected this criticism of earlier policies. As the deputy director (1967:14) stated:

> . . . his department could claim to have had, over the years, considerable experience with persons of Aboriginal extraction. *This experience has been gained in providing comprehensive child and social welfare services to all people of the State rather than from special concentration upon Aborigines and differentiating this group of people from other citizens of the State.* . . . It was further stated that it would be reasonable to suggest a similar policy should be adopted in the case of services for Aborigines and that Departments such as Education, Child Welfare and Social Welfare, Health, Housing and Police, each of which has dealings with Aborigines, should diversify their activities and provide, over and above a general service to the community, any special services required. *People of Aboriginal descent form part of this State's population and their problems differ only in degree from those of other sections of the community.*

Accordingly, following the report's findings, policies were no longer formulated with regard to the *qualitative* needs of Aborigines through *particularistic* policies and practices but were to be brought into line with policies *universally* applied to meet the *quantitative* needs of all welfare recipients throughout the state.

The critique of the total institution formed the basis for the redeployment of state intervention through the deterritorialisation of power from one centralised site to a number of specialised sites of control. The abolition of the AWB did not bring about the suspension of state control of Aborigines but dispersed such power from one site, the total institution, to a multiplicity of sites, specialised social welfare agencies. In effect, the 'special needs' of Aborigines were to be treated as differences of *degree* rather than differences in *kind* from other members of the wider society. Such policy changes were a continuation of the process of cultural homogenisation. Aborigines in the state were given the same rights and access to the agencies of the state's bureaucracy as other members of society. The rights were demanded for Aborigines in terms of formal egalitarianism as the abstract and ahistorical 'rights of man' not as the rights of Aborigines as products of a specific and concrete history.

7.3. Formal Egalitarianism as Assimilation

The most significant consequence of the shift in government policy was the major and rapid change in the residential patterns of Aborigines throughout the state. On the whole this was in keeping with the criticisms levelled at the total institution and segregation. The committee report (1967: 14) recommended that 'in due course all Aboriginal reserves should disappear'. Furthermore, it recommended and implemented a policy that 'no further housing should be constructed on reserves now set apart for Aborigines except on town blocks' (ibid.) and that 'future housing should be at least of Housing Commission standard and should be scattered throughout the town and not concentrated in any one street or area' (p. 12).[6] What occurs here is a process of atomisation, or the breaking up of those collective residential sites within which Aborigines reproduced a collective community identity. In consequence, by 1980 some 90.6 per cent of Aborigines in NSW were living in urban areas (Parliamentary Report 1980: 130). The state effectively retained nominal control over residence patterns, in this case by determining where they could not rather than where they should live.

The initial implementation of such policy had varying consequences for the Aboriginal communities in the Macleay Valley. Whereas the 'fringe camp' at Greenhill had been a central point of opposition to government control, it was now officially sanctioned. The building of 22 new three-bedroom houses in 1965/6 transformed the 'fringe camp' into 'town blocks'. Similarly, Bellbrook reserve had been entirely rebuilt with 15 'modern type' houses erected in 1963/4 (AWB report 1964: 4). These houses had three bedrooms, a combined kitchen/dining-room and a bathroom/laundry. Both these developments had occurred as a continuing part of AWB policy prior to the 1967 report, so the initial consequences of the abolition of the AWB had little effect on either of these communities. For Bellbrook residents it largely meant the end of European managers. In the long term, however, it has meant that overcrowding has continued and that Aborigines have had to find accommodation elsewhere. This is indicated by the fairly constant population figures in both communities between 1967 and 1978 (see Table 7).

For the Aboriginal residents of Burnt Bridge, however, the abolition of the AWB meant the closing of the station, which had immediate consequences. At this time, Burnt Bridge had 33 dwellings, two communal blocks, a communal laundry block and a public hall (AWB report 1967: 388). The AWB classified this type of housing as 'pre-war'. As evidence before the Joint Parliamentary Committee stated, 'most dwellings on the station were sub-standard, from the construction, provision of facilities and the number of occupants to each' (ibid.). (See Chapter 4 for details of construction and nature of housing.) Members of the MDWC were more forthright when they described the conditions on Burnt Bridge as 'shocking' and added that 'Kempsey is getting a bad name as a result of press publicity' (MDWC Annual Report 1967/8).

6. As Docker (1964) shows, there was a major change in press reports on AWB housing policies from the 1950s to early 1960s which moved from approval to significant criticism. By the mid-1960s housing of Aborigines on stations was not presented in the press as a positive policy.

Table 7. Aboriginal Population

Year	Greenhill (1960–68)	Burnt Bridge (1960–68)
1960/1	n.a.	262
1961/2	n.a.	274
1962/3	63	270
1963/4	46	239
1964/5	200	162
1965/6	202	155
1966/7	234	226
1967/8	215	192

Sources: AWB reports 1962: 15; 1964: 13; 1966: 12; 1968: 21

As early as 1959, a survey of the health conditions on the reserves in the Macleay Valley had found that improved 'sanitation, water, better housing were essential for the Aborigines if we wanted to improve his hygiene and health conditions' (MDWC Minutes, July 1959). The beneficiaries of these reports would appear to have been the communities of Bellbrook and Greenhill as both communities were completely rehoused. In relation to Burnt Bridge, however, between 1964 and 1967 the MDWC continually exchanged correspondence with the AWB over the issue of rehousing the population. Consistent with the MDWC's policy of assimilation, committee members recommended that residence be found within the town (MDWC Annual Report 1967/8).

In July 1969 the station at Burnt Bridge was officially closed. It was expected that the residents would gradually find accommodation elsewhere. Statistical information provides some evidence of how the changes in policy affected the pre-existing patterns of Aboriginal housing. It would appear that the establishment of Greenhill as a 'town settlement' enabled some of the residents to move from Burnt Bridge station in the mid-1960s (see Table 7). The evidence indicates that a significant decline occurred in the Burnt Bridge station population which coincided with a subsequent increase in the population at Greenhill.

The major change in residential patterns of Aborigines on Burnt Bridge occurred after the closure of the reserve. According to research carried out by Kitaoji (1976: II–52) in 1971, of the original 33 dwellings on Burnt Bridge only 'seven dwellings and 52 persons' remained. By that year, Kitaoji reports that the majority of Aborigines lived in the municipality of Kempsey (see Table 8). In other words, within three years only 52 Aborigines remained on Burnt Bridge. By 1979, the figure had marginally increased to 74 persons (*Aboriginal Quarterly* 1979: 43). Similarly, the population at Greenhill marginally increased to 251, and the Bellbrook population remained fairly constant at 139 (ibid.) (see Table 8). The major growth in Aboriginal housing occurred in the

Table 8. Aboriginal Housing: Kempsey Shire[7]

District	No. of Houses 1971	1979	Population 1971	1979
Kempsey South	19	49	118	n.a.
Kempsey West	21	47	138	n.a.
Greenhill	27	27	211	251
Burnt Bridge	7	8	52	74
Bellbrook	15	15	113	139
South West Rocks	–	5	–	49

Sources: (i) *Aboriginal Quarterly* 1979
(ii) Ngaku Housing Cooperative
(iii) Kitaoji 1976

municipality of Kempsey where the number of houses increased from 40 in 1971 to 96 in 1980 (see Table 8).

The relationship of formal egalitarianism (and the policy framed by both the local and state government) sought to 'scatter' Aboriginal housing 'throughout the town' as part of a programme to disperse the community within the wider society. This programme was taken up by the NSW Housing Commission (HC), which took over the major responsibility for Aboriginal housing from the AWB in 1968. The two main programmes available to Aborigines, HC rental and Homes for Aborigines (HFA), automatically adopted a policy of dispersal by dealing with Aborigines only as individual families. The records from the HFA programme (1984 figures) clearly show the scattering of Aboriginal housing in Kempsey (see Table 9). The pattern of dispersal of the 43 residents reveals that policies seen to be best suited for the assimilation of Aborigines in 1967 continued to be adhered to throughout this period.

At least in the short term, this policy of dispersal has not broken inter-family ties. Aborigines in the Macleay Valley have generally become more mobile through the use of cars and tend to visit relatives and friends frequently. In addition, for economic reasons government-assisted housing tends to be concentrated in particular areas (see Map 7), which ensures that the distances between family and friends are relatively short. Furthermore, recreational activities, such as football, netball, bingo and drinking, provide recognised meeting places for Aboriginal interaction. The increased use of organised sites for recreation reflects a shift away from a situation in which informal and personal interactions govern collective expressions of identity towards

7. For the sake of clarity I have combined Kitaoji's figures for South Kempsey and East Kempsey (17 dwellings/123 people and 2 dwellings/5 people respectively) under the heading South Kempsey; and West Kempsey and Central Kempsey (17 dwellings/128 people and 4 dwellings/10 people) under the heading West Kempsey (Kitaoji 1976: 2/18; see also Map 7).

Table 9. Kempsey Municipality: Distribution of HFA Houses (1984)

Street	No. of Houses	Street	No. of Houses
Alb. st.	3	K.M. st.	2
Blo. st.	1	Lei. st.	1
Coc. st.	2	Lor. st.	2
Cre. st.	1	Mid. st.	3
Dan. st.	1	M.B. st.	2
E.K. st.	2	Nic. st.	1
Elr. st.	1	R.E. st.	2
F.S. st.	1	R.T. st.	3
G.H. st.	2	Toz. st.	1
G.N. st.	5	Wes. st.	6
J.C. st.	1		

Source: Housing Commission figures, June 1984

one in which particular formal sites are set aside for specific activities. This shift conforms to the pattern in the dominant society where the provision of sanctioned sites for *public* recreation make it easier to order and control collective activities.

Consistent with such patterns of formal social interactions is a cultural ordering of social space between public and private, which exists within the dominant society. In part, the structuring of leisure activities reflects the control and direction of social space, which is a central aspect of the process of cultural homogenisation. This is more evident in the social ecology of suburban housing, which *reinforces* the autonomy of nuclear families, than in the maintenance of transfamilial ties, and it relocates community interactions into a separate and distinctive realm. In this realm, the social ecology of the *collective life* of the 'total institution' varied significantly from that of the *individuated* patterning of suburban housing. There are significant shifts in the borderlines of private/public life which carry with them cultural significations in terms of the organisation of social space, which are, in turn, premised on different modes of social control. This shift can be highlighted by looking at the social organisation of the Dhan-gadi as it took shape within the 'total institution' in the period between 1937 and 1968.

The main criticism of institutionalisation was that it sustained rather than removed a sense of collective identity amongst Aborigines. For Aborigines this was constituted externally, as I discussed in the previous chapter, in the experience of segregation and in their opposition to institutional and wider forms of social oppression. At the same time, however, such discriminatory practices had pressed the Aborigines of the Macleay Valley into two small stations and a major fringe camp which produced an intensification of relations between community members. This had much to do with the establishment of *discrete* and

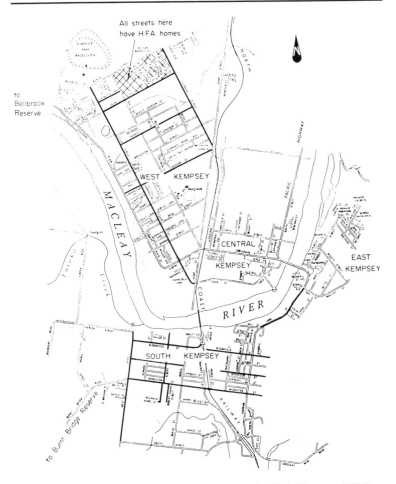

Map 7. Municipality of Kempsey: Streets with HFA Houses (1984)

immobilised communities in which the complex and specific rules associated with kinship were overlayed by more diffuse and generalised rules
of social interaction. As one man put it on moving to a fringe camp,
initially 'you were glad to get away from 'em, go and work somewhere
until you got used to 'em'. Getting 'used to 'em' involved establishing
personalised relations, an extension of the same forms of reciprocal
relations that underpinned kinship ties. Institutionalisation, paradoxically, sustained these close textures of social relations within these
communities.

The physical setting of the 'total institution' then, had provided the site for the reproduction of collective sentiments and solidarities. The social boundaries created by social segregation, the physical environment created by close-packed housing and the relative homogeneity of community members (Kempsey and Urunga) shaped and sustained transfamilial forms of solidarity and mutual interdependence in economic and social spheres. In the formal sphere, community members fostered a sense of local loyalty through organising their own dances, balls, annual baby shows, marching girl teams and football matches. Many of these activities served not only to entertain but to raise money for community needs, such as school clothing for the children. At a more informal level, institutional life created only narrow distinctions between the private and public domains of social life. Under the manager's regime, there had been an attempt to privatise cooking and eating habits by relocating such activities within houses and away from the camp fire. In effect, this was an attempt to expand the private domain. Nevertheless, despite the presence of stoves in homes on Burnt Bridge in 1965, 'a good deal of cooking was done at outside fire places' (Long 1970: 47). To eradicate the more pervasive, less conspicuous, taken-for-granted aspects of social interactions within the confines of the 'total institution' was an even more difficult task for the managers.

I am referring here to the use of public and private space within the setting of a homogeneous domain. This homogeneity was based on the stability of the station's population and the degree of familiarity and regularity that this brought to everyday interactions. In addition, most social interactions occurred in the station's communal areas. Both formal and informal activities and collective and individual interactions were conducted within a homogenous public domain, rather than as specialised activities in spatially and functionally discrete domains. Within the same space children played, men or boys organised 'scratch' teams for rugby league or cricket matches, or people merely congregated to talk. At night, the sites of social interaction were people's verandahs, where fires (in four-gallon kerosene tins punctured with holes and elevated on bricks) provided the focal points for informal gatherings. The enclosed private domains of family homes were not the principal sites of social interaction. The *private* area was highly restricted, in part because people did not stay alone in their restricted area for any length of time and in part because of a cultural emphasis on gregariousness. In effect, despite the intrusions of the manager and matron, public space remained the primary site of social interaction. This pattern of social interaction was no doubt reinforced by the rudimentary nature of the two-room cottages, which had no inside water, electricity or toilets.

It is, I would argue, through this use and categorisation of public/private space that life in the 'total institution' differed significantly from the wider society and provided the basis for distinctive patterns of social interaction. In other words, the social identities of community members were largely moulded and given form by the interactions that took place in public space. Public space remained largely predictable in terms of who was using it and what was occurring. The constancy and regularity of such interactions within the public domain reaffirmed the reality of *distinctive* community relations.

Furthermore, the homogeneity of the public domain generated and guaranteed its own communal forms of social control. It provided a 'natural' setting for observation, speculation, evaluation of, or intervention in (for the purposes of censure or support) a wide range of social activities. Underpinning this was the limited use of private space (the privatised domain of the family unit) and the extensive use of public space as the principal domain of social interaction. This division between public and private facilitated communal surveillance as the main medium of social control. *Being seen* provided the constant factor in regulating social life. It is this specific division which is associated with the use of *shaming* as a regulatory practice based on external communal authority. As I suggest in Chapter 6, shame regulation is associated with *acting* differently (or *being* different) and with the transgression of *public* codes, rules or rituals of conduct. The essentially closed community of the total institution did much to perpetuate such forms of social control through communal surveillance.

Institutionalisation as a means of retraining Aborigines for life within the wider society had therefore contained a major paradox. Attempts to reconstruct the private sphere of family life through segregation, monitoring and surveillance had also preserved transfamilial ties and community solidarities. In this respect, the Joint Parliamentary Committee (1967), discussed earlier, was partially correct in identifying 'the congregation of Aborigines on reserves' as the main factor 'retarding' (as it put it) assimilation. This was not because any group of people who are segregated 'fix their own standards quite different from the rest of the community' but because in this case institutionalisation allowed them to preserve forms of social interaction and social control that pre-dated the total institution (see Chapter 4). It is necessary to distinguish between the different kinds of monitoring and surveillance to understand their differences and similarities. The communal control was exercised in a diffuse way as a *democratic* form of surveillance and intervention from *within* the community. The surveillance and intervention by state functionaries, by contrast, was institutionalised in a *specialised* and *hierarchical* form imposed from *above* or *outside* the community. For example, the role of the manager/matron tended towards the *abolition* of private space, insofar as social and personal relations were always open to the scrutiny of those in authority, but the limited scope of private life amongst the Dhan-gadi also ensured a certain regularity of conduct.

The point I want to stress is that Aboriginal collective identity in the 1937–1968 period was constituted in part through continuing the distinctive cultural practices that pre-dated the total institution and in part through resisting the segregating policies associated with institutionalisation. This degree of continuity was made possible because of the aberrant use of the total institution as a means of retraining a specific group of people. Institutionalisation, as an instrument of government intervention, sought to change *isolated families* rather than *isolated individuals*. This is demonstrated by the 'diminished responsibility' of the institutionalised inmate not being associated with the individual, but collectively ascribed to the race. Yet, the general rationale behind the confinement of people in asylums, hospitals or prisons, and the regimes of control and reform applied in such institutions, are all geared towards the treatment of people as individuals in what Goffman (1961) calls, the 'three spheres of life', sleep, work and play. As Goffman points out, however, this is contingent on *separating* individuals from 'family life' and subjecting them to the 'solitary life' of institutions. But, as we have seen, this separation of individuals was never comprehensively applied. As a result, institutionalisation effectively provided the Dhan-gadi with a continuity of social experience which was separate from that of the wider society and was reinforced by their isolation as a bounded territorial unit.

Changes instituted in 1967 meant that when the Aborigines from Burnt Bridge were rehoused in municipal Kempsey, they moved into a social environment radically different from that of the reserve. For a start, the suburban housing was designed for very different configurations of public/private space. It was built to provide privatised, individuated space for the autonomous nuclear family, with public space sharply demarcated from private space. The intimate domain of the family took on a wider yet more isolated role in the reproduction of social life, while the function of public space diminished as it gave way to public thoroughfares for traffic and selected park areas beyond the immediate gaze of most inhabitants. The continuity of public/private space, along with a specific form of social control, had been broken and family autonomy reinforced. The public domain had become uncontrolled and heterogenous – the domain of the stranger. On Burnt Bridge station, as the *Hastings Shire Gazette* described it, 'there had been no attempt to subdivide the area into streets and allotments as in an ordinary village or town' (cited Kitaoji 1976: II–30). In Kempsey, by contrast, the house and yard provided an enclosed and isolated domain in which surveillance was limited to selected visitors within the private domain. Public/private space was no longer an integrated totality, but consisted of separate, unconnected spheres.

The formal egalitarianism of government policies in the post-AWB period was more effective than earlier policy in establishing housing conditions that were conducive to assimilating Aborigines in the dominant society's patterns of consumption. By guaranteeing the right to a certain minimum standard of living, formal egalitarianism ensures that the norms that are assumed are those of the dominant society and that the objectifications of Aborigines implicit in such bureaucratic interventions are in terms of deviations from such norms. The attempt to improve the material and social conditions of Aborigines' sub-standard housing and overcrowded conditions is also a process of cultural homogenisation. It is not that conditions have not needed improving but rather that the state has exercised unilateral control over the general thrust (and the specific details) of the improvements that have been sought. The Aborigines have had no input of any significance in these matters. The exercise of power has been in making them conform to a number of culturally-specific assumptions about the nature of familial ties, social relations and interaction.

Central to bureaucratic intervention in Aboriginal housing is a culturally-specific view of familial relations as constituted in the self-enclosed, autonomous nuclear family. In the first place, elegibility for a house is determined on the basis of a single family. Universalistic criteria are uniformly applied in the selection of all applicants on the grounds of families in need. Recipients must show that they 'have a housing need; be otherwise unable to gain accommodation and . . . that he/she can be a responsible tenant (pay rent, care for house)' (*Aboriginal Quarterly* 1981: 34). On the basis of demonstrable need, all applicants are treated equally with uniformity and consistency as the main component of policy. Similarly, the same conditions of responsibility apply universally to all welfare recipients. The Housing Commission became the authority that determined the rules of normality. In terms of residence, the nuclear family provides the benchmark of normality and the means for regulating the composition of familial and transfamilial use of private (domestic) space. As the Housing Commission stated (*Aboriginal Quarterly* 1981: 36) with regard to Aboriginal tenants:[8]

> Family size does not matter, but the commission discourages permanent overcrowding because it is unhealthy and causes undue damage to the house. A tenant can apply for a larger house in the case of a permanent increase in the size of a family. Families can still accommodate extra residents for limited periods such as school holidays, family crises, or other temporary circumstances.

8. The information was provided specifically for Aborigines in *Aboriginal Quarterly* 1981, vol. 3, no. 4. The article, 'NSW Housing Commission – Questions and Answers', sought to clarify any 'misconceptions about the policies . . . as they affect Aborigines' and 'to set the record straight' (p. 33).

The only legitimate permanent residents are members of the immediate nuclear family. In this way, the Housing Commission assumes a regulatory role over tenants and effectively controls and regulates transfamilial associations within the domestic sphere.

In this activity, the role of the Housing Commission is similar to that of other welfare agencies that intervene to ameliorate social hardship. Donzelot (1979), however, states that such intervention is the articulation of the *normalising discipline* of the carceral or total institution into the social domain of family life. Following Foucault, he argues that the power exercised through welfare agencies is not a negative form which seeks to exclude or repress but rather a more positive form which seeks through regulation to change and transform. It is through 'normalisation' that power is exercised. As can be seen from the above, what is sought is the self-regulation of an *autonomous nuclear family*. Any other *extra residents* are regarded, at best, as *temporary* and condoned only in extraordinary circumstances. Autonomy can be guaranteed only by conforming to these prescribed standards. The aim of such policies is twofold: (a) to regulate the spatial dispersement of Aboriginal families as individuated units and, (b) to regulate the internal functioning of Aboriginal families. This indirect form of policing underpins the change from regulation through institutionalisation to the more subtle forms associated with formal equality.

Donzelot (ibid. pp. 91–2) argues that such normative requirements are linked to the maintenance of certain economic/moral behaviours. 'Liberty' is secured only, 'on condition that you turn it to your advantage in order to better ensure your autonomy through the observance of norms that guarantee the social usefulness of the members of your family; or else, losing that autonomy, you will fall back into the register of tutelage'. The initial criteria for Housing Commission rental (that families have a housing need and be 'unable to gain accommodation') waives the rights of these individual families to regulate their social lives without hierarchical surveillance. As Donzelot (ibid. p. 92) puts it, 'the demand for assistance . . . [is] an indicator of immorality'. In this regard, however, they are not so much condemned as managed and regulated until they achieve the optimum functioning of family members, for example by not making any more demands for assistance.

Such normative requirements also involve particular economic/moral behaviour identified with the efficient utilisation of internal family resources. The collection of rent places a *regular* demand on family resources and indirectly provides an opportunity to monitor the 'progress' of Aboriginal families' economic/moral behaviour associated with the reproduction of autonomous family units. As the Housing Commission (*Aboriginal Quarterly* 1981: 36) states:

It is recognised that Aboriginal people sometimes have difficulty in budgeting, but there has only been one HFA eviction in the past two years. If a family misses one or two rental payments the Commission contacts them. It would not be helping the tenant to let the arrears mount up. Once the causes of a tenant's problems are known (unexpected bills or a funeral) extra help is often arranged from other sources, and a reasonable arrangement for payment of arrears negotiated. Only as a final resort is eviction action started.

The families are 'punished' by eviction for not fulfilling their financial obligations only as a 'final resort'. The exercise of power in this context is not repressive but rather 'positive' in as much as it seeks to manipulate and correct 'deviant behaviour' in terms of a particular social norm. Their failure to preserve family autonomy, either through inefficient use of their internal economic capacities or by failing to control or regulate their needs, i.e. 'budgeting' within the private sphere, will, however, lead to greater intervention and regulation by the state authorities.

This exercise of power is part of a process of cultural incorporation. Conformity to such economic/moral behaviour effectively cuts across kinship-related ties. Economic/moral relations amongst the Aborigines in the Macleay Valley stand in direct contrast to European norms (see section 7.4 below) in that they are grounded in transfamilial obligations to provide mutual aid and support. An explicit example of this can be seen with regard to funerals. The cost of a funeral in 1980/1 was $800 (for a local death) and $1,200 (if the body had to be brought from other parts of the state). With people living mainly on social security payments, this places severe economic hardship on the community. As payment is required in advance, many funerals are delayed until 'pension day' (each Wednesday fortnight) when money can be raised through kinship and friendship networks. Rather than a specific response to an economic crisis, the ability to mobilise kinship and community ties is based on a generally-accepted set of economic/moral behaviour patterns. Such social relations are organised and maintained extensively beyond the autonomous, individual family. As I indicate later, kinship and other close relationships are essentially defined by the amenability and responsiveness of people to needs in a number of social and economic contexts.

The exercise of pedagogic power forced Aboriginal families to conform to a number of culturally-specific assumptions about the nature of familial ties and wider patterns of sociality. It is by means of such 'normalisation' that, through its welfare departments, the state controls Aborigines in the contemporary period. The agents of the state become the regulators of family life and decide which behaviour is deviant and what constitutes the norm. Family autonomy can be retained by conforming to such socio-cultural norms.

7.4. The Quantification of Aboriginality

The shift to specialised bureaucratic management opened the way for many more quantitative studies (through survey sociology) on most aspects of Aboriginal life. Many of these were triggered off by the constitutional change in 1967, which included Aborigines in the Australian census. The subsequent period yielded numerous survey studies by government departments and academics on Aboriginal employment, income, crime, housing, health and education (see Rowley 1973; 1978; Lippmann 1973; 1981; Schapper 1970; Broom and Jones 1973; Long 1970; Henderson 1974; Kitaoji 1976; Altman and Nieuwenhuysen 1979; Treadgold 1980; Young 1982; Western 1983). My concern is not with the methodological aspects of survey sociology but with its ideological dimension. Such studies form part of the specialisation and scientisation of government policies, as they reproduce the forms of knowledge and discourse that provide the basis for government intervention. At the same time, they provide new objectifications of the Aborigine as an 'abstract, universal man' with his or her quantifiable needs.

This knowledge directly relates to government intervention and provides a discourse for assimilation. It identifies a number of interrelated variables which contribute to the overall situation of rural Aborigines – the cycle of poverty associated with poor education, poor health, lack of skills and training and discrimination conceived of in terms of prejudice. (The latter is discussed below.) In these studies employment is seen as the main welfare indicator in assessing the socio-economic position of Aborigines within the wider community. It is also, however, taken as an index of other variables, such as health standards and educational qualifications, which are seen to have economic consequences. This conclusion derives from the belief that in 'settled Australia' Aborigines 'participate in the market economy and compete with white labour' (Altman and Nieuwenhuysen 1979: 121). Their educational qualifications are believed to have given them the credentials with which to compete for positions on the job market and, with the acquisition of improved technical skills and education, they are expected to be able to climb up from the bottom rung of the employment and income ladder.

A comparison of the available survey data between 1965 and 1980 reveals a significant decline in Aboriginal employment (Young 1982: 23). Young's figures (p. 22) show that males earning a wage dropped from 56.5 per cent of the surveyed population in 1965 to 41 per cent in 1976, and to 28.7 per cent in 1980 (see also Altman and Nieuwenhuysen 1979: 10–16). More specifically, most of the studies point to the low occupational status and level of employment of Aborigines in the private sector, especially in agriculture. Drawing on Rowley (1973 and

1980), Young (1982: 18) points out that, whereas in 1965 some 80 per cent of the men were employed as unskilled agricultural workers, this had dropped to 4 per cent in 1980. Several writers suggest that this should be understood in the light of the Aborigines having historically occupied marginal and unskilled positions in the work-force (Altman and Nieuwenhuysen 1979: 127; Young 1982: 16). Under these circumstances, however, 'it becomes more essential for Aborigines to acquire skills which will allow them to compete in the shrinking job market' (Young 1982: 18).

The studies reveal major quantitative differences between Aborigines and Europeans, with Aborigines having abysmally low standards of health and education and very little employment. All the studies point to the need for continued state intervention *but do not consider the forms of intervention*. They are also all basically functionalist in approach, in that they see state intervention as a means of ameliorating personal hardship by guaranteeing a socially-defined minimum standard of living to all members of the state – i.e. formal egalitarianism is synonymous with the guarantee of a right of all to a minimum standard of living. This is not meant to suggest that such studies are uncritical, but that they overemphasise the content of policy, i.e. the quality of the state's services, and ignore the wider socio-political, ideological and economic spheres, of which welfare intervention is but a part. For example, Altman and Nieuwenhuysen (1979: 42) are critical of 'piecemeal policies'; Henderson (1974: 141–8), in a more comprehensive review, objects to the way in which policy is implemented and calls for more consultation with Aborigines so that it can be applied more effectively; and, in their sociological studies, Broom and Jones (1973) merely reproduce the standard internal bureaucratic critiques. For example, they argue (p. 73) that whereas:

> The development of coherent social policies involves descriptions, explanation, evaluation and utilisation . . . [there is] a need to clarify the true status of Aborigines because such information is a precondition to efficient progress towards betterment. It is also necessary to record in a systematic and orderly way the form, magnitude and trend of investment by state and commonwealth governments in Aboriginal betterment.

To sum up then, these critiques lead to internal bureaucratic reviews which assert the need for reform but also foster bureaucratic control and expansion. Survey sociology brings to the 'problem' of Aboriginal inequality the individualising logic of bureaucratic intervention which takes the form of voluntaristic solutions. The solution is sought in improved education or better job training to increase the *individual's* bargaining power in the job market through improved educational credentials and/or job skills. As Lippmann (1981: 148) states:

> The number of years of formal education does not necessarily equip with 'success' from an individual's standpoint, but lack of adequate schooling takes away the choice of life-style to which all Australians should be entitled. Knowledge is political and adds to the power and capacity of those who hold it: the insights which it brings can be translated, where desired, into action.

The transformative potential of knowledge is primarily perceived as an *individual acquisition*. The determination of such individualistic and voluntaristic solutions is not through the *content* of such 'knowledge and skills' but through the structures of pedagogic practices which impart knowledge as an individual rather than collective acquisition[9] (cf. Chapter 9). For it is the 'performance' of each *individual* which is evaluated and ranked according to his or her *individual* ability to conform to a set of normative standards. It is the individual's attainment of formal qualifications which is seen to benefit *individual* Aborigines in gaining employment. These studies ideologically maintain the hegemonic incorporation of Aborigines by defining and reproducing the parameters of ideological and political action established by the state in the contemporary period.

Most contemporary survey sociological research on 'non-traditional' Aborigines is firmly grounded in the liberal ideology of the wider society. The major success of liberalism in this regard has been the achievement of legal equality through a sustained critique of discriminatory and restrictive legislative practices, both at the local and state level, associated with ideas of biological racism. There is, however, a *profound paradox*, which emerges in the relations between liberalism and the Aboriginal 'problem', or, more specifically, between the critique of racist ideology and liberal notions of 'freedom' and 'equality'.

The liberal critique of racism is underpinned by a culturally-specific view of the individual. The rejection of racism is very much on the grounds that the individual is reduced to an *anonymous member of a collectivity*. In effect, the critique of racism is that it divests the 'individual' of particular 'character', 'abilities' and 'personal identity' and condemns the stigmatised individual to an anonymous status ascribed by race. What is seen to be denied is egoistic existence. By contrast, what is asserted in liberal discourse is that all identities are, or should be, egoistic identities. The universal 'rights of man', i.e. formal egalitarianism, are ideologically structured in opposition to the establishment of all collectivities and deny collective notions of identity. The

9. Both Broom and Jones (1973: 87–9) and Lippmann (1981: 149) are aware of the ideological 'bias' in the *content* of educational curricula and that it often expresses the culture and history of the dominant society. Both seek to redress this by recommending more Aboriginal input into the curricula and participation in schools, for example teachers or teachers' aides. What is missed is that it is not simply the *content* but the *practices* by which such forms of knowledge are acquired that are equally ideological, or, more accurately, constitutive in patterning social behaviour.

recognition of minority, as opposed to individual, rights effectively constitutes a partial attack upon this essentially liberal position.[10]

There is a uniformity in the liberal critique of racism, the 'equality' associated with formal egalitarianism and the accompanying forms of bureaucratic intervention in terms of the same culturally-specific view of the universal individual. The modern state has been premised on the separation of the political state from particularistic distinctions in terms of which such distinctions can manifest themselves only outside the realm of the political state. It only recognises universal 'man' who has shed all particularities. As Marx (1963: 12) puts it:

> The state abolishes, after its fashion, the distinctions established by *birth, social rank, education and occupation*, when it decrees that birth, social rank, education, occupation are *non-political* distinctions; when it proclaims, without regard to these distinctions, that every member of society is equal in popular sovereignty, and treats all the elements which compose the real life of the nation from the standpoint of the state. But the state, none the less, allows private property, education, occupation, to *act* after their own fashion, namely as private property, education, occupation, and to manifest their *particular* nature. Far from abolishing these effective differences, it only exists so far as they are presupposed. It is conscious of being a political state and manifests its universality only in opposition to these elements. (Original emphasis.)

According to Marx, the abolition of the particular, for example race or religion, is the condition of universal equality within the state. The assertion of the particular in the case of Aborigines, therefore, poses a major dilemma for the state. It is resolved by asserting the quantitative needs of the Aboriginal population in terms of a quantitatively measured level of inequality. The qualitative aspects of inequality, however, are rendered peripheral both within discourse and the discursive practices initiated by the state. This new objectification of Aborigines in a scientific or mathematical discourse is capable only of representing Aborigines in terms of quantitative deviations from statistical norms.

The quantification of differences, in effect, has continually and systematically effaced the Aboriginal experience of inequality. Indeed, the very notion of inequality assumes a norm of equality from which it can be measured and, in turn, demands a scientific (mathematical) project in order to quantify such inequalities. This equivalence and

10. Rand (1964: 172) provides the most logically consistent position in this regard. She describes racism as, 'the lowest, most crudely primitive form of collectivism. It is the notion of ascribing moral, social or political significance to a man's genetic lineage – the notion that a man's intellectual and characterological traits are produced and transmitted by his internal body chemistry. Which means, in practice, that a man is to be judged not by his own character and actions, but by the character and actions of a collective of ancestors.' Rand advocates a return to this more 'genuine' form of liberalism. In its clearest form 'there is no such thing as a collective or racial achievement. There are only individual minds and individual achievements' (ibid. p.174).

equality are premised on notions of an 'abstract, universal man' whose needs are quantifiable and presumes the universality of atomised individualism. Such statistical approaches treat as unproblematic the forms of knowledge that are produced, forms of knowledge which constitute Aborigines as individual subjects. Likewise, they encourage forms of intervention which constitute Aborigines as objects for the individualising technologies imposed upon them as welfare recipients. The logic of state intervention ensures that both nuclear family and individual success are made possible, while the qualitative aspects of group success are systematically ignored. Equality is another form of cultural incorporation in which expressions of cultural racism are embedded in the universalistic forms of bureaucratic intervention.

In the same way as 'equality' for Aborigines provides the basis for hegemonic incorporation at the level of the state, the forms of freedom accorded Aborigines perform a similar function. The 'freedom' they are afforded is the same as that available to all other members of society and hence is simply a formal admission to equal status. The universal recognition of Aboriginal equality is also a denial of fundamental aspects of the history of Aborigines, their conquest, domination and, more specifically, their loss of political sovereignty. The 'freedom' to express a particularistic history, however, is not denied or politically repressed, as it was in the past, but restricted to the realm of civil society and kept outside the political state. Assertions of Aboriginality can be expressed as a personal identification or through voluntary associations of like minded individuals, in the same way as other individuals in society may express themselves as members of a religious group, political party, or in affirmation of a particular ethnic identity. 'Sovereignty', in this respect, can be expressed, but only outside the realm of the political state. The particular remains an egoistic expression restricted to civil society. The state merely has a judicial role to guarantee such individuals freedom of association.

The 'freedom' to assert particularistic individual allegiances or to join a voluntary association remains contained, primarily, within the domain of civil society. Beyond the level of personal ascription, the freedom to express effective differences is equally restricted to civil society. Given the low economic status of Aborigines, the financial self-sufficiency required to develop alternative socio-cultural forms of organisation in areas such as education and housing ensures that the development of such projects requires patronage from a private economic benefactor. Such patronage, in effect, engenders another form of structural dependency. This is most clearly seen in the relatively recent establishment of an Aboriginal Academy on the upper Nulla Nulla Creek (near Bellbrook reserve), which is funded from private interests by members of a fundamentalist Christian church. In 1980, the Aboriginal Academy had 20 students, ranging from eight to 15 years, taught primarily by two Aboriginal women. What is perhaps most evident is that the economic inequalities within 'civil society' are closely connected to other social inequalities in as much as they relate to the power to make decisions and therefore the ability to satisfy individual or group (for example religious or educational) interests. In this respect, the development of this alternative Aboriginal school is heavily influenced by fundamentalist church doctrine whereby people are expected to be vegetarian, to refrain from drinking alcohol and certain beverages, smoking and dancing, and to reject the religious and ritual practices of the past as 'satanic'.

Chapter 8

Racism as Egalitarianism: Changes in Racial Discourse

8.1. Egalitarianism: the Totem of Equality

Changes in state policies towards Aborigines in the post-1967 referendum period brought about shifts in the local European population's
ideological constructions of Aborigines. The forms of racism prevalent
since the beginning of the 1980s have gained significance through their
opposition to the socio-scientific objectifications of Aborigines associated with welfare interventions. The basis for social welfare stresses
no inherent essence but regards the environment as the source of the
Aborigines' social being. The forms of intervention are egalitarian in
that they seek to guarantee a minimum standard of living and/or
ameliorate the social conditions of inequality. By contrast, the constructions within the local community identify Aborigines as inherently
inferior because of their dependency upon social welfare and their
perceived utilisation of the 'tax payer's money'. Aborigines are pejorat-
ively defined by their place within, or in relationship to, state apparatuses. Further, Aboriginal dependency upon social welfare is alleged
to reveal the inherent essence of Aboriginality. In effect, these assessments present an image of Aboriginal personhood in opposition to
their rights as citizens.

The reconstitution of relations between Aborigines and Europeans in
the Macleay Valley requires a reassessment of the nature of race
relations. Analyses of racism have increasingly been adopting comfortable pedagogical moral critiques of 'prejudice' or 'exploitation', which
tend to instruct rather than illuminate. These moral critiques passively
lead us through the subject matter and become substitutes for an
analysis of the concrete specificities of racism. In effect, studies of
racism lose any disconcerting critical edge as their analysis assumes the
comfortable predictability of a predigested subject.

The significant feature about racial attitudes in Kempsey is that they
are grounded in the universal and moral imperatives of an egalitarian

ethos. This was summed up in a local newspaper editorial (*MA*, April 1980)[1] about the exclusion of an Aboriginal man from a local hotel, which argued that, 'A man in his cups – whatever his colour – is no asset to any person or place. A man in his cups who is also aggressive and disorderly – whatever his colour – can't bring down the wrath of this or that person upon a publican who wants order and acceptable behaviour on his premises.' Presented in such a way, it is difficult to come to a different conclusion. Yet, in achieving this, the statement drains the incident of all the particulars of time and place and recognises only the equivalence or egalitarianism of the individual. In a more general sense, historical and social experience is homogenised, and an illusory unity is created between individuals. Social determinants are replaced with a universal, psychologistic notion of 'human nature' governed by individual preferences judged to be rational or irrational. This form of egalitarianism effectively provides a vehicle for the creation of new expressions of domination.

In the contemporary period, racial tension is expressed in incessant and unrelentingly negative gossip about state assistance to Aborigines. The logic of the *formal egalitarianism* of state interventions, which stress environmental factors as the source of inequality, is rejected and replaced with a *populist egalitarianism*, which stresses that 'all men are created equal' and make their own way according to natural abilities. Dumont (1972) argues that in the modern state biological egalitarianism is the fundamental basis for universal citizenship. In this, it is not the group, but individuals who 'become the measure of all things' before the state. The state protects the civil and political rights of individuals to operate freely. At the same time, to be recognised as a social individual, i.e. a citizen who is a bearer of rights and responsibilities, one must also be assessed as capable of making rational choices (Turner 1986: 7). The predominance of biological racism as a social discourse was closely linked to the denial of Aboriginal equality before the state. Biological racism categorised Aborigines as existing 'outside the family of man', as biologically inferior. Biological difference is attributed as the ontological basis for hierarchy and discrimination.

The construction of Aboriginal identity has always been in part an exploration of their humanness (see also Lattas 1986). Such evaluations crystallised around the relationship of personhood to citizenship rights. In the policies of exclusion and the proposals for their domestication, the evaluations of Aboriginal humanness have held a central place. A similar process is revealed in the competing egalitarian depictions of Aborigines in the present. Both egalitarian representations are united in an essentially humanist epistemology which celebrates the

---

1. The editorial won the Non Metropolitan Newspapers Award for outstanding journalism in 1980.

human being as an individual. The totem of equality is built on this basis and in a manner which dispels or ignores human particularities. (See Chapter 6 for an account of formal egalitarianism in this regard.)

In the populist account, this has led to a reformulation of the categorisation of Aborigines as not fulfilling the criteria of 'abstract universal man' through obstensibly cultural, rather than racial, constructions of their humanness as an inversion of the conventional economic/moral values of the dominant society. The existence of racism is denied as a thing of the past, identified with previous institutional forms of segregation and expressions of biological inferiority. The removal of such 'artificial barriers' to Aboriginal 'success' is seen to reveal their 'true nature'. The obsessive concern amongst Europeans with levels of government assistance to Aborigines provides confirmation, while denying overt racism, that Aborigines are indeed neither capable of acting 'rationally' nor of having equivalent rights and responsibilities.

8.2. The Decline of the Rural Economy

Several writers have addressed the issue of the changing face of the rural economy of NSW and its consequences for Aborigines (see Chapter 6). Such studies seek quantitative assessments. Their emergence coincides with quantitative forms of state intervention and policies of equal opportunity which seek a more equitable distribution of Aborigines throughout the social hierarchy. The issue of racism, as understood by such writers, is in terms of an artificial barrier to individual Aboriginal mobility exacerbated by rural decline. Racism is reduced to a phenomenon which can be quantitatively measured. The disproportionate concentration of a particular group, in this case Aborigines, is seen as an indicator of discrimination and exploitation. The magnitude of racism is reduced to a mathematical formulation. While such studies may be important in pointing towards quantitative forms of inequality, they do not look at the particularities of the contemporary racial discourse.

Racism is assigned an a priori meaning and reduced to a singular, unitary and transhistorical phenomenon, which is informed by an essentialist theory of prejudice in human nature. Racial prejudice is conceptualised as an individual and essentially non-rational response based upon ignorance or misconception. In the first place, racism is condemned in advance as an aberration which may be remedied by education. Increasingly, the 'objectivity' of quantitative analyses fulfil this function. Secondly, racism is reduced to overt discrimination motivated by individual prejudice. For example, Rowley (1973: 343) argues in relation to the economy that 'the Aboriginal worker will tend to be the "last on" and "first off" the job'. Here, racism is reduced to a random pattern of intolerant behaviour by 'unscrupulous employers' (ibid.). It is both simplified and mystified. My analysis of race relations in the Macleay Valley is directed towards a critique of such perspectives and starts by summarising some of the historical developments discussed elsewhere in this book.

Race relations in the Macleay Valley are based on both *formal political segregation* and *informal economic segregation*. Historically Aborigines occupied a particular niche within the rural economy. At the beginning of the century they moved into specific areas of the economy, which Europeans had abandoned as they moved on to more materially-rewarding and stable occupations (see Morris 1983). The economy was characterised by conspicuous segmentation, whereby Aborigines and Europeans generally operated as economically non-competing groups, i.e. the Aborigines were temporary agricultural labourers, while the Europeans were share farmers, dairymen, or small or large land-owners. Contrary to Rowley's argument, Dhan-gadi men and women held marginal and temporary, but stable, positions within the local economy (in bush work, fencing, corn pulling and cattle mustering) for a full three generations.

Expressions of racism were not premised on a random pattern of intolerant behaviour but rather inscribed into a systematic pattern of inclusion and exclusion. Historically, Aborigines secured employment in the undesirable and marginal areas of the economy. Equally, they were systematically excluded from dairying, the dominant economic activity of the region. This exclusion from dairying was not arbitrary, but consistent with other forms of political exclusion from various spheres of social life; for example the public schools, cinemas and local hospital were all segregated (see Chapter 5). Discrimination was not a random or arbitrary phenomenon, nor could it be reduced to simple notions of exploitation. What was encoded in such patterns of segregation was a racism associated with notions of pollution. The political and economic patterns of segregation provided concrete forms through which the hegemonic unity of Europeans was sustained and reproduced.

In the contemporary period, these relations have been transformed and reconstituted in new forms, but the hegemonic unity of the European community has been sustained, and its superiority over that of the Aborigines remains unquestioned. These forms of racism gained their specificity from the restructuring of the local economy, which reduced Aboriginal employment in the private sector to a token presence and concomitantly resulted in the Aborigines' increasing dependency upon the state. This restructuring of the rural economy has resulted in a marked reduction in general labour participation through the abandonment of those labour-intensive occupations that they had occupied in the past (see Morris 1983). Whereas Aboriginal dependency had previously been maintained through political and legalistic controls, in the contemporary period such controls are achieved indirectly through the economic coercions generated by their displacement from the local economy: that is, in terms of their transition from underemployment to unemployment.

The structural changes in the local economy occurred as a result of increasing specialisation of production and the switch from labour-intensive to energy-intensive production techniques. Such structural changes have meant the virtual collapse of the two-tier economy of large/middle-range pastoralists and worker–owner dairy farmers. The latter, as an economic unit, no longer exist on the upper Macleay and only in a modified form on the lower Macleay. In the period between 1948/9 and 1978/9 dairy stock numbers have dropped dramatically: in 1948/9 there were 37,695; in 1958/9, 31,550; 1968/9, 27,305; and 1978/9, 11,658 (Curtin 1980: Appendix I). This is matched by a similar decline of dairy farms in the corresponding period: 1945/6, 686; 1956–61, 513; 1968/9, 322; 1978–79, 118 (ibid. p. 7).[2] On the upper Macleay River, dairy farms declined from 123 farms in 1954 to 13 in 1969 (Neil 1972: 86) and ceased altogether in the following year with the closure of the cooperative butter factory. Similarly, on the lower Macleay, the structurally-related industries also contracted, and now only one butter factory and one liquid milk supplier continue to operate.

The dramatic decline in the dairy industry, which had been the core of the local economy, was accompanied by wider structural changes in those areas of production associated with the diversified economy of the pre-war years. Both pig and corn production have also steadily declined (see Table 10). The sustained contraction in these agricultural activities is reflected in the more general figures of participation and production within the local economy. The figures available on the number of rural property owners reveal the degree of structural change that has occurred in the economy.

In social terms such changes have brought about significant population shifts within the Macleay Valley. The Macleay Shire, the geographical area covering rural farm land, has undergone a significant drop in population. The post-war peak occurred in 1950/1 when the population reached 9,080 (SRNSW 1951: 427) and 9,170 (SRNSW 1952/3: 616) respectively. By contrast, in 1974 and 1975 (the Shire was amalgamated with Kempsey municipality in 1975) the population progressively dropped to a low of 7,270 (ABS 1975: 27) and in the following

---

2. The circumstances could have been far more drastic had political changes not been brought about in the liquid milk trade. Under the terms of the Dairy Industry Authority, Macleay suppliers were excluded from the 'milk zone' which supplied local and large metropolitan markets. In 1971, Macleay suppliers became engaged in the local liquid milk trade of which some 52 of the remaining 118 suppliers were currently employed (Curtin 1980: 4).

Table 10. Contraction in Agricultural Activities

PIGS

Year	Numbers	
1948	7,972 (1949:57)	
1949	8,530 (1950:57)	
1978/79	4,427 (1980:59)	
1979/80	4,443 (1981:31)	

CORN

Year	Area	Yield
1948/49	1,692 h (1949:214)	4,635 t (1959:24)
1949/50	1,965 h (1959:216)	4,248 t (1950:224)
1978/79	414 h (1980:59)	1,104 t (1980:59)
1979/80	not assessed	465 t (1981:31)

OWNERS

Year	Owners	Land in Production
1952/53	833 (1952/53:10)	173,771 h (1952/53:94)
1955/56	900 (1956:169)	198,810 h (1956:169)
1978/79	508 (1980:59)	162,123 h (1980:59)
1979/80	572 (1981:31)	163,522 h (1981:31)

h = hectares
t = tonnes
Sources: SRNSW and ABS

year to 7,250 (ABS 1976: 31). In effect, there had been a loss of approximately 2,000 people over a period of 25 years.

The other tendency in the Macleay Valley has been towards the expansion of beef production through specialisation and capitalisation. Beef production is the only area of growth. Stock numbers between 1945/6 and 1959/60 ranged from between 39,288 and 45,866 head (Curtin 1980: Appendix I). In the 1960s, however, beef production increased rapidly. Between 1960/1 and 1969/70 cattle numbers fluctuated between a record low of 36,033 (in three drought-affected years) and a record high of 66,708 by the end of the decade. In the following decade this growth continued. Between 1970/1 and 1978/9 the number of head of cattle fluctuated between 72,754 and 83,000 (ibid.).

In sum, then, increasing specialisation has brought with it a shift from labour-intensive to capital- and energy-intensive production. The results of such changes are reflected, for example, on an upper Macleay property which was once a major employer of Aborigines. Whereas for most of his life the present owner used to employ between 10 and 20 men, and a number of these full time, he now employs only two

Europeans. Three generations of Aboriginal men from Bellbrook reserve had worked on his property over the years. Now its original 6,070.5 hectares have been reduced to 2,023.5 hectares of the best land. The alluvial flats, which had been used for maize production, have now been sown with grasses for fattening cattle. Whereas he once engaged in diversified agricultural production – pigs, maize, dairy and beef production – he now specialises only in the latter. Furthermore, a $25,000 tractor now does any clearing of land required, and a spray unit attached to the back of the tractor is used to prevent the growth of noxious weeds and shrubs. The pastures are maintained and improved through aerial spraying with superphosphate.

The structural changes that have occurred in the post-war period have meant that local control and participation in the economy have receded. The worker/owner aspect of the economy is now a minor sector. Similarly, there has been a quantitative contraction in labour-intensive employment. The consequences of such structural shifts on the local population are clearly seen in the endemic unemployment within Kempsey and throughout the mid-north coast region. The unemployment figures for Kempsey by the mid 1970s were considerably higher than the corresponding figures for the state, and this trend has continued. Between 1974 and 1977, unemployment in Kempsey rose from 6.0 per cent to 16.2 per cent, while in NSW as a whole it rose from 1.6 per cent to 7.5 per cent (NSW North Coast Region 1978, Part II: 76). In January 1980, the Kempsey Commonwealth Employment Service had 1,173 unemployed people on its books (*MA*, March 1981: 1). The unemployment figure, as an overall percentage of the population rather than of the work-force, was 16 per cent. The combined figure for Kempsey and the two adjacent districts was the second highest in the state. The highest was also on the north coast.[3]

The restructuring of the local economy has meant that the Aborigines of the Macleay Valley have been displaced from their agricultural niche. The other sectors of the economy (the commercial/retail sector and the small industrial sector), apart from a few exceptions, only employ Europeans. The commercial/retail sector of Kempsey contains three large supermarkets, two large clothing stores, five banks, six hotels, nine motels, a local tri-weekly newspaper and a range of small retail outlets (such as coffee shops, chemists and fruit shops) in a number of arcades. In 1980/1, one Aboriginal girl had employment in a local bank, and only four Aborigines were employed in the industrial sector. According to my informants, they were in three of the five largest firms, each of which employed between 30 and 100 workers with an overall total of 310. Town employment has traditionally been a European

---

3. The adjacent region, Lismore, recorded the highest number of unemployed people in the state, 3,552 (*MA* 1981: 1).

preserve. One of the main campaigns by the Macleay District Welfare Committee in the early 1960s was to secure employment for '*one* Aborigine in the town'. It was commonly known amongst Aborigines which individuals had jobs in the private sector of the economy because there were so few of them.

Most employment for Aborigines in 1980/1 was in the public sector. The Council, with 180 positions, was a major source of employment in the valley, but it engaged only four Aborigines – a machine operator, an electrician, a library assistant and a general labourer. Similarly, the local hospital, with a total staff of 284, employed only five Aborigines, four as general staff and one as a nurse (amongst 150 nurses). Government departments provided employment for another eight, and government-funded community organisations (the medical centre, legal aid, the housing cooperative and cultural and educational research) employed another 12. On Bellbrook reserve, which had a population of 139, only two people (a husband and wife) were in full-time employment (as a handy-man and a community health worker), and both were government funded.

At present, most Aborigines in the Macleay Valley are part of a pool of chronically unemployed people. Those who are employed are concentrated in the public sector and rely heavily on limited forms of government intervention to generate employment opportunities. Aborigines now compete with Europeans for the same jobs and, in this context of structural change and direct competition with Europeans, are likely to find themselves in the situation Rowley (1973) describes as 'last on/first off'.

The patterns of segmentation have not disappeared; they have merely changed. Aborigines are now virtually excluded from working in the private (commercial/retail, industrial and agricultural) sectors of the economy, and several recent studies (mentioned earlier) report the same kind of deterioration in employment in other rural districts. The only real chances of finding employment are in the public sector of the economy. That jobs for Aborigines have to be politically created in this sector is an indication that race continues to be important in determining whether or not people are able to find work within the local economy of the Macleay Valley. The virtual absence of Aborigines from the private sector of the economy and their concentration in the public sector reveals the nature of the racial redistribution of employment opportunities in the contemporary period.

8.3. The Shifts in the Meaning of Racial Discourse

The change from political and legalistic control to the economic coercions of a declining rural economy also changed the emphasis and meaning of racism. The biological and cultural criteria which had for the most part informed racial discourses on Aboriginal inferiority and social segregation were no longer emphasised. The political practice of racial exclusion, which had been synonymous with racial inferiority, was also no longer overtly evident. In fact, during the course of the 1960s the political domination of Aborigines by repressive and discriminatory legislation was removed (see Chapter 6).

The relationship between racial inferiority and political exclusion was bluntly stated by a witness appearing before a Parliamentary Committee inquiring into Aboriginal welfare (1967: 384), who justified continuing the exclusion of Aborigines from cafés, restaurants and hotels on the grounds that they were unhygienic. As he put it, 'you can *smell* them'. He was simply rather crudely reiterating a medical discourse associated with 'pollution', which had constituted the politics of exclusion for most of this century. Since the removal of all discriminatory and repressive legislation, Aborigines formally have the same rights of access to public places as Europeans. The rescinding of discriminatory legislation has removed one of the important elements maintaining the hegemonic domination of Europeans: the political proscription of Aborigines from areas of social life.

Although assertions about the genetic or cultural inferiority of Aborigines are no longer expressed in the public/political domain, such attitudes still persist as private convictions or personal beliefs. For example, one woman explained to me that after a lifetime of observing Aborigines and being in personal contact with them (her mother had Aboriginal women in regularly to do her washing), she believed that Aborigines were intellectually inferior to whites. Her one qualification was that 'Aborigines are not stupid though, they're cunning, you know, like monkeys'. On another occasion I was told that 'full bloods' were alright but that it was those who had become mixed with whites (genetically) who were the problem. This problem of the half caste was due to the union between lower class whites and Aborigines. As he put it, 'they get the bad' from whites combined with their own Aboriginality. Ontological difference is expressed in terms of biological determinism, where the personality and behaviour of social groups is hereditary.

For the most part, however, such assertions did not predominate in the construction of Aborigines as 'symbolic failures'. Most expressions of Aboriginal inferiority today relate to notions of individual deviance associated with the conventional morality of an autonomous self-regulating individual. This can be seen in the constant assertions that Aborigines are drunken, lazy and live off the taxpayers' hard-earned money. The dominant position of such overt expressions reveals that racism has undergone a number of fundamental shifts in emphasis and changes in content. In the absence of political segregation to provide concrete referents of European moral and intellectual hegemony, the 'knowledge' of a transhistorical Aboriginal inferiority is constructed out of their 'deviance' within the private/personal domain.

The metaphysical scaffolding on which previous racial discourse was erected, through standardised notions of biological or cultural inferiority, seems less evident. The decline of political and institutional forms of racism, under the increasing weight of a liberal critique, had rendered the biological expressions of racism problematical. In the contemporary period, the raw materials for constructing Aborigines as symbolic failures are drawn from the perceived deviant personal behaviour of Aborigines and their misuse/abuse of personal property/ possessions. The deviant personal behaviour was asserted by Europeans in a number of areas and in numerous ways. The failure of Aborigines to work was seen as an indication that they were lazy, or that they don't want to work, or that they just don't stick at anything, or as an indictment of the corrosive effects of social security payments – 'they just won't work since they got the welfare payment'. The construction of knowledge within these negative, pejorative characterisations seeks legitimacy for an a priori notion of Aboriginality which grounds its claim to authenticity in empirical evidence, i.e. Aboriginal unemployment.

The criticism of Aborigines as welfare recipients is, of course, also applied to Europeans. Dependency is axiomatic with subordinate status. It is a central tenet of populist egalitarian sentiment. Indeed, the possibility of such an understanding is associated with the cultural habits of a class-related capitalist culture. As Heller (1988: 2–4) argues, it is the capacity to stratify society along the functional lines of the division of labour, i.e. institutionalised function performance, which has given the forms of life and cultural patterns their class relatedness. Dependency, in this sense, may well be extended to the status of the young (prefunctional) and the aged (postfunctional), to use Heller's terminology, and understood in terms of capacities developed through natural maturity and decline. Subordinate status is synonymous with absence of self-autonomy.

Towards the unemployed, dependency is linked to the view that status is reflected in the remuneration that people receive from using their natural abilities and skills. Populist egalitarianism does not deny hierarchy, but constitutes it as natural. As everyone is born equal, social hierarchy is established through the use of natural skills and abilities. Criticism of the unemployed is part of a class-related discourse which links assistance through welfare payments to the notion that there is a loss of self-motivation and self-respect for those on government 'handouts'. Such assertions are part of a general stigma, attached to recipients of welfare payments, that associates welfare assistance with individual deviance.

In the case of European 'dole bludgers', however, it is regarded as an individual aberration, atypical of Europeans in general. Such deviant behaviour by Aborigines was generally considered to have a uniformity and consistency which pervaded the *whole* Aboriginal community: the absence of self-motivation and self-respect is seen as innate. Ontological difference, mobilised as a vehicle for racism, is not expressed in terms of genetic or phenotypical traits, but rather as an inversion of conventional moral values. Difference is, nevertheless, ascribed as ontological and asserted as the basis for hierarchy. Such assertions, obviously, were not applied to Europeans. As an Aboriginal woman put it, 'If a whitefella does something wrong, he's wrong, [but] if a blackfella does something wrong, we're all wrong.' Aborigines are well aware, in this contemporary period, that the chronic unemployment in their community is transformed into a general characteristic associated with Aborigines outside this specific context. As it was put to me, 'You wanta go up and have a look so you can really see what the Aboriginal people have done [land clearance associated with bush work]. They'll [Europeans] say "Oh white man done that". White man never done that, it's the black man who did it.' Or again, as an inversion of the moral critique, when 'there was work, they were willing to work, but the wages were low, very low.' The European evaluation and understanding of Aborigines is as a *group* in which selective elements are utilised to ascribe general characteristics that exist outside time and place.

Other European evaluations were based on observing Aboriginal gambling and drinking. The public display of drunkenness usually provided the reference point for the perceived high incidence of drinking amongst Aborigines. More often, however, the primary criticism was that most of the money they received from government handouts, as they were inevitably called, went to the local pub or TAB (state government betting agency) and that whereas 'most whites would only have small bets, Aborigines place bets in $50 notes'. Similarly, it was suggested to me that if I really wanted to research Aborigines in Kempsey I should sit on the library steps opposite the pub that Aborigines frequented and count how many went in. Then, I was assured, I would know what Aborigines were really like. What is explicit in these characterisations is that Aborigines are wasteful, indulgent and misusing the taxpayers' money. But they are saying something more than this.

Such depictions of personal behaviour underpin an ontological view of Aborigines as irrational beings incapable of controlling the quantitative allocation of welfare money. They are, in effect, beings who cannot calculate. Such characterisations suggest that Aborigines exist primarily through sensations, through satisfying their desires. This is seen to be all they are capable of doing.

Here there is a unity linking the assertions that Aborigines are incapable of work and are drunks and spendthrift gamblers, with notions derived from an inversion of the conventional moral values of the dominant society. It is through these cultural lenses that Aborigines are constructed as 'symbolic failures'. Central to this is the notion of work, for it is through work that individuals become independent entities capable of controlling their own existence. Furthermore, work is a regular, disciplined and purposeful activity which stands in direct contrast to the consequences of receiving 'handouts', considered to be money for 'doing nothing'. The conventional values associated with the idea of work are not simply instrumental values relating to the satisfaction of wants but associated with moral values of acting rationally and responsibly. This self-conscious rational being, a being with conscious purposes who consciously shapes his or her own existence, is juxtaposed against the irregular and undisciplined behaviour of Aborigines whose unrestrained desire seeks to satisfy only the most ephemeral and immediate wants.

In terms of consumption, personal deviance is associated with the failure to comply with cultural notions of deferred gratification. The contrast is with a more restrained and calculative form of pleasure, such as the small bet, which implies the harnessing of desire to reason. Notions of dignity and self-esteem are seen here to be maintained through a continual opposition to the fragmenting tendencies of desire and impulse.

A similar unity in the evaluation of Aborigines by Europeans is found in characterisations of Aboriginal housing, which also build up a picture of Aborigines as irrational beings who misuse or abuse their personal property or possessions. The expressions of deviant behaviour assert that Aborigines are drunken, noisy or continually fighting and that their children are uncontrolled. In effect, Aboriginal families are constructed as incapable of leading ordered and responsible social lives. Similarly, there is the chorus of complaints that Aborigines do not look after their houses properly. Aboriginal housing, almost by default, is considered to fall into disrepair through neglect or abuse, and the interiors are invariably assumed to be dirty.

A striking expression of this was in an account of an Aboriginal family who allegedly chopped a large hole in the floor of their house so that they could drop all their rubbish and food scraps through to the pigs living underneath. Chicken-wire had been run around the foundations by the occupiers to enclose the pigs. The themes of abuse of personal possessions (and the unhygienic and polluting properties of pigs and rubbish) are self evident. Also important, however, is the satirising of Aboriginal rationality as primitive or naïve, which is posited in the inappropriate use and violation of private space. The critique embodied in this anecdote was founded on a clear-cut demarcation of inside/outside space, a norm which the Aborigines were regarded as having violated. The pigs which should be located in outside space are attached to inside space and, likewise, the rubbish and foodscraps which should be despatched to outside space remain within inside space. The Aborigines in this anecdote had, in primitive and irrational style, privatised elements of outside space. What is signified here is the belief that Aborigines are incapable of understanding the most rudimentary cultural codes associated with domestic life.

The distinguishing feature of such a racial discourse about Aborigines is the claim to legitimacy through 'empirical verification'. Such claims are asserted on the grounds of personal experience, observation, or the communicated personal experience of others, for example, those who had lived next door to an Aboriginal family, who had occupied a house after the family had moved out, or who had been given information by servicemen who had made calls to repair appliances. If the pejorative characterisations of Aborigines are inaccurate, it does not necessarily follow that they are illusory. The raw materials are drawn from the present and are structurally reinforced by the Aborigines' present circumstances. Both the selection of elements and the interpretation (which is unified and given meaning by particular cultural codes) are mystified by such empirical or 'commonsense' verifications.

The connection between empirical evidence, inaccuracy and illusion is made apparent in the degree of welfare assistance ascribed to Aborigines. Apart from a secondary-school allowance provided for Aboriginal children ($2.50 per week), Aborigines in Kempsey receive the same range of welfare payments and pensions as members of the European community, yet local Europeans perceive the level of 'handouts' as far in excess of those available to them. As one European woman put it:

> I think there will always be prejudice while ever there is the big handouts given to Aborigines. . . . I feel the white people are the people discriminated against, not the Aboriginal people. . . . We see cases where Aboriginal people are given handouts for their children to attend school, and in lots of cases the money never reaches the school, it doesn't go to their education, it goes to the local hotel and this is why until something is done about this system of this handout – I'm sure a lot of Aboriginal people don't want these handouts – but I feel there is this handout and this abundance of money that there'll always be prejudice and this is a sad thing.
>
> (Talkback Radio, Kempsey, 1980)

This theme of the 'big handout' and 'abundance of money' is quite common in discourse among Europeans in the Macleay Valley. There is an exaggerated view of how much financial assistance individual families receive from the government. I was, for example, told that if Aborigines abuse their homes or cars, the government pays for the repairs, not to mention the financial installments on houses, cars and television sets. This is consistent with the view expressed that 'Aborigines received a cheque every second day for some form of allowance' (ibid.).

Such exaggerated claims could be said to demonstrate the social distance between Aborigines and the rest of the community. I would argue, however, that this is not a matter of ignorance but that such 'inaccuracies' are ideological statements of Aboriginal inferiority. The structuring of this racial discourse is grounded in an opposition to those points of bureaucratic intervention associated with formal egalitarianism. These expressions of racism gain their significance through their opposition to the socio-scientific objectifications of an Aborigine as an 'abstract, universal man' with quantifiable needs. Within the context of the negative perception of welfare, the assertions of such overwhelming welfare dependency continually act to provide a symbolic index of the degree of Aboriginal inferiority and confirm their incapacity to manage and control their own affairs.

Therefore, the abolition of judicial forms of racial discrimination from the domain of the political state has not abolished racism but only engendered a number of changes. What has emerged is a secular form of racism where the 'objectivity' of personal observations, or of personal knowledge, provides 'empirical' verification. Underpinning such assertions is a *culturally constituted* and transhistorical view of Aborigines as irrational beings incapable of calculative reason. They cannot control the quantitative allocation of taxpayers' money nor appreciate other benefits from government services. Such typifications sustain the hegemonic unity of the European community. They also deny the political efficacy of government policies and the socio-scientific objectifications of Aborigines that accompany them.

At the moment Aborigines are caught between two extremes. At the local level they are never regarded primarily as *individuals*, but almost always as *Aborigines* who are insensible to ethics and negate the society's values. At the other extreme government policy, which is based on formal equality, structures relations with Aborigines in terms of a universal human nature which demands universal equality for all. This contradiction is captured in the following account (Sartre 1972: 57) of the different ways in which an anti-Semite and a democrat relate to a Jew. 'The former wishes to destroy him as a man and leave nothing in him but the Jew, the pariah, the untouchable; the latter wishes to destroy him as a Jew and leave nothing in him but the human, the abstract, universal subject of the rights of man and the rights of the citizen.' At the local level, the Aborigines of the Macleay Valley have a common situation and a common bond because the community they live in typifies/treats them as Aborigines and because anti-Aboriginal sentiment is a pervasive and permanent aspect of the community in which they live. At the level of the state, political emancipation reduces

Aborigines to individuals, to an ensemble of universal traits, which denies them the historical and experiential aspects of their everyday existence.

Chapter 9

The Politics of Identity: from Equal Rights to Land Rights

The Aboriginal people of New South Wales are the *true* owners of this state. We are entitled to be compensated for the loss of this land by theft, for the loss of its use, the loss of its natural resources. *We are entitled to develop our own communities in accordance with our own traditions and aspirations.* We are entitled to self determination; to freedom from government control and interference in our lives, our future. *We are entitled to our heritage; our sacred sites, our traditional foods, our sovereign status.* We demand recognition of these rights by the government of New South Wales. We will not stop calling for land rights until these demands are met.

> (NSW Aboriginal Land Council, cited Wilkie 1983: 12)

The emergence of political organisations such as the NSW Aboriginal Land Council introduced a radical new dimension to relations between Aborigines and the state. 'For the first time in history', the state was 'faced with counter definitions of aboriginal ethnicity from themselves' (Weaver 1984: 183). The Aboriginal political organisations of the past had demanded equality, the right to be treated as equally human. The secessionary logic of the new demands sought a different solution to the relations of domination, which had always forced Aborigines to experience themselves in terms other than their own. This issue, the politics of a distinctive identity, has mutually influenced national, regional and local struggles, through which Aborigines aim to gain control over their own social and cultural identity, and has been emphatically expressed in the state-wide political movement towards land rights in NSW which emerged in the early 1970s (see Wilkie 1985).

The growing significance of an Aboriginal voice in the political arena, which is being expressed through non-governmental political organisations, has been matched by a corresponding recognition of Aboriginal representation in the government's policy-making organisations (see Weaver 1983, 1983a).[1] The recognition that Aborigines and Aboriginal

---

1. Discussions about incorporating Aboriginal groups into national policy formation are

groups are entitled to participate in policy making, and the attention being given to land rights by non-governmental political organisations and the media, have changed the former non-dialectic nature of relations between Aboriginal groups and the state (see Cousins and Nieuwenhuysen 1984; Jennett 1984; Jones and Hill-Burnett 1982; Weaver 1984). The frozen dialectic that gripped relations in the past is giving way to a confrontation between the state, various interest groups and Aboriginal organisations' competing claims and forms of knowledge.

Resistance to acceptance of Aboriginal identity subsumed within a national sovereignty provides a unique challenge to contemporary Australian polity. The revival of an Aboriginal voice is, by definition, a political act which challenges, to borrow Jacoby's (1975) term, a more general 'social amnesia'. The dominant society's 'collective forgetting' of the Aborigines' sovereign rights is and has been a precondition of their domination, not only in the sense that domination is 'naturalised', but also in that the possibilities of challenging such historical representations are absent from the political agenda. The politics of indigenous rights in Australia do not begin with the same assumptions that inform the Canadian (nor the US) situation – where limited sovereignty and residency rights on reserves accompany Indian status. The existence of treaties between these nation states and the respective Indian nations has long provided them with a distinctive legal status. [2] The Aboriginal people of Australia have no such legal status. Australia became subject to British sovereignty in the judgement passed down by the British Privy Council (1788) and, at the time of initial colonisation, the land was 'practically unoccupied without settled inhabitants or settled laws' (Detmold 1985: 58).[3] This judgement formed the basis of the non-recognition/denial of the sovereign rights of Aborigines (see also Hookey 1984; and Lumb 1988). In the two main cases to challenge this judgement, (Milirrpun versus Nabalco Pty Ltd (1971) and Coe versus Commonwealth of Australia (1979)), the validity of the British Crown's claim to sovereignty was upheld.

The validity of the British claim to sovereignty stemmed from the judgement that Australia was, according to the rules of international

---

found in Stevens (1980); Lippmann (1981); Weaver (1983 and 1983a) and Beckett (1983). Weaver has given an extensive and comprehensive history of the emergence of Aboriginal advisory bodies and explores their ambiguous status as advisory bodies cum pressure groups. An analysis of such processes is beyond the scope of my discussion here.

2. In the US, 'between 1778 and 1869, 370 treaties were made between the United States and various Indian "nations"' (Powell 1978: 86). Much of this land was expropriated between 1887 and 1930 through the introduction of the General Allotment Act or Dawes Act (1887). The Act authorised the president to 'divide Indian reservations into individual holdings and assign a parcel of land to each inhabitant, leaving the "surplus" available for orthodox homesteading by all-comers' (ibid.).

3. I am indebted to Chris Charles for drawing my attention to Detmold's excellent discussion of the constitutional aspects of the status of Aborigines.

law operating in the eighteenth century, a 'settled colony', i.e. *terra nullus* (unoccupied), rather than a 'conquered colony', where limited forms of indigenous rights and sovereignty were granted, as, for example, in the US and Canada. The demonstrable historical falsity of such a legal claim has produced, as in the High Court case of Coe versus the Commonwealth of Australia (1979), a view of history that argues that legal theory takes precedence over historical evidence. As Blackburn J., the presiding judge stated, 'once made, practice or judicial decision *will not be disturbed* by historical research . . . what is important is the legal theory, and for this purpose *historical fact may give place to legal fiction*' (cited Detmold 1985: 60). In short, the judgement affirmed the status quo, namely that, constitutionally, the non-recognition of the rights of Aborigines as an *indigenous* people remained unaltered.

Nevertheless, the status of Aborigines has recently undergone some important changes, which have occurred as part of the higher profile the Commonwealth government has taken in Aboriginal welfare servicing. In the 1970s and early 1980s, the Commonwealth performed only a limited and auxiliary role in welfare servicing compared with the regional state governments. The provision of specific policies, however, rehabilitated the notion of an Aboriginal collectivity expressed in terms of special services (medical, legal, cultural) and land rights. These government initiatives are part of a shift from an assimilationist to a cultural pluralist programme, cast within the idiom of 'self determination'.

The cultural pluralist programme attempts to resolve the anomaly the original inhabitants pose for the modern state, but without acknowledging their sovereign status. The present solution to the Aboriginal 'problem' is sought through the recognition of cultural differences rather than the specificities of colonial dispossession and domination. This stress on cultural distinctiveness is not arbitrary, but grows out of the 'legal fiction' on which the constitutional sovereignty of the nation state is based. When the constitutional basis of pluralist policies is separated from its political rhetoric, 'self determination' reflects more the expansion of the welfare system into Aboriginal affairs than a recognition of indigenous rights.

This view is echoed in a number of studies that focus on a process of domination sustained by relations of dependency (see Paine 1977; Collmann 1979; Howard 1981 and 1982; and Beckett 1983). Mechanisms of control are not confined to the political and economic arenas. The analysis needs to be extended to the terrain of ideology and culture, where the hegemonic forms that power assumes are associated with the struggle over the politics of identity.

In Foucauldian terms, the politics of identity refers to an aspect of power whereby a subjugated group is turned into an object of knowledge. With respect to cultural pluralism, in the production of knowledge about the past of minority groups, the state becomes the possessor and producer of the collective representations of transgenerational knowledge. In effect, minority groups lose the right to speak for themselves as the production of their past, their history, is invested in experts and authorities and mediated by institutions of the state system. The hegemonic process ascribes to Aborigines a position within state ideology which nullifies the particularity of the Aboriginal past. They are defined as the 'first Australians' rather than as the indigenous people. Aborigines become the 'first immigrants', the first of a series of waves of immigrants, who make up the multi-cultural composition of modern Australia.[4] History is emptied of the past, the past reduced to a series of cultural/historical moments of migration and settlement – English, Irish, German, Italian, Greek – leading to the triumph of the present. The appropriation of Aborigines as cultural/historical figures mystifies the relationship that exists between this new ideological representation of Aborigines and their constitutional/legal status. It provides the basis for the ideological struggle between the Aboriginal understanding of the past and the production of the past by the state.

9.1. The Ideology of Cultural Pluralism

Paine's (1977: 3) notion of *welfare colonialism* provides a conceptual tool for penetrating the contemporary circumstances of fourth-world peoples in liberal democracies. The process of continuing domination, he argues, is facilitated through the development of relations of dependency between indigenous minorities and welfare departments in the relatively permissive context of a partial recognition of such groups as a collectivity. The relationship is 'solicitous rather than exploitative, liberal rather than repressive'. Such policies reflect the success of liberalism over previous racial and discriminatory practices, but also its limitations. As Beckett (1983: 3) aptly reminds us, it is the colonisers who make the decisions, even if they are supposed to be for the good of the colonised. In this connection, the critical probing into contemporary policies, initiated by Paine, has brought into focus the subtle forms of political and economic control associated with apparently 'non-demonstrative colonialism'.

---

4. Under the title, *A Land of Immigrants*, the Department of Immigration & Ethnic Affairs (1985: 1) produced the following representation of Aborigines: 'At least 40,000 years ago, humans first set foot on the Australian landmass. Probably originating in mainland South-East Asia, *they were the first Australians – our earliest immigrants* . . . From Australia's north-west, the newcomers are believed to have spread along the coast and up the major river systems . . . *By the late 18th century, when Europeans arrived to settle*, an estimated 250,000 to 300,000 Aborigines were living in Australia.'

Colonialism ceased to function in any demonstrable sense in the 1960s, when legislative changes (discussed below) brought an end to race and racial discrimination as the central dynamic in the state control of Aborigines. In NSW, as in other states, colonial relations were expressed through the idiom of race, and race provided the morality for discriminatory practices. From the assimilation policies of the late 1960s, the Aborigines emerged as a 'deprived social group' with special quantitative needs. They were seen as deviations from a statistical norm, and this led to their incorporation into the state's general welfare system. Their admission was in keeping with the historical expansion of quantitative forms of specialised welfare intervention in health, education and housing in the post-war period.[5] During the 1970s, however, the policy of multiculturalism resulted in some recognition of Aborigines' qualitative needs. Under this new doctrine, ethnicity provided the morality for special services to Aborigines.[6]

This new emphasis emerged as the Commonwealth government became more involved in Aboriginal affairs following the amendments to the Australian Constitution after the 1967 referendum. This enabled the Commonwealth government to assume responsibilities for Aborigines previously carried out by various state departments. Specifically, this involved changes to Section s.51(26), which empowered the Commonwealth government to enact special laws for Aborigines. As Hanks (1984) points out, the constitutional power of s.51(26) had originally been intended to support discriminatory legislation associated with a 'white Australia' immigration policy. Under s.51(26), the Commonwealth government had the 'power to make laws for the peace, order and good government of the Commonwealth with respect to . . . the people of any race, other than the Aboriginal race in any State, from whom it is deemed necessary to make special laws' (cited Hanks 1984: 20). The removal of the reference to Aborigines in the referendum enabled the transfer of legislative controls to the Commonwealth parliament.

The referendum promoted the incorporation of Aborigines into Anglo–Australian society. The view enshrined in the 'white Australia'

5. This was especially so between 1945 and 1978 when the number of employees in the NSW public service changed from 30,315 (including teachers) to 77,000 (excluding teachers): an average increase of 4.33 per cent per year (NSW North Coast Region 1978, Part II: 269). Encel (1962: 219–20) provides comparable employment figures for the 'administrative revolution' of both Commonwealth and state bureaucracies between 1939 and 1959.

6. As Brown (1984) points out, there is a distinct analogy between racist ideologies (with their emphasis on inherent biological factors) and interpretations of 'ethnicity' associated with inherent cultural forms. The moral underpinning that ethnicity provides in Aboriginal policy may be seen in the functioning of the Land Rights Act (Northern Territory) (1976), in which access to land is regulated by (1) a demonstrable traditional link to the land and, (2) its being unoccupied crown land (land not utilised by Europeans). The legislation enshrines a static rather than a relational and processual view of culture which dehistoricises the colonial context.

policy, which sought to preserve the homogeneity of Anglo–Australian culture, sanctioned an expanded assimilation programme for Aborigines (see Chapter 7). It continued to equate homogeneity with the imperatives of peace, order and good government and heterogeneity with the seeds of social divisiveness and potential conflict. The powers of s.51(26) were not used until a new government was elected in 1972.[7] Special government laws from this period were interpreted to include *positive* forms of discrimination. While the constitutional changes were ultimately to have far-reaching consequences, they did not exclude the use of negative or positive forms of discrimination. The use of s.51(26) validated the recognition of cultural differences within constitutional bounds. The changes bestowed *validity* in its legal sense, rather than questioning the *legitimacy* of the ultimate power of the Commonwealth in relation to the indigenous population.[8]

Nevertheless, government legislation in the 1970s provided the basis for the limited development of Aboriginal control and staffing of legal services, medical centres, pre-schools and economic enterprises, such as housing cooperatives and pastoral stations.[9] In effect, the government endorsed the growth of some degree of authority within Aboriginal communities. Perhaps the most significant example of this was the granting of Aboriginal land rights (1976) to groups under the jurisdiction of Commonwealth control in the Northern Territory.[10] Similarly,

7. The government remained firmly committed to the assimilation policy. As the minister for immigration stated, 'We must have a single culture. If migration implies multicultural activities within Australian society, then it was not the type Australia wanted. I am quite determined we should have a mono-culture with everyone living in the same way, understanding each other and sharing the same aspirations. We do not want pluralism' (cited Kalantzis, Cope and Hughes 1984/5: 195).

8. The terms are drawn from Detmold (1985: 49), who points out that, 'legitimacy is not the same thing as validity. To say a law is valid implies that it is authorised by a higher law. Legitimacy relates to the highest law, the point where no question of validity can arise: the ultimate power of the Commonwealth is not valid but legitimate. . . . Lawyers, quite at home with questions of validity, are often uneasy when questions of legitimacy are canvassed. Such questions are political in the strictest sense; that is, they are concerned with the power of a polis (or Commonwealth, to use our word)' Not unnaturally, the issues that have received the most anthropological interest concern Aboriginal local organisation or land tenure. They have followed largely from the impact upon anthropology of the Gove Land Case (1971) and the Land Rights Act (1976) (see, amongst many others, Gumbert 1981; Maddock 1983; Keen 1984 and, more recently, Williams 1986). The questions that are primarily raised are those of recognition in terms of *validity* within the existing legal system. By contrast, the same attention to the political implications of the Coe versus Commonwealth of Australia case (1979), which deals directly with the question of *legitimacy*, has not yet occurred.

9. The significant legislation passed in the 1970s included the Aboriginal Loans Commission Act (1974), which enabled a statutory commission to advance loans for Aboriginal business enterprises, the Aboriginal Land Fund Act, corporations and Aboriginal land trusts to acquire land, and the Aboriginal Councils & Associations Act (1976), which provided for Aboriginal community councils and Aboriginal associations (non-profit or business enterprises) (Hanks 1984: 25). The other significant legislation was the Aboriginal Land Rights Act (Northern Territory) (1976).

10. Several authors have written on the development and consequences of the land rights' movement (see especially Maddock 1983; Weaver 1984).

despite the earnest endeavours of the assimilation policy for migrants, the large numbers of immigrants of non-British origin who settled in Australia in the post-Second World War period changed the social composition and the political character of Anglo–Australian society. Martin (1978) and Kalantzis, Cope and Hughes (1984/5), in their respective considerations of post-war immigration, show that there has been an evolution in immigration policy which paralleled that in Aboriginal affairs. Government recognition of land rights and ethnic rights occurred simultaneously in the 1970s.

The limited nature of the reform intended by cultural pluralism is apparent in the final (1975) report of the Commonwealth Committee on Community Relations (cited Martin 1978: 56):

> Pluralism, as defined here, implies first and foremost mutual tolerance and respect for cultural differences by all the members and institutions of Australian society . . . It is in striking a balance between the pressures and requirements of a wider range of ethnic groups and the host society that a fine line divides cultural pluralism from structural pluralism . . . Separatism and segregation become characteristic of (such) a situation which allows a society to develop 'plural structural units' and enshrines the potentiality of conflict and tensions between these units. *Institutional differences will inevitably prevent common sharing and participation in a universalistic value system and sharing in key social institutions . . . However, the viewpoint of 'cultural pluralism', as advocated by this Committee, does enable ethnic groups, if they so desire, to establish their own structures and institutions usually of a cultural and social nature, for example, the media, clubs and restaurants, shops and community organisations . . .* While recognising the utility and value of ethnic structures in achieving the ends of pluralistic integration, it has to be borne in mind that an excessive emphasis on self interest programs may be harmful both to ethnic groups and the host society. These inherent dangers of structural pluralism can be avoided if the interaction between all groups is sustained at all levels and in particular through their common participation in the shared and universalistic structures of the wider society.

The committee recommends the restructuring of community relations. Nevertheless, the report, which preceded the establishment of a commissioner for community relations, sought to remove fears of any secessionary logic associated with cultural pluralism. While the 'universal value system' and 'universal structures' of the wider society were to remain unaltered, specific or additional domains were to be demarcated for expressions of cultural distinctiveness.

These principles guided the implementation of new structures and services for Aboriginal communities, catering to their special needs. The processes of control in this seemingly solicitous form of government intervention are twofold. In the first place, economically and politically the state controls the extent and scope of pluralist practices.

Secondly, while the state no longer suppresses cultural and social differences, it does domesticate them by controlling the domains in which they can be 'legitimately' expressed. Control here is more ideological than political (in the narrow sense) or economic. I have already suggested that to understand this social phenomena it is necessary to understand the historical/social relations between Aborigines and the sovereign order of the state: the relations one is concerned with here are colonial relations. These, it should be stressed, are real; they are historically specific social realities. As a process of mystification, hegemonic domination is constituted in the identification and selection of particular symbolic representations of Aboriginality. In guaranteeing expressions of 'ethnic difference', both historically and culturally, the state attempts to centralise and manage the production of the representations of identity.

To begin with I will consider the auxiliary nature of the government-funded projects (and hence the perpetuation of the 'universal structures' of the wider society) established for Aborigines in the Macleay Valley. Significantly, most Aboriginal families were still living in some form of Housing Commission accommodation in Kempsey, the major town in the valley, in 1980/1. The establishing of an Aboriginal housing cooperative in 1978 had made little impact upon the housing needs of Aborigines in Kempsey. Its shortcomings were expressed to me in terms of 'too little to help the people, band-aid treatment: six houses a year when you need 20. All it does is get the community fighting'. At one level, this reflected the nature of external control associated with the allocation of funding; that is, the number of houses that could be built and the number of people employed. Such structural forms of dependency conformed to external controls associated with welfare colonialism.

Control was not, however, restricted to this external form but also penetrated the internal workings of the cooperative, which had to conform to the rational and codified rules and regulations associated with bureaucratic forms of organisation. For example, monies allocated for housing had to be strictly used for such purposes. In one year, the houses were completed within the allocation, and the surplus was spent by the cooperative on acquiring better machinery and a truck. Such expenditures were regarded as being outside the allocation and had to be returned to departmental revenue. Furthermore, to increase funding for housing and employment, the cooperative applied for monies from another Commonwealth scheme. The application was granted but subject to direct supervision. The building team, which had been working together since 1978, was placed under the supervision of a 'white fella' who was required to be 'on the job for eight hours a day'. Thus, the universal application of rules and regulations took precedence over internal structures of authority defined in terms of 'self-determination'. Above all, the cooperative had to reproduce the same organisational model that applied to welfare programmes in general.

The recognition of Aborigines as a collectivity by the Commonwealth government is limited both in the scope of autonomy associated with 'self determination' and the overall allocations of resources provided for communities. Where the particularity of Aboriginal concerns in the Macleay Valley have been acknowledged, it is in a manner unlikely to threaten overall policy. Similarly, in education, the vast majority of Aboriginal children of school age in 1980/1 were incorporated into the local state school system. At the secondary school level, there were 106 Aboriginal children in a school population of 1,150 pupils.

In general, government policy has facilitated the incorporation of Aboriginal children into the local school system. The Commission of Inquiry into Poverty (1977) found that, in 1967, 42.5 per cent of Aborigines over the age of 15 had not been educated beyond primary school level (Altman and Nieuwenhuysen 1979: 121), which reflected the level of education attained in state-controlled segregated schools on reserves in the past. Rowley's (1973 and 1982) studies of country towns in NSW reveal a marked improvement in the formal attainments of Aborigines within the state school system. In 1965, only 13.4 per cent of Aborigines over 15 years remained at school, while in 1980 the figure had reached 35 per cent (cited Young 1982: 16). Such government practices were politically motivated to achieve equality of opportunity and sought a more equitable distribution of Aborigines throughout the social hierarchy of the dominant society.

In the contemporary context, government policy has predominantly addressed the individual needs of children. In Kempsey, Aboriginal teachers' aides are employed to ease the problems of those who have difficulty fitting into an overwhelmingly European context. Similarly, financial assistance is provided to improve the educational performance and credentials of individual Aborigines by encouraging them to remain at school at secondary level. (In 1980 the Aborigines Secondary Grants Scheme was giving students attending high schools a text book and uniform allowance of $2.50 a week.) Such policies have sought to redress the considerable quantitative differences between Aborigines and Europeans. (The corresponding figure for non-Aboriginal children remaining at secondary high school is 56 per cent (Young 1982: 16).) As a government spokesman in Kempsey explains:

> The reason why we have special measures for Aboriginal children is that for over the past 100 years or so they have fallen so far behind the white community in general. If you ever look at the statistics, I think one Aborigine became a lawyer, none ever became a doctor, none became a dentist, engineer, few became teachers and so on. That's a situation a modern country like Australia cannot continue to have. . . . The governments, both state and

federal, have decided to try and give some opportunities, not handouts or favours, to Aboriginal kids.

(Talkback radio, Kempsey, 1980)

Such policies gain their importance here as an atonement for past policies, but they do not necessarily promote 'self determination'. The concern expressed here is with the *quantitative* differences between Aborigines and non-Aborigines.

To reiterate the point made in Chapter 8, the individualising logic of bureaucratic intervention fostered here takes the form of voluntaristic solutions to an Aboriginal 'problem'. The solution sought in improved education, or better job training, is to increase an *individual's* bargaining power in the job market. Education is understood in terms of an instrumental or means/end logic: its transformative potential is translated into an *individual acquisition*. The determination of such individualistic and voluntaristic remedies is not only contained in the *content* of such 'knowledge and skills', but also in the structures of the pedagogic practices, which impart knowledge as an individual rather than collective acquisition. The 'performance' of each individual is evaluated and ranked according to his or her *individual* ability to conform to a set of normative standards. The pedagogic procedures focus upon the individual attainment of formal qualifications which may help individual Aborigines gain employment.

By contrast, the only government programme that allowed local Aboriginal groups to function independently of the state school system consisted of funding a mini-bus to take young boys to bush locations so that they could be educated in the knowledge of traditional bush skills. (This is discussed more fully later.) While a cultural and educational programme was also established, it was as part of the state school system. During its rather short period of funding (two years), the programme did produce spin-offs for the community through the participation it generated, but, in that its aim was to collect information about 'traditional culture' for inclusion in the local primary school curriculum, even this involvement of Aborigines in the Macleay Valley was within the 'universal structure' of the dominant society. *Qualitative* differences had in effect been given partial recognition and a subordinate role in overall policy. Furthermore, Aboriginal culture was reproduced in a fetishised form: it was presented as an aspect of the past that was separate from everyday existence. The accent on 'traditional' culture suspends contemporary cultural forms, privileging those of the past. To push the point further, such separation aestheticises Aboriginal culture into an essentialist form.

The economic and political dimensions of welfare colonialism give only limited recognition to Aborigines as a collectivity. This is also true at an ideological level. In general terms, through multiculturalism the state attempts to create the institutional and social spaces in which 'divergent' cultural forms can be given complementary expression within the state. The emphasis on 'cultural differences' in itself signals that we are dealing with 'deviations' from the dominant Anglo–Australian core culture. As Neuwirth (1969) points out in the North American context, such labelling shows that members of the core culture continue to monopolise certain kinds of political and economic power and their 'ethnic values' constitute the 'norm'. The dominant cultural forms are valorised as 'universal' rather than historically and culturally relative. The concessions implicit in the ideological structuring of such cultural relations legitimates the existing order and perpetuates its dominance.

In the absence of any relativising of the dominant culture, fictional notions of equivalence mask inequality. Cultural pluralism represents 'culture' as a reified form which exists outside power relations. It is, as Bauman (1985: 13) suggests, a vision of a multiplicity of equivalent 'cultures' after the pattern of the market place. This relativising of values does reflect an ideological break from assimilation models, which upheld the privileged and absolute values of the dominant society and its educative (civilising) role. The valorisation of the institutional forms of the dominant society as 'universal structures' reveals the partial recognition that notions of cultural equivalence mask. My earlier discussion of the individualising and voluntaristic solutions provided for Aborigines in education policies points to the fact that they are cultural rather than simple political solutions to the Aboriginal 'problem'. In addition, it draws attention to the role of such institutions in reproducing the cultural norms of the dominant society. The individualising strategies of pedagogic practices and the constructions of knowledge in terms of a means/end logic manifested in credentialism both conform to the central cultural values of the dominant society.

9.2. The Politics of Identity

To ascribe to events and actions the label 'politics' is to elevate their social significance. The use of the word invests certain events with a critical importance which separates them from the innocuous or mundane events of the everyday. This flows from their election or alignment with the privileged domain of organised politics, as a dynamic moment in the processes of social and political change. The meaning attributed to 'politics' involves the separation of the organised politics of the public arena from the private sphere of daily life, as if the political and the personal can be treated as unattached domains. Yet, in the daily lives of the Dhan-gadi, the public and the private spheres have continually been dissolved into one precarious ground for the negotiation of identity. Conversely, historical and social change has continually reached the most intimate areas of social and personal life. The contemporary changes in the social circumstances of the Dhan-gadi do not lessen the view of the personal as political.

'Getting the rights' in 1967 removed many of the discriminatory laws and practices that had limited Aborigines' movements and activities in the wider society. The patterns of everyday interaction that had sustained distance and signalled Aboriginal subordination were removed. Formal exclusion could no longer be publicly sanctioned, and informal expressions of Aboriginal inferiority were also rendered more problematical. Here, I refer specifically to those areas of potential or actual contact, particularly in privately-owned shops or businesses, where contact had been avoided by simply denying Aborigines service – 'you couldn't get a feed in Kempsey' and 'you couldn't get a taxi'. In shops where interaction did occur it was usually within the context of an established etiquette which reinforced the Aborigines' inferior status. As one woman put it, 'It got that way, say now you were going to the shop, you gotta wait your turn. See all the whitefellas they'd be served first, you could wait'. Shopkeepers found such exchanges with Aborigines particularly problematic because of the subordinate position they, as the providers of a service, assume in such transactions. They tended to deal with this difficulty by constructing customer hierarchies that affirmed the superior status of both the European customer and the shopkeeper.

Today, by contrast, Aborigines have equal access to shops, and the informal etiquettes have largely disappeared. The development of self-service supermarkets has also considerably reduced the need for uncomfortable interactions. More importantly, though, 'getting the rights' has heightened Aboriginal consciousness and determination with regard to such issues. As the same woman stated, 'Today, you wouldn't want to get in my road. I'd up and tell ya, "Get out of my road, I'm here before you!" But you weren't to do that before'. The removal of the excessive powers of the police over the Aborigines has been another important factor. It was pointed out to me that policemen now have to knock before they enter, which was something they did not do before. Furthermore, as one man stated, today:

> You'd stand up and have an argument. You'd be askin' him, 'What you come here for?' You wouldn't do that before, not on your life. He's just a man today. He was a policeman to us. The kids today, if the policeman come in they'll come out and look up in your [his] face. They don't even run away. Times change.

In effect, many of the overt interpersonal patterns of domination inscribed in bodily gestures of deference and subservience have changed significantly in recent decades, but, in some cases, have been and still are consciously resisted.

Conversely, as a result of the state's social integration policies, the majority of Aborigines are spatially dispersed throughout the municipality of Kempsey and have been given equal access to government institutions and services previously denied them. Today the Dhan-gadi people live in European-style housing, eat European food, wear European-style clothing, drive European cars, attend European schools and speak a distinctive form of English as their only language. They are also involved in many European sports and leisure activities.

The dynamics of this situation have generated a more conscious awareness of collective identity amongst the Dhan-gadi. In this context, the normative values and behaviour associated with a cultural emphasis on sharing assume a greater social significance in expressions of collective identity. The maintenance of daily patterns of interaction (called 'togetherness'), which underpin kinship obligations of mutual aid and support, signify a distinctive aspect of a shared identity. As one man expressed it:

> Our people don't care who's there, they help themselves as much as they like to eat. They're happy to see their people come, we call it given given. They'd be real happy. People come and (ah!). You put the kettle on or whatever you got to boil and have a feed and; you'd be right. . . . They reckon one old lady used to cut her head with tomahawk [she'd be so happy]. I never went that far [laugh].

'Sharing' and 'togetherness' characterised not only distinctive behavioural traits but a set of virtues and values which commonly expressed a sense of collective distinctiveness and cohesion by members of the community.

The shift from a Manichaean world, to use Fanon's term, based on a clear-cut racial dichotomy of social worlds, enforced by laws and the political practices of exclusion, to a situation of formal equality and social integration has markedly transformed the political context. To consider the Aboriginal community as an isolated social and physical entity was (and is) impossible and analytically inappropriate. At the same time, to assume that the construction of a distinctive community identity by the Dhan-gadi is an 'imaginary' representation of their 'real' social experience was (and is) equally inappropriate. The expressions of a subservient consciousness and 'habits of subalternity', described in earlier writings (see especially Reay and Sitlington 1948; and Fink 1955 and 1957), are no longer evident. Instead, a new politics of identity has emerged, in which *self*-affirmation underpins expressions of collective cultural identity and acts in tandem with a political rhetoric of self-determination. In the earlier situation, resistance was related to individual and collective forms of praxis in the everyday life of the total institution (see Chapter 5). Political/racial exclusion, by default, had provided the basis for a collective identity.

In the absence of the relative simplicity of the earlier period, it is not so much the external determinant of *race*, but a more symbolic emphasis on particular *cultural forms* internal to the community which signify identity and membership. The significance of such cultural forms as symbols of distinctiveness have to be understood as part of a cultural resistance to the continuing attempts to construct and control Aboriginal identity. By this, I mean the objectifications of Aborigines, as we have seen earlier, in welfare policy and in the dominant racial discourse of the local European community. Notions such as 'sharing' and 'togetherness', relating to kinship obligations, gain new significance as a distinguishing characteristic of their own humanity. They are also a means of establishing cultural distance between themselves and what is seen as the self-appropriating and self-possessing nature of Europeans. The conscious articulation of a distinctive cultural identity asserts a control over community identity.

Importantly, the notions of 'sharing' and 'togetherness' assert that being born into the community is not enough to sustain membership. One must also socially identify and participate in the activities of the community. Nominally, membership of the community is recognised at birth if one parent is Aborigine. This does not provide so much a biological referent of parental association but a social one of connectedness to a network of kin relations. Men and women generally possess an extensive knowledge of the genealogies of their own family and of other families in the Macleay Valley. What is clear, however, is that the categories the Europeans applied to Aborigines, for example octoroon, quadroon, half-caste, and full-blood, have no relevance to community membership at all. People may describe others as 'half-white' but it is in much the same way as they speak of other Aborigines as being 'half-Dhan-gadi'. Such assertions relate to the scrupulous accuracy with which people map out their genealogical relations rather than to any grid of social acceptability. The major significance is placed on the maintenance of close familial and social ties.

An important contrast to this can be seen in the perception of those Aborigines who have gone 'white fellas way'. They are regarded as having severed or minimalised such familial and social ties with members of the community (either by moving away or making relations unwelcome) and, thereby, of having rejected 'sharing' and 'togetherness' as significant aspects of social interaction. In the case of a woman, brought up on Bellbrook reserve, her marriage to a local European entailed the complete distancing of herself from her family, relatives and friends. From the time of her marriage she did not visit or talk to relatives, and even chance meetings in the street were met with non-recognition and avoidance. Similarly, there is a certain disdain for people who have been able to 'pass for white' but who found 'they had some blackfella in 'em after we got "the rights"' 'cause they thought there might be somethin' in it for 'em'. Those who had 'gone whitefellas way' were described by younger people as 'coconuts' – black on the outside but white on the inside. Such a nominal identification with being Aboriginal by birth alone is rejected. In effect, those who deny notions of mutual aid and support and close ties grounded in familiarity are seen to behave like Europeans.

Social identity is based upon webs of resemblances. Past and present relationships are not perceived in terms of a biological model but are defined primarily in terms of cultural notions of interconnectedness. Relationships are grounded in continuity and duration. Social legitimacy is established through maintaining the emotional bonds that give expression to social connectedness.

The central importance of notions of togetherness and sharing in the contemporary situation, however, is that they perform a dual function – they act as symbols of *distinctiveness* and of *resistance* to the processes of individuation and incorporation within the wider society. The notions of sharing and togetherness provide a counter-critique of the perceived materialism and egoism of the dominant society. As one woman put it, 'Blackfellas always sharing, whitefellas even let their own starve before they'd help 'em.' For this woman, relationships between Europeans are egoistic in nature because they are informed by a concern to satisfy only one's own wants and the setting apart of oneself to the exclusion of others. To satisfy one's needs is to place primary importance on the private domain and to ignore wider social relations. The major criticism levelled at Europeans, and the distinction drawn between them and Aborigines, is that their outlook is focused upon the self-interestedness of the enclosed, individuated family at the expense of wider social relations.

The same criticisms of the self-enclosure which dominated relations between Europeans was expressed in an assessment of the means by which Europeans dealt with conflict. As one man put it, the resolution of conflict differed significantly between the two communities, 'They'd [Aborigines] have a fight and after a set to they'd be good again or they'd have a good row and they'd be friends again. They don't keep their quarrels not like white people. When they [Europeans] get a set on another whitefella, he's finished, forever. They [Aborigines] are too soft hearted they are.' Conflicts between Aborigines were characterised by temporary ruptures, passionate and personalised, which brought about a resolution of conflict but, more importantly, a resumption of social relations in as much as 'they'd be good again' or 'friends again'. What it means to be 'soft hearted' is to be malleable or responsive with regard to close familial or community ties. To be 'soft hearted' corresponds to a moral ordering of sociality which emphasises mutual support and concern.

By contrast, what is seen as abhorrent amongst Europeans is that conflict results in the permanent rupture of social relations 'finished, forever'. Once again, it is the self-contained and egoistic nature of European relations which is juxtaposed with the importance attached to the maintenance of social relations by Aborigines. To be European is to be 'hard hearted' which is to adopt modes of behaviour associated with instrumental and impersonal forms of social interaction. The individualised and depersonalised nature of social relations between Europeans is rejected here.

Underpinning such notions is a construction of self in which primary importance is given to *personal relations*. In this concept of self the individual is perceived, not as a unique entity, but as associated with a particular social status grounded in personal relations and attached to certain obligations. The Aborigines' comprehensive knowledge of genealogies should not be regarded as a lifeless historical archive or instrumental by-product of the regulation of marriages. Such 'domestic histories' are 'accounts for insiders, told anecdotally, assuming much knowledge of the genealogical intricacies and individual foibles' (Barwick 1981: 77). Social connectedness is based on remembrance grounded in intimacy and duration and given expression in the form of personalised knowledge of the contingent and particular. Furthermore, personalised histories are told by reference to family names in the absence of any explicit chronological ordering except as indicated by genealogical levels of the people involved (ibid). Simultaneously, these 'atemporal histories' express the possibilities and limitations of one's own existence as each individual's experience is rendered commensurable through time. The objectification of genealogical ties across generations today is given concretised expression through photographs, which are invariably given a prominent place in Aboriginal homes. These photographs of relatives and friends provide symbolic representations of the network of personal relations into which individuals are embedded.

The concern with genealogies relates to forms of knowledge which provide the basis for an alternative construction of self to that of an autonomous, self-regulating individual: that is, in terms of the former, an objectification of self which is articulated through personalised relations which extend beyond the immediate family. The interconnectedness of self to others is related to those with whom one is familiar: those with whom one is related, one grows up with or, more specifically, those with whom one engages in relations of mutuality; in anthropological terms, relations conducted through the idiom of kinship where notions of generalised reciprocity shape and inform daily interactions. This is primarily reflected in the continuing affiliation of

Aborigines today to the communities they were born in and/or grew up in, i.e. Bellbrook, Greenhill and Burnt Bridge, and the differentiation of local Aborigines from outsiders, i.e. *Aborigines who are unknown.* Such moral and social connectedness provides the constitutive basis for the forms of knowledge associated with extensive genealogies, which are intimately linked to a social construction of reality.

We are dealing with what McKinley (in a personal communication) calls the 'philosophy of human obligations' – the basis of extended kinship relations, where moral obligations within the immediate family are analogically extended to close kin and friends. This is the direct opposite of what pertains in situations or societies where 'altruistic' relations are confined to the nuclear family and differentiated from the contractual relations (which are dissolvable at will) which characterise dealings in the wider social domain. There is an absence of the bridge between domestic and wider social relations, which is characteristic of kinship relations amongst Aborigines. A homology may be seen to exist between the structure of nuclear family relations and a construction of self based on individual personality development (McKinley, personal communication). By contrast, the genealogies the Aborigines possess and preserve are knowledges of self as situated within a network of moral and social relations both within and across generations. The maintenance of such extended kinship relations is a constant self-affirmation of a collective identity.

The emphasis on personal relations is seldom reflected in the structuring of relations between the Dhan-gadi and particular government personnel. The establishment of an Aboriginal medical centre in 1977 provides an anomaly to this pattern. The centre began in the rudimentary conditions of a room in an old weatherboard building which was replaced in 1980 by a newly constructed, fully equipped medical centre. The centre is staffed and administered by Aboriginal people with the exception of the doctor. (Two Aboriginal health workers and a nursing sister have been employed by the NSW Health Commission.) The Aboriginal medical centre has an auxiliary function in relation to the local hospital and other specialist medical services within Kempsey. The most significant result attributed to the establishment of the medical centre has been the dramatic drop in the admissions of Aboriginal children to the local hospital:

> There was an abrupt decrease in the number of admissions of Aboriginal children to Kempsey District Hospital from 1976 to 1977, with further decreases in 1978 and 1979. For the three years 1974 to 1976, the average number of Aboriginal children admitted during the August to October period was 110. This dropped to an average of 74 for the three years 1977 to 1979, a reduction of 33 per cent. The 'bed-days' average declined by 46 per cent from 793 in 1974–1976 to 429 in 1977–1979. Over the same period the number of admis-

Table 11. Admissions of Children to Kempsey District Hospital (1974–1979)

Year	Admissions (Aboriginal)	'Bed-Days' (Aboriginal)	Days in Hospital (Aboriginal)	Admissions (Non-Aboriginal)
1974	98	638	6.5	140
1975	108	619	5.7	134
1976	123	1,121	9.1	132
1977	83	472	5.7	153
1978	78	460	5.9	135
1979	62	354	5.7	162

Source: Copeland 1980: 5.

sions of non-Aboriginal children remained fairly constant. (Copeland 1980: 5)[11]

While the number of admissions of Aboriginal children dropped, the level of admission for non-Aboriginal children has remained the same (see Table 11).

The medical reason for such a sudden change is in the early intervention achieved by the new Aboriginal medical centre. As Copeland (ibid. p. 6) states, 'Aborigines bring their children to the service in the early stages of their illness, rather than waiting until their children are severely ill and then presenting them at the hospital' and 'children with gastroenteritis and chest infections in particular are being treated earlier, and hospital admissions are often avoided'.[12] In social terms it could be argued that the alienating aspects of racism in the wider society had made Aborigines reluctant to use the medical facilities available to the general public. This is no doubt a factor, but the personalisation of relations, which has resulted from the establishment of the medical centre, has also provided a positive element. As Copeland (ibid. p. 5) points out, one of the principle reasons for the shift towards early intervention is 'because the service is staffed and run by *local Aboriginal people* apart from the doctor'. This situation, I should also add, applied to the doctor as well, because he was informally spoken off as 'Doctor Dick', i.e. by his first name rather than his surname.

The personal relationships at the medical centre stand in marked

11. The author is the medical practitioner who has been employed at the medical centre since its beginnings.
12. The significance of this in quantitative terms can be measured in the differences between hospital separations for Aboriginal and non-Aboriginal children under five years in the country towns of NSW. In 1977, the general figures for Aborigines showed that hospital separations for respiratory diseases (bronchitis, emphysema and asthma) were an appalling 549 per 1,000. The rate was seven times higher than for non-Aboriginal children (*Aboriginal Hospital Morbidity in New South Wales* 1979: 15). Parasitic and infective diseases (enteritis and diarrhoea) had a rate of 262 per 1,000, which was eight times higher than among non-Aboriginal children (ibid. p. 16).

contrast to the impersonal and anonymous professional relationships at the local hospital, where competence and qualifications are the primary criteria. This more personal form of care at the auxiliary medical centre was largely responsible for the dramatic decline in the hospitalisation of young children. Conversely, the absence of such relations must be seen as a significant factor in the parents' reluctance to seek medical attention for their children, except in unavoidable situations. The alienation reflected in such patterns is associated with the organisational techniques of bureaucratic apparatuses, where an impersonal rationalised hierarchy of experts dominates interpersonal relations.

Culturally, the presence or absence of personal relations is a distinguishing feature in the patterning of Dhan-gadi social existence. Personal relations provide the maps of meaning for interpreting the social world, which is itself partially shaped by such social patterns of interaction. At the Aboriginal Academy in the Macleay Valley, conscious attempts are made to mediate the institutional forms of relationships and, with the exception of one man, the teachers and other staff are all Aborigines. The staff 'know the life of Aboriginal Australians from their own experience of it', and it is equally important that the teachers are seen to be 'more like uncles and aunts than authority figures' (*MA*, November 1980).

In a more complex way, this counter-critique of the dominant society effectively rejects both the *quantification* of social relations within the general European community and *quantitatively-based* forms of state intervention, such as housing and education. In terms of the latter, the critique of the process of atomisation that accompanies the allocation of state housing was expressed in a locally-produced Aboriginal magazine: 'freedom of movement is restricted . . . we are closed in by walls, by fences, by traffic in the street and so on' (*Bread and Wine* 1981). Such spatial housing patterns serve the needs of an atomised family existence, but inhibit social interactions and fragment social relations based on notions of mutual aid and support.

Similarly, 'sharing' symbolises a rejection of the quantified relations of exchange which serve as the primary means of ordering social interactions. The notion of 'sharing' rejects the behavioural attributes associated with the rational, calculating individual which are seen to reduce European interactions to quantitative, measured relations of exchange. They are viewed as a contrast to the qualitative nature of relationships and the generalised forms of exchange that exist in the Aboriginal community. The individual acquisitiveness of Europeans is related to objectifications of self, articulated through *personal possessions* (for example, property or individual qualifications) rather than *personal relations*.

'Togetherness' symbolises the inverse of the self-enclosed, self-sufficient individual family. It is a denial of the egoistic aspirations of a 'familial culture', or 'culture transmitted in a particular family': in other words, the cultural variation constituted in each family through familial preferences in things such as moral attitudes, material possessions, and patterns of eating and drinking (Reay 1963: 37). Difference is constituted through egoistic preference and through families being structured in opposition to or in competition with other families. This 'subjective', egoistic construction of the private domain is juxtaposed to the impersonal contractual relations of the wider (mass) society. Such social patterns of individuation and atomisation are consistent with constructions of a self-possessing and self-appropriating individual. They stand in opposition to the relations of mutuality which codify for the Dhan-gadi the movement from self to socially-distant others in a manner that extends beyond the closed personal domain.

The construction of a distinctive social identity is not simply an expression of different cultural forms from those of the wider society; it is also a rejection of continuing cultural domination. The assertion of different virtues, values and patterns of behaviour rejects the moral and intellectual hegemony that has characterised the varying forms of colonial domination. The shift in the relations of domination has conditioned a shift in the expressions of a culture of resistance to the bureaucratic and local forms of racism that have recently emerged. Political struggle for these Aborigines is synonymous with a cultural struggle, which is embedded in a resistance that sustains distance from the dominant society. Whether the dominant discourse amongst Europeans about Aborigines was based on biological racism or cultural racism, the fact remains that it has continuously constructed them as 'symbolic failures'. The recent granting of equality to Aborigines has achieved full citizenship status and an end to formal aspects of racial discrimination. However, the predominant forms of state intervention also deny the cultural specificities of Aboriginal existence and, seemingly by default, endorse and perpetuate through various forms of government intervention a continuing cultural/political domination.

9.3. The Politics of the Past

As it aestheticises 'deviant' cultures, cultural pluralism dehistoricises. The particularity of Aborigines' social and historical experience – their conquest, domination and loss of sovereignty – is reduced to a recognition of a reified and restricted notion of cultural particularity, an exaggerated essence. Thus decontextualised, Aboriginality is removed from the contemporary experience of Aborigines in NSW – a contemporary experience which includes an interpretation of the recent past. Nevertheless, such an aestheticisation constructs a form of Aboriginal particularity which is compatible with the new nationalism of multiculturalism.[13] That is, the state appropriates it as a unique aspect of the 'ancient history' of the national heritage which separates Australia from other regional nations.

The cultural pluralist production of the past by the state provides for the ideological incorporation of Aborigines. The conflation of culture as history or history as culture mystifies the historical relations of domination by replacing them with cultural representations of Aborigines in an essentialist form which exist outside time and space. In effect, the legislative guarantees of cultural pluralism provide for expressions of 'ethnic difference', but at the same time enable the state to control and centralise the constructions of these symbolic representations. It is not so much *access to* knowledge but rather the production of knowledge itself that constitutes this hegemonic form of power.

For the Dhan-gadi, an understanding of the 'past' and its uses is derived not only from the immediate contingencies of government policies but also from the meanings and values generated by their own forms of knowledge and experience. The oppositional forms that expressions of collective identity assume can be made apparent if we consider the meanings attributed by Dhan-gadi people to notions of a 'separate heritage'. This is not simply expressed in terms of cultural equivalence, but in opposition to it. The stress in the political rhetoric of cultural pluralism upon equivalence reduces the particularity of Aboriginal 'culture' to one amongst a multiplicity of cultures recognised by the state. For the Dhan-gadi, the meaning of a separate heritage is one that differentiated them from *all* other members of society because it pre-existed European occupation. The focus on being 'the original inhabitants' provides a form of resistance to the globalising aspects of cultural pluralism.[14] This was made apparent to me at a meeting held in Kempsey on Aboriginal education, at which a hapless education officer was praising the more enlightened attitude to *ethnic groups* in the school system. He was immediately challenged by a woman who stated that Aborigines were not an 'ethnic' group but the original inhabitants. The dangers inherent in the recognition of ethnic groups by the state is that such cultural equivalence threatens to subsume the historical particu-

13. The most explicit expression of this 'new nationalism' was made by the prime minister in 1982 (cited Kalantzis, Cope and Hughes 1984/5: 195–6). 'We cannot demand of people that they renounce the heritage they value, and yet expect them to feel welcome as full members of our society. . . . Multiculturalism . . . sees diversity as a quality to be actively embraced, a source of social wealth and dynamism. . . . The [Galbally] report [has] identified multiculturalism as a key concept in formulating government policies and recognises that Australia is at a critical stage in its development as a multicultural nation.'

14. This opposition to the globalising aspects of multiculturalism is also reflected at a state level in the non-participation of Aboriginal groups in the annual folkloric festival. The festival is held in Sydney and symbolically expresses the ethnic diversity of Australian culture. It is celebrated in a parade that winds its way through the streets of Sydney where different national/cultural origins are displayed through music, dance and dress.

larities of Aboriginal existence. For Aborigines in the Macleay Valley, cultural pluralism has generated a process of ethnogenesis. This process has been defined as 'the generating of new forms of social life – dialectically related to the spirit, but not duplicating the letter of the past' (Diamond 1974: 23). Cultural pluralism has provided the basic conditions for Aborigines to articulate a more sharply-defined cultural identity through their dealings with state apparatuses (for example, the legal system, medical care and housing). At the same time this is heightened by the political necessity of differentiating themselves from other ethnic groups. Elements of the past are drawn upon to assert this distinctiveness. For example, as a locally-produced Aboriginal magazine states, 'The Aboriginal people have retained the spiritual values of our Dreamtime; togetherness and sharing is still a natural part of our lives; but we no longer share our campfires, only our micro-wave ovens!!!' (*Bread and Wine*, 1981). Continuity with the past is stressed here as the unifying source of identity. Social identity is preserved in the perpetuation of inner values, untouched by a material world largely shaped and dominated by a European presence. In this context, the symbolism of the 'Dreaming' evokes an identification with values that pre-existed and survived the impositions of the new sovereign order.

At the same time, the importance of maintaining a distinctive social identity is expressed in terms of regaining what has been lost and a need to get back to earlier and superior forms of social life. For a number of people this was to be achieved by what was spoken of as a 'cultural renaissance' through the revival of the initiation ceremonies. During the period of my research, the surviving initiated men were placed under increasing pressure to put the young men 'through the rule'. In effect, the demand was for a more conspicuous and institutionalised expression of cultural distinctiveness which characterises the assertiveness now attached to public aspects of collective identity. For young men, a return to the integrity of Dhan-gadi identity is to be achieved through the revival of such ceremonies.[15]

The use of government funding to purchase a minibus, with which to transport young boys to bush sites, was another expression of this phenomenon. Ostensibly, the aim of the excursions was to provide a formal context in which older men could transfer their skills and knowledge about bush foods to the young boys. The meaning of such a practice was, however, conceived to extend beyond the mere transfer of technically-usable knowledge. Indeed, the learning of bush skills was simultaneously equated with the acquiring of men's esoteric knowledge. The absence of women from such excursions, particularly in a social domain where they would normally have been included,

---

15. No initiation ceremonies were held during the period of my fieldwork. However, in late 1985, after a 50-year break, such a ceremony was held.

emphasised that the transfer of knowledge involved both secular and esoteric forms of knowledge restricted to men. This not only involved the young boys in learning what was called 'men's dancing', which included public performances, but also the acquisition of 'inside knowledge'.

Nevertheless, the 'revival' of the past was not unproblematical; neither was it universally approved of within the community. For some, it was felt better to 'leave it alone' – a concern determined less by a desire to forget or to turn away from the past than from a recognition that they were dealing with dangerous mystical forces.[16] The 'past', in this context, is not a lifeless ensemble of habits, beliefs and artifacts. The transfer of knowledge 'not for women's eyes' involves an engagement with mystical forces which is potentially dangerous for those participating. Therefore, the capacity and expertise of those in authority to manipulate and constrain such forces to the safety of those involved and perhaps the community in general, was a major point of discussion.

The excursions reflected organisational principles and engaged forms of knowledge that were different from the pedagogic practices of the state. These principles were premised on differential, rather than universal, access to knowledge. In addition, the participation of those in the minibus excursions reflected differential selection based upon the mobilisation of kinship and other social affiliations. This also applied to those seeking to revive the initiation ceremonies. The state's practices, by contrast, are associated with universal access to knowledge embedded within a cultural logic which assumes the equivalence of individuals as independent units. Concomitantly, such knowledge realises its full potential in a person's ability to mobilise it in a strategising manner or, more generally, as technically-usable knowledge. The efficacy of knowledge is constituted as a resource and is chiefly conceived of within a cultural logic associated with instrumental or purposive rationalism. Social differentiation is linked to a model based upon the strategising individual. The constitution of knowledge, as referred to above for the Dhan-gadi, realises its full potential in the ability to differentiate between the 'illusory' and 'truth', which is determined by the possession of secret knowledge.[17] The perpetuation of the possession of exclusive understandings determines the organisation of knowledge and provides an important basis for social differentiation.

These social activities are marginal in terms of overall government

16. Another example of this was expressed to me in an anecdotal story about a man living in the community whose father had been a 'cleva fella'. When his father had died his 'dilly bag' containing dangerous substances used in sorcery had been hung over his grave. His son had never ventured near it fearing the harm it would do him.
17. I draw this point from a private communication with Andrew Lattas.

policy. Their importance is that they reveal differences in a context where the Dhan-gadi themselves exercise a large degree of control. In them, we are dealing with cultural differences objictified in a relatively unmediated context. There is an objectification of internal differentiation that reveals a structure of shared assumptions. It is difference rather than opposition to the organisational forms of the state that is expressed here, although the distinction between difference and opposition is never complete. That such practices occur 'in the breach rather than as the rule' directs attention to the hegemonic nature of cultural pluralism.

Conversely, the oppositional practices of the process of ethnogenesis are produced within this structural relationship. It draws our attention to an essential feature of ethnogenesis; that is, the regaining of control over the production of knowledge of ones own cultural and political identity. By definition, this requires the establishment of some form of social closure (see Neuwirth 1969; Dolgin and Magdoff 1977). Commonality is established through the identification of a special relationship between specific social practices and values and a collective notion of self. The concepts of group and person are metonymised.

In this context, 'bush tucker' has gained a greater significance. Previously, the effects of domination had rendered problematical what Europeans called 'dirty blackfella food'. Even today, this legacy is revealed in the ambiguous way people will delight in describing the eating of different bush foods while reassuring me (a European) as to how clean such cooking is. Nevertheless, despite these problematical vestiges, 'bush tucker' is one of the sources for the demarcation of a distinctive identity. Thus, as stated earlier, a community bus was purchased to teach young boys, amongst other things, knowledge and skills related to bush foods. Ideologically, what is reaffirmed through such practices is a special relationship expressed in terms of access to, and control and understanding of, a body of knowledge and skills not available to others. In effect, those capable of participating in and understanding such a relationship are also differentiated. The reintroduction of young boys, in a formal context, to such practices gains new significance as an important aspect of the reclamation of identity.

This is often extended further in assertions that 'white fella' food is a big problem affecting Dhan-gadi people. It is said that Dhan-gadi men, for example, were 'bigger and stronger' in the past because they were healthier through eating 'bush tucker'. As one man put it, 'You only gotta look at the mens in them days, womens [too] all big. I tell 'em today they're not worth looking at, they're skinny. Since they got on the white man's food, they went to pieces.' The body is used here as a metonym of the social condition of the Dhan-gadi. Central to such ideological statements is the relationship between food and a collective notion of self. The relationship asserted here is between culturally-specific items of food and the images of the Dhan-gadi themselves.[18]

The ethnogenesis of the Dhan-gadi is indicative of a major shift in the politics of opposition. For most of this century, expressions of Aboriginality have been a distinct social and political disadvantage. Previously, the political opposition of Aborigines has been constructed in terms of the political idioms of the dominant society, i.e. appeals to egalitarianism based on equal rights or human rights. Such a political response sought to expose the hypocrisy of the dominant society by challenging it in the context of its own ideology. The distinguishing feature of opposition in the contemporary context is contained within the overt expressions of a collective identity drawn from a common past and associated with a distinctive social identity.

The legitimacy of their right to speak and articulate their own experiences underpins an increasing awareness of the politics of identity. The metonymic connection of Dhan-gadi identity with a specialised body of knowledge in effect denies Europeans the capacity to gain *authentic* access to, and understanding of, matters Aboriginal. The oppositional aspect of the politics of identity is directly linked to the politics of representation itself. Such a cultural politics moves away from the redistributive politics of equal rights and egalitarianism to the politics of difference. The emergence of the politics of culture is linked to what Jameson (1984) calls the struggle of the 'inner colonised' – indigenous minorities, ethnic groups, deviants, other marginals and, differently, women. I would argue, following Foucault (1980a), that these are the groups and individuals most subjected to the gaze of experts and authorities and, hence, to modes of objectification outside their control. Domination is not necessarily constituted through restrictions to access to knowledge; it can also be constituted through control of the production of knowledge itself, i.e. through the establishment of a hierarchy which denies the legitimacy of such groups to speak for themselves except through some mediated form.

Fundamentally, the assertions of a distinctive identity provide a challenge to those forms of hegemonic power. The rejection of the validity of constructions of identity by others is not simply a question of 'understanding', but, more specifically, a rejection of the forms of control that such objectifications sustain. As Aborigines in Kempsey pointed out, they did not want to be studied 'like animals' or 'like plants in a green house' or, stated more directly, 'you are here to steal our secrets'. What such statements refer to are the relations of power associated with being turned into an object of knowledge. An explicit connection is seen to be made between Aborigines and lesser forms of life, such as animals and plants.

18. See Carter (1983) for a more comprehensive development of the use of the body as a metaphor of Aboriginal identity in another NSW community.

Perhaps, more importantly, what is identified is a relationship in which they lose control of their own identity. Thus, the politics of identity is an expression of resistance to attempts to make Aborigines experience themselves in the terms defined by the dominant society.

The politics of cultural pluralism has generated two conflicting processes. At the same time as the state attempts to encourage expressions of cultural distinctiveness, it also attempts to centralise and control them by demarcating particular institutional sites for their expression. Conversely, they provide a focus for notions of separate identity which exist beyond those constructed by the state.

This is evident in the development of the main issue of the late 1970s for Aboriginal groups – land rights – which opened up a new site of major political concern. In 1977, for example, the NSW Aboriginal Land Council was formed to struggle for the recognition of land rights in the state (see Wilkie 1985). This was an independent body organised and controlled by Aborigines and open to all Aboriginal communities. It was formed shortly after land rights had been granted to groups in the Northern Territory the previous year.

Between 1977 and 1981, the Aboriginal Land Council received ten land claims from regional groups to submit to the NSW government (see *Land Claims in NSW* 1981). Furthermore, the claims for land rights were outside the ambit of the Commonwealth legislation, which required demonstrable evidence of comprehensive religious links with the land as the sole criteria (see Maddock 1983). The report of the New South Wales Parliamentary Committee on Aboriginal Land Rights (1980: 62) recommends four bases for claims to land – need (spiritual, social and economic); compensation (both monetary and land); long association; and traditional rights.[19] The boundaries established for land rights under Commonwealth legislation were redefined and expanded within these recommendations. My point is that the cultural pluralist environment has also led to the empowerment of the political practices of Aboriginal groups and facilitated the process of ethnogenesis.

Through its attempts to control the construction of Aboriginality, the state has also provided an arena in which such ideological constructions can be contested. As I mention earlier, the ideological aspect of cultural pluralism is found in the mystification of historical relations

19. In 1983, the NSW parliament passed the Aboriginal Land Rights Act, which provided for the establishment of regional land councils to be funded from 7.5 per cent of state land tax revenues for 15 years. However, the Act provided little scope for land rights. The regional land councils could only make claims for unwanted crown lands: this excluded private property and crown land held by, or in the future subject to use by the government. In effect, they could only have land that the dominant society could find no use for. What was considered the most cynical exercise, however, was the simultaneous introduction of the Crown Lands Act (1983) validating previous illegal revocations of Aboriginal reserves and stations (see Wilkie 1983).

between Aborigines and the dominant society. In the 'plagiarised' expressions of Aboriginal culture, they are 'assimilated' as 'cultural/ historical' figures who symbolically represent the ancient heritage of the modern Australian nation. They originated in mainland South East Asia; they developed a rich, complex and distinctive culture, finely tuned to their environment, and their oldest art pre-dates the prehistoric cave paintings of Europe (see footnote 4). The heritage of the 'first Australians' is given a unique place as the national heritage, which both separates from and unites multicultural Australia with its regional neighbours.

The processes that facilitate the production of Aborigines in this emblematic form generate a series of contradictions which emerged most clearly at local community level. The complexities of this interplay can be seen in the relations that developed between the Aborigines and the National Parks and Wildlife Service (NPWS) in the early 1980s. Under the National Parks and Wildlife Act (1974), this agency was empowered to administer the Act and identify, record and protect Aboriginal places of significance and *relics*. The control, protection and acquisition (if deemed necessary) remained in the hands of the director of the NPWS (Act no. 80: 57). Such relics were 'deemed to be the property of the crown', and the director was empowered to take legal action against those who disturbed or removed them (ibid. pp. 75–9). In effect, the intention of the state was to record, protect and preserve those *remaining* objects/features of an Aboriginal heritage as an aspect of the state's history. An important aspect of this, based on an initiative of the NPWS, is the identification of sacred sites primarily as artifacts or relics of an Aboriginal heritage. The policy implemented was to fence off such sites and to erect public signs to explain their significance for Aborigines, as well as the penalties that would be incurred for interference, destruction or removal (ibid. p. 78).

The Act provides the only legislation for the protection of sites and artifacts identified as significant by Aborigines in NSW (see Haigh n.d.), and the NPWS has played a major part in protecting important Aboriginal sites. Its most successful venture has probably been saving the sites at Mumbler Mountain in southern NSW from the encroachments of an international wood-chipping operation (see Egloff 1979). As an institution, the NPWS has also performed an important role in actively encouraging Aborigines to participate in this work. Through its policies of protection and participation, the NPWS has provided both a focus for and a stimulus to the sense of identity developing in many Aboriginal communities. However, the ideological frame in which the legislation operates is what concerns us here, for the terms of the protection and preservation of the Aboriginal heritage are couched in the cultural logic of the dominant society. In the first place, the legislation deems the sites, as well as other *relics*, worthy of control so that they might survive to be appreciated by *all* members of the state and succeeding generations.[20] This secular/temporal understanding of the sites reduces them to historical artifacts, things of the past.

For initiated men, however, both the Dhan-gadi and the Gumbaing-irr, the control of and access to such sites poses a major dilemma. As one man put it:

> *In the old days we looked after our sacred sites ourselves without letting white people, white men and white women taking care of them. We know what to do and that's why I always say they should never interfere with our sacred things.* If there were a lot of things that weren't sacred that's alright for them to go and see. Kiddies of ours, even young men, we wouldn't let them go past our sacred sites, trees even, that was anywhere in the bush or sacred site rocks. We wouldn't let 'em go because they wasn't men. They had to be initiated *before* they could go to these things and they are sacred to us, *very sacred things.* We don't say nothing to anybody because we look after these things ourselves. That's why we don't like white women or white men coming to ask different things about our things or they should do this or that. . . . That's our sacred places. Our young people, young men, they should never be there either because its not right. It's not right at all. They should be all initiated before they get the job on the Parks and Wildlife to do these jobs.

In effect, the dilemma arose out of conceptions of access that were markedly different from those framed in the legislation. Differential access to the sites had been changed to egalitarian access in the legislation. Indeed, the NPWS's practice of fencing off and signposting such sites was premised on notions of public, egalitarian access. For these Aboriginal men, however, the principle is one of restricted and differential access, as such sites are part of a body of secret/sacred knowledge. They distinguish between members within the Aboriginal community as well as 'white men and women'.

Authority and care of such sites is conditional on control of a particular body of knowledge gained through initiation ceremonies. Such sacred sites are not invested simply with a secular historical significance but are associated with mystical sanctions and mystical powers. They do not symbolically represent a past heritage but are sites where mystical power resides in a concretised form. As one man put it, 'you can't act the goat with our law, it'll kill you'. This statement was made in the course of discussing a transgression of ritual in an earlier period, when, it was asserted, a young initiate had violated eating taboos. In this, he had eaten a 'wild' turkey in defiance of ritual sanctions; in the result 'feathers and bones [turkey's] came out his knees'. The ritual

---

20. It should be noted that the head of the NPWS's Aboriginal and Historical Resources Unit has made a similar point: 'We consider that we should remove the word "relic" from the Act. It denotes culture no longer exists and belies the fact of Aboriginal culture today' (cited Wilkie 1985: 103).

sanction is conceptualised here in terms of an analogical transfer of properties attributed to the agency of mystical force. Such analogical thought reflected the retention of a more anthropomorphic view of the world in which all elements 'are bound up in a world of efficacy' (Cassirer 1956: 157).

The influence of this mystical connection, where analogical thought and action are evident, is apparent in the case of an Aboriginal man who developed cancer whilst recording sites for the NPWS. The young man involved had previously been initiated as a *Dilkirr* (see Chapter 3). Yet, when he developed cancer, it was said that this was due to his work on sacred sites which were too powerful for him. The logic of the construction of the illness was connected with an analogical transfer through direct contact with such sites. As forms of knowledge and understanding of the social world, they differ significantly from those that prevail in the wider society.

It is not contended that this apprehension of reality in itself provides an independent and homogenous world view that sustains a clear-cut distinction between the Dhan-gadi and the wider society. The causal relationship between a mystical agency and illness and death is no longer held as a totalising world view. Indeed, the effectivity of a mystical agency is seen to be active largely upon those participating in the now specialised and restricted domain of religious activities. Generally, illness in everyday life is considered to be a pathological condition of the body as it is in the wider society; but, as in the specific case above, it can still be considered to be causally related to an independent object associated with a mystical agency which may enter and damage the body. The perception of social relations and the classification of social experience retain distinctive differences from their counterparts in the wider society. Such an apprehension of the world stands in direct contrast to the secular historical view that underpins the state's appropriation of Dhan-gadi sacred sites.

These cultural forms condition opposition to the hegemonic appropriations of Aboriginal 'history' and 'heritage'. The processes of cultural incorporation serve to heighten an Aboriginal sense of identity, which challenges rather than utilises the conventional political idioms of the state. The conscious articulation of a collective social and cultural history stresses the uniqueness and particularity of an Aboriginal identity, which had pre-existed European occupation. As one man stated:

> . . . before the white people came over here from pommie land or England . . . to come and take over our country, they [Aborigines] carried on as before they [Europeans] ever came across here. They [Aborigines] carried out business in their own way. They did it properly. . . . It all belong the Aborigines of Australia. You fellas, the white fellas, have come here and tell us what to

do, do it this way and do it that way.

The essential contradiction of European occupancy is emphasised here. It is their dispossession, domination and loss of sovereignty that provides the foundation for the development of the modern state. By locating the 'otherness' of Aborigines within its own institutional sites, the state has attempted to contain and control the *possible sites* and expressions of 'otherness'. They have also provided new areas of struggle in the construction of identity which resist such hegemonic relations of power.

Appendices

Appendix I: Article published by Burnt Bridge resident, George Davis (n.d.)

The Aborigines of Australia

Their Birthrights and Lines of Life

The women are divided into four lines: –

1. Gargungunie
2. Gourangunie
3. Wongungunie
4. Wirrgungunie

The men are also divided into four lines: –

1. Wizongunie
2. Gurbungunie
3. Muszongunie
4. Wombongunie

These are the birth lines of women: –

The daughters of Gargungunie (1) will be Gourangunie (2)
The daughters of Gourangunie (2) will be Gargungunie (1)
The daughters of Wongungunie (3) will be Wirrgungunie (4)
The daughters of Wirrgungunie (4) will be Wongungunie (3)

These are the birth lines of men: –

The sons of Wizongunie (1) will be Gurbungunie (2)
The sons of Gurbungunie (2) will be Wizongunie (1)
The sons of Muszongunie (3) will be Wombongunie (4)
The sons of Wombongunie (4) will be Muszongunie (3)

A Wizongunie boy (1), on coming of age, marries a Gargungunie woman (1).
A Gurbungunie boy (2), on coming of age, marries a Wirrgungunie woman (4).
A Muszongunie boy (3), on coming of age, marries a Wongungunie woman (3).
A Wombongunie boy (4), on coming of age, marries a Gourangunie woman (2).

All births are born under what is known as Bugghar (totem) living, or eatable.

————

There are two classes of Kangaroos, the red and the grey.
The red is called Moolong, the grey, Womboyne.

230

There are four classes of Wallabies: –

    1. Bulcoon   = Forest Wallaby
    2. Murrong = Scrub Wallaby
    3. Birriga   = Rock Wallaby
    4. Birraigun = Wallaroo

There are two native names for the Scrub Paddymelon, viz: –

    Mucoong and Booyong

There are three classes of Opossums: –

    1. Whatoo   = Forest Opossum
    2. Kindang = Scrub Opossum
    3. Bookaree = Sugar Opossum, whose habitation is
                           where there is a scrubby patch

There is only one kind of Native Bear, called Goola or Yurri, and only one kind of Porcupine, called Thurakil.

If there is a death, any of the four lines is forbidden to eat any of the above for a period of from one, two, three, four, or five years, in honour of a near relative.

———

No man was permitted to take a woman unto himself before he had passed through the Law, and not under five years after he had passed through. The woman had to be handed over to him by the Chief of the Heads of the Tribe. If he takes a woman without their consent, the penalty is Death. He would be put into a circle, known as a Gourrai, and there openly put to death.

A young woman must be a certain age before she can be handed over to her man that has the right to her by the Law. The age must be twenty-two, or over. She must be fully developed, called in the native language, Gnubbong.

———

The age of a boy was judged by his hair, (native name, Gethung).

The four lines of men and women were judged by their hair:–

    A Gurbungunie has straight, coarse hair
    A Muszongunie has straight, fine hair
    A Wizongunie has coarse, curly hair
    A Wombongunie has fine, curly hair

The women were judged in the same way. They were known, in any part of Australia, by any of the tribes, by their hair.

The way they used to tell the years was by the shedding of the bark of different trees, once a year. One of the trees is a grey gum, called Thurriburbung. Another is the Eucalyptus, called Yarrabung. The blue gum or flooded gum is called Gulaibung. The black butt is Yumbulabung.

Also, trees in bloom: – Tallowwood = Garlybung; Bloodwood = Ghuribung;

Ironbark = Burragirbung; Sallywattle = Cooperongbung.

These are the main trees by which they tell the years.

Names of Places in the Native Tongue

Euroka was a place, that was dense scrub, with a clear spot, where the natives used to go in the morning, when the sun shines, to get the sun. They therefore called it Yoorooka, meaning sun.

Dondingalong = Thundengulung = Apple tree flat
Dungay = Thungair = Forrest Iguana
Mooparaba = Morparabung = a tree that grows by the creek, or scrub, bearing a red fruit or red blossoms
Yarrahappini = Yurriyuppinni = a bear rolling down a hill
Kurri Kurri means 'be quick'
Kunderang Station = Kundorang = a male Wallaby
Taree = Thurrimy = Forest Gum Tree
Toorooka = Thurookul = Stones in the river bed, where they used to go to practice pelting one another with stones, turning them off with their shields
Warbro Station = Wopra = a male Kangaroo

All mothers-in-law in the four lines of women are called Boring or Buccai. All sons-in-law are Buccais. They must not speak to one another while life remains, or even look at each other, according to Law or Birth-lines. These Birth-lines must be strictly kept, until they die.

These are the lines of life in the early days in this great land of Australia.

The author of above particulars is

GEO. R. DAVIS
Burnt Bridge, Macleay
River, NSW

Appendix II

List 1: Mid-North Coast Reserves established between 1880–1908*

*Lower Macleay River***

(1) Shark Island, No. 10187, 360 acres, 23.11.1889, Parish of Arakoon, County of Macquarie. Occupied Billy Taylor, Rob Roy. Revoked 3.9.1920.

(2) Little Shark Island, Whisky Island, No. 17537, 25 acres, 15.4.1893, Parish of

* Compiled from oral history sources and official records.
** Three other men, Ned Hoskins, Charlie Douglas and Albert Woodlands, are known to have lived on land at Belmore River on the Lower Macleay. In both official records and local accounts, the land and farms are mentioned but its location to my knowledge has not been officially recorded.

Clybucca, County of Dudley. Revoked 25.4.1919.

(3) Kinchela Creek Reserve, No. 173a also 59762, 11 acres, 2 roods, 28.7.1884, Parish of Kinchela, County of Macquarie. Occupied by 'Big Bob' (1890). Revoked 28.2.1969.

(4) Kinchela Reserve, No. 174, 2.75 acres, 23.4.1883, Parish of Arakoon, County of Macquarie, locality Long Reach on river. Occupied by William Drew.

(5) Kinchela Reserve, No. 57397, 26 acres, 29.8.1924 (Kinchela Boys Home), Parish of Arakoon, County of Macquarie. Occupied and cleared William Drew (1880). Not revoked.

(6) Pelican Island, No. 251, 80 acres, 25.11.1885, Parish of Arakoon, County of Macquarie. Occupied by Fred Drew, George Drew and Thomas Mark (1883). Revoked 21.11.1924.

(7) Fattorinni Islands, No. 252, 14 acres, 25.11.1885, Parish of Kinchela, County of Macquarie. Occupied by John Moseley (1883). Revoked 20.3.1925. No. 253, 27 acres, 25.11.1885. Occupied by James Linwood (1883), Bob Moran (1886). Revoked 20.3.1925.

(8) Burnt Bridge (Euroka Creek), Nos. 20865, 20866, 172 acres, 9.6.1894, Parish of Kalateenee, County of Dudley. Occupied by John Moseley, Albert Moseley, Thomas Moseley, George Davis, Eugene Miranda, William Richie, Richard Dungay and William Dungay. Revoked 16.4.1956. No. 27273, 365 acres, 19.2.1898. Revoked 17.7.1956.

(9) Sherwood Reserve, No. 12998, 146 acres 3 roods, 29.11.1890, Parish of Kullatine, County of Dudley. Revoked 3.2.1919.

Upper Macleay

(10) Bellbrook Reserve, No. 49982, 40 acres, (1885); 65 acres, (1892); 90 acres, (1914). Dick Kelly, Harry Callaghan, Bill (Wombo) Murray, Billy Holton, Alick Thompson, Harry Vale, Jack Scott, Billy Mills, Ralph Quinlan, Gilbert Duckett, George Mackie, Harry Parry, Jimmy Jackie and George Crawford, Parish of Nulla Nulla, County of Dudley. Not revoked.

Hastings River

(11) Brill Brill Creek, No. 2598, 87 acres, 30.10.1886, Parish of Cogo, County of Macquarie. Occupied by Jim Davis, Dick Dungay, Murray with families.

(12) Cairncross Reserve, No. 19474, 10 acres, 13.1.1894 – located at Ballangarra, Rollands Plain (Wilson River) – Parish of Cairncross, County of Macquarie. Occupied (1914) Percy Moseley. Revoked 20.11.1964.

Bowraville/Nambucca

(13) Stuarts Island, No. 140, 70 acres, 14.5.1883, Parish of Nambucca, County of Raleigh. Revoked 22.4.1955.

(14) Deep Creek/Cow Creek, No. 31243, 40 acres, 28.7.1900, Parish of Valley Valley, County of Raleigh. Occupied by Fred Buchanan 15.3.1916 (hut extension). Revoked 4.4.1952.

(15) Allgomera Creek, No. 38625, 20 acres, 10.12.1904, Parish of Allgomera, County of Raleigh. Revoked ?.10.1962. No. 39584, 28 acres, 26.8.1905, Parish of Allgomera, County of Raleigh. Occupied J. Donovan. Revoked 7.5.1920.

(16) Wirrimbi Island, No. 42775, 9 acres, 3.6.1908, Parish of Bowra, County of Raleigh. Occupied by the Dottai family (2-roomed hut) 30.3.1916. Revoked 1924.

Urunga

(17) Urunga Island/Yellow Rock, No. 12679, 250 acres, 24.10.1891, Parish of South Bellingen, County of Raleigh. Occupied by Norman Binalong. Move from Urunga Island to Yellow Rock, 7.12.1921. Officially closed to Aborigines May 1937. Revoked 17.12.1954.

List 2: Aboriginal Farmers on the Macleay River (from Official Records)

Fattorinni Island

1883	John Moseley, wife and 5 children	14 acres
	Jim Linwood, wife and 2 children	27 acres
1886	Bob Moran moved onto island with Jim Linwood	
1891*	John Moseley, 5 men and 5 women	
	Jim Linwood, 1 man and 11 women	
	Bob Moran, 5 men and 6 women	

Pelican Island

1883	Fred Drew	14 acres
	George Drew	14 acres
	Thomas Mark	11 acres
1890	Fred Drew	16 acres
	George Drew	15 acres
	Thomas Mark	16 acres
	Ned Anderson (Cook?)	9 acres
	Clarence Jimmi	9 acres
1891*	Fred Drew, 2 men and 4 women	
	George Drew, 2 men and 2 women	
	Thomas Mark, 1 man and 2 women	
	Ned Cook, 2 men and 2 women	
	Mark Drew, 1 man and 2 women	
	Clarence Jimmi, 1 man and 1 woman	

Shark Island

1890   Billy Taylor
                         Rob Roy

1891[*]   Billy Taylor, 5 men and 3 women
                         Jimmy Taylor, 2 men and 5 women

Kinchela

1884   William Drew 10 acres, had already been there
                         for 4 years

1890   William Drew

1891[*]   Billy Stewart, 7 men and 4 women

References

Altman, J.C. and J. Nieuwenhuysen 1979. *The economic status of Australian Aborigines*, Cambridge: Cambridge University Press.

Amin, S. 1973. *Neo-colonialism in West Africa*, London: Monthly Review Press.

Andrews, A. 1979 (1920). *First settlement of the Upper Murray*, Sydney: Library of Australian History.

Barwick, D.E. 1972. 'Coranderrk and Cumeroogunga: pioneers and policy', in T. Epstein and D. Penny (eds), *Opportunity and response*, London: Hurst & Company.

——1981. 'Writing Aboriginal history: comments on a book and its reviewers', *Canberra Anthropology*, 4 (2), 74–86.

Bauman, Z. 1985. 'On the origins of civilization: a historical note', *Theory, Culture and Society*, 2 (3), 7–14.

Beckett, J. 1958. 'A study of a mixed-blood Aboriginal community in the pastoral west of New South Wales', M.A. thesis, Australian National University, 296 pp.

——1964. 'Aborigines, alcohol and assimilation', in M. Reay (ed.), *Aborigines now*, Sydney: Angus & Robertson.

—— 1965. 'Kinship, mobility and community among part-Aborigines in rural Australia', *International Journal of Comparative Sociology*, 1 (1), 7–23.

—— 1982. 'The Torres Strait Islanders and the Pearling Industry: A Case of Internal Colonialism,' in M. Howard (ed.), *Aborigines and Power in Australian Society*, St Lucia: University of Queensland Press.

—— 1983. 'Internal colonialism in a welfare state', paper presented at American Anthropological Association, Chicago.

Bee, R. and R. Gingerich 1977. 'Colonialism, classes and ethnic identity: native American and the national political economy', *Studies in Comparative International Development*, 12 (2), 70–93.

Bell, J. 1959. 'Official policies towards the Aborigines of New South Wales', *Mankind*, 5 (8), 345–55.

—— 1964. 'Assimilation in New South Wales', in M. Reay (ed.), *Aborigines now*, Sydney: Angus & Robertson.

Belshaw, J. 1978. 'Population distribution and the pattern of seasonal movement', in I. McBryde (ed.), *Records of times past*, Canberra: AIAS.

Berndt, R. 1976. 'Territoriality and the problem of demarcating socio-cultural space', in *Tribes and boundaries in Australia*, Canberra: AIAS.

Blainey, G. 1966. *The tyranny of distance*, Melbourne: Sun Books.

——1975. *Triumph of the nomads*, Melbourne: MacMillan.

Bleakley, J.W. 1961. *The Aborigines of Australia: their history, their habits, their assimilation*, Brisbane: Jacaranda.

Blomfield, G. 1981. *Baal Belbora: the end of the dancing*, Chippendale: Alternative Publishing Cooperative Limited.

Bowle, J. 1974. *The imperial achievement*, Sydney: Penguin.

Brenner, R. 1977. 'The origins of capitalist development: a critique of neo-Smithian Marxism', *New Left Review*, 104, 25–92.

Broom, L. and F.L. Jones 1973. *A blanket a year, Aborigines in Australian society*, Canberra: Australian National University Press.

Broome, R. 1982. *Australian Aborigines*, Sydney: Allen & Unwin.

Brown, K. 1984. 'A bad year for avocados: Blainey and immigration', *Arena*, 67, 70–7.

Butlin, S. 1968. *Foundations of the Australian monetary system 1788–1851*, Sydney: Sydney University Press.

Calley, M. 1957. 'Race relations on the north coast of New South Wales', *Oceania*, 15 (4), 296–323.

Campbell, I. 1978. 'Settlers and Aborigines: the pattern of contact on the New England Tableland 1832–1860', in I. McBryde (ed.), *Records of times past*, Canberra: AIAS.

Campbell, J.F. 1968, *'Squatting' on crown lands in New South Wales, 1835–1847*, Melbourne: Melbourne University Press.

Campbell, V. 1978a. 'Ethnohistorical evidence on the diet and economy of the Aborigines of the Macleay River Valley', in R. McBryde (ed.), *Records of times past*, Canberra: AIAS.

Carter, J. 1983. 'The body: sources of mediation of Aboriginal identity', paper given to AAS Conference, Adelaide University.

Cassirer, E. 1956. *The philosophy of symbolic forms, mythical thought*, vol. 2, London: Yale University Press.

Castle, R. and J. Hagan 1978. 'Dependence and independence: Aboriginal workers on the far south coast 1920–75', in A. Curthoys and A. Markus, *Who are our enemies?*, Neutral Bay: Hale & Iremonger.

Clark, D. 1975. 'Australia: victim or partner of British imperialism', in E. Wheelwright and K. Buckley (eds), *Essays in the political economy of Australian capitalism*, vol. 1, Sydney: Australia & New Zealand Book Company.

Clark, M. 1984. *A short history of Australia*, Melbourne: MacMillan Press.

Cochrane, P. 1980. *Industrialisation and dependence*, St Lucia: University of Queensland Press.

Coleman, J. 1981. 'A new look at the north coast: fish traps and "villages"', in S. Bowdler (ed.), *Coastal archaeology in eastern Australia*.

Collmann, J. 1979. 'Fringe camps and the development of Aboriginal administration in central Australia', *Social Analysis*, 2, 38–57.

Copeland, R. 1980. 'The effect of an Aboriginal medical service on admissions of children to hospital in a NSW country town', *Medical Journal of Australia*, special supplement on Aboriginal health, 1 (1), 5–6.

Cousins, D. and J. Nieuwenhuysen 1984. *Aborigines and the mining industry*, Sydney: Allen & Unwin.

Creamer, H. 1977. 'Malaise and beyond', in P. Stanbury (ed.), *The moving frontier*, Sydney: A. & W. Reed Pty Ltd.

Curr, E.M. 1886. *The Australian race*, vol. 3, Melbourne: Ferres.

Curtin, W. 1980. *Situation statement, dairying in the Macleay District 1980*, Kempsey: District Livestock Office.

Deleuze, G. 1977. 'Nomad thought', in D. Allison (ed.), *The new Nietzsche*, Delta Press.

Detmold, M. 1985. *The Australian Commonwealth*, Sydney: The Law Book Company.

Diamond, S. 1974. *In search of the primitive*, New Brunswick: Transactional Books.

Docker, T. 1964. 'The popular image: Aborigines and the newspapers', in M. Reay (ed.), *Aborigines now*, Sydney: Angus & Robertson.

Dolgin, J. and J. Magdoff 1977. 'The invisible event', in J. Dolgin, D. Kemnitzer and D. Schneider (eds), *Symbolic anthropology*, New York: Columbia University Press.

Donzelot, J. 1979. *The policing of families*, New York: Pantheon Books.

Douglas, M. 1984. *Purity and danger*, London: Ark Paperbacks.

Dumont, L. 1972. *Homo hierarchicus*, London: Palidan.

Duncan, A.J. 1969. 'A survey of Aboriginal education in New South Wales', M.Ed. thesis, University of Sydney.

Dunn, M. 1975. 'Early Australia: wage labour or slave society', in E. Wheelwright and K. Buckley (eds), *Essays in the political economy of Australian capitalism*, vol. 1, Sydney: Australia & New Zealand Book Company.

Egloff, B. 1979. *Mumbulla mountain: an anthropological and archaeological investigation*, Sydney: G. West, Government Printer.

Eliade, M. 1965. *Rites and symbols of initiation*, New York: Harper & Row.

Elkin, A.P. 1933. 'Studies in Australian totemism', *Oceania*, 4 (1) 65–90.

—— 1936. 'Native education with special reference to Australian Aborigines', *Oceania*, 7 (4), 459–500.

—— 1940. Fieldnotes.

—— 1944. *Citizenship for the Aborigines: a national Aboriginal policy*, Sydney: Australasian.

—— 1951. 'Reaction and interaction: a food gathering people and European settlement in Australia', *American Anthropologist*, 53, 164–86.

—— 1974. *The Australian Aborigines*, Sydney: Angus & Robertson.

—— 1975. 'R.H. Mathews: his contribution to Aboriginal studies', Part II, *Oceania*, 46 (2), 126–52.

—— 1976. 'R.H. Mathews: his contribution to Aboriginal studies', Part III, *Oceania*, 46 (3), 207–34.

—— 1977. *Aboriginal men of high degree*, St Lucia: University of Queensland Press.

Encel, S. 1962. 'Power', in P. Coleman (ed.), *Australian civilisation*, Sydney: F.W. Cheshire.

Enright, W. 1899. 'The initiation ceremonies of the Aborigines of Port Stephens', *Journal of Royal Society of NSW*, 33, 115–24.

—— 1932. 'Social divisions of the Birripai', *Mankind*, 102.

Evans, R., K. Saunders, and K. Kronin 1975. *Exclusions, exploitation and extermination*, Sydney: Australia & New Zealand Book Company.

Evens, T. 1987. 'Psychologism and ethnocentrism in anthropological interactionism', *Social Analysis*, 22, 61–72.

Fanon, F. 1976. *The wretched of the earth*, Harmondsworth: Penguin Books.

Fink, R. 1955. 'Social stratifications – a sequel to the assimilation process in a part-Aboriginal community', M.A. thesis, University of Sydney, 137 pp.

—— 1957. 'The caste-barrier – an obstacle to the assimilation of part Aborigines in north west New South Wales', *Oceania*, 28 (2), 100–10.

Fitzpatrick, B. 1969. *British imperialism and Australia, 1783–1833*, Sydney: Sydney University Press.

Fletcher, B. 1976. *Colonial Australia before 1850*, Sydney: Thomas Nelson (Australia) Ltd.

Foucault, M. 1970. 'Orders of discourse', *Social Science Information*, 10 (2), 7–30.

—— 1977. *Discipline and punishment*, Harmondsworth: Penguin Books.

—— 1977a. 'The political function of the intellectual', *Radical Philosophy*, 17, 12–14.

—— 1978. *The archaeology of knowledge*, London: Tavistock Publications.

—— 1980. *Power/knowledge: selected interviews and other writings 1972–1977* (ed. C. Gordon), Sussex: Harvester Press.

—— 1980a. 'Intellectuals and power', in D. Bouchard (ed.), *Language, counter-memory, practice: selected essays and interviews*, Ithaca: Cornell University Press.

—— 1982. 'Afterword: the subject and power', in H. Dreyfus and P. Rabinow, *Michael Foucault: beyond structuralism and hermeneutics*, Sussex: Harvester Press.

Fredrickson, G. 1985. 'Redemption through violence', *New York Review of Books*, 38–42.

Friedman, J. 1983. 'Civilization cycles and the history of primitivism', *Social Analysis*, 14, 31–52.

Genovese, E. 1974. *Roll, Jordon, roll, the world the slaves made*, New York: Pantheon Books.

—— 1975. 'Class, culture and historical process', *Dialectical Anthropology*, 1, 71–9.

Godelier, M. 1972. *Rationality and irrationality in economics*, London: Monthly Review Press.

Goffman, E. 1961. *Asylums*, Harmondsworth: Penguin Books.

Goodall, H. 1982. 'A history of Aboriginal communities in New South Wales, 1909–1939', Ph.D. thesis, University of Sydney.

Gramsci, A. 1982. *Selections from prison notebooks* (eds Q. Hoare and G. Nowell Smith), London: Lawrence & Wishart.

Guillaumin, C. 1980. 'Idea of race and its elevation to autonomous scientific legal status in sociological theories', in *Sociological theories, race and colonialism*, Poole: UNESCO.

Gumbert, M. 1981. 'Paradigm lost: an analysis of anthropological models and their effect on Aboriginal land rights', *Oceania*, 52 (2), 103–23.

Gunson, N. 1974. *Australian reminiscences and papers of L.E. Threlkeld*, vol. 2, Canberra: AIAS.

Haigh, C. n.d. 'Some special Aboriginal sites', in *The Aborigines of New South Wales*, Sydney: NPWS.

Hall, S. and T. Jefferson (eds) 1977. *Resistance through rituals*, London: Hutchinson & Company.

Hanks, P. 1984. 'Aborigines and government: the developing framework', in P. Hanks and B. Keon-Cohen (eds), *Aborigines and the law*, Sydney: Allen & Unwin.

Hardy, B. 1976. *Lament for the Barkindji*, Sydney: Rigby Ltd.

Hartwig, M. 1965. 'The progress of white settlement in the Alice Springs district and its effect upon the Aboriginal inhabitants, 1860–1894', 2 vols, Ph.D. thesis, University of Adelaide, 669 pp.

—— 1978. 'Capitalism and Aborigines: the theory of internal colonialism and its rivals', in E. Wheelwright and K. Buckley (eds), *Essays in the political economy of Australian capitalism*, vol. 3, Sydney: Australia & New Zealand Book Company.

Hausfeld, R.G. 1963. 'Dissembled culture: an essay on method', *Mankind*, 6 (2), 47–51.

Heller, A. 1980. 'The power of shame', *Dialectical Anthropology*, 6, 215–28.

—— 1988. 'Existentialism, alienation and postmodernism: cultural movements as vehicles of change', in A. Milner, P. Thomson and C. Worth (eds), *Postmodern conditions*, Clayton: Centre for General & Comparative Literature (also 1989, Oxford: Berg Publishers).

Henderson, J. 1851. *Excursions and adventures in New South Wales*, 2 vols, London: W. Shoberl.

Henderson, R.F. 1974. *Rural poverty in northern New South Wales*, Australian Government Commission of Inquiry into Poverty, Canberra: Australian Government Publishing Service.

Hiatt, L. 1965. *Kinship and conflict*, Canberra: Australian National University Press.

Hirst, P. and P. Woolley 1982. *Social relations and human attributes*, London: Tavistock Publications.

Hodgkinson, C. 1845. *Australia from Port Macquarie to Moreton Bay*, London: T. & W. Boone.

Holmer, N.M. 1967. *An attempt towards a comparative grammar of two Australian languages*, vol. 2, Canberra: AIAS.

Hookey, J. 1984. 'Settlement and sovereignty', in P. Hanks and B. Keon-Cohen (eds), *Aborigines and the law*, Sydney: Allen & Unwin.

Horner, J. 1974. *Vote Ferguson*, Sydney: Australia & New Zealand Book Company.

Howard, M. 1981. *Aboriginal politics in south western Australia*, Nedlands: University of Western Australia Press.

—— 1982. 'Aboriginal brokerage and political development in south western Australia', in M. Howard (ed.), *Aboriginal power in Australian society*, St Lucia: University of Queensland Press.

Howitt, A.W. 1904. *Native tribes of south eastern Australia*, New York: MacMillan & Company.

Jacoby, R. 1975. *Social amnesia*, Sussex: Harvester Press.

Jameson, F. 1984. 'Periodising the 60's', in S. Sayres, A. Stephanson, S. Aronowitz and F. Jameson (eds), *The 60's without apology*, Minneapolis: University of Minnesota Press.

Jeans, D. 1972. *An historical geography of New South Wales to 1901*, Sydney: Reed Education Publications.

Jennett, C. 1984. 'Aborigines, land rights and mining', in E. Wheelwright and K. Buckley (eds), *Essays in the political economy of Australian capitalism*, vol. 5, Sydney: Australia & New Zealand Book Company.

Jones, D. and J. Hill-Burnett 1982. 'The political context of ethnogenesis: an Australian example', in M. Howard (ed.), *Aboriginal power in Australian society*, St Lucia: University of Queensland Press.

Jorgensen, J. 1974. *The sun dance religion*, Chicago: University of Chicago Press.

Jorgensen, J. et al. 1978. 'Energy, agriculture and social science in the American west', in J. Jorgensen et al. (eds), *Native Americans and energy development*, Massachusetts: Anthropology Resource Center.

Kahn, J. 1981. 'Explaining ethnicity: a review article', *Critique of Anthropology*, 16

(4): 43–52.

Kalantzis, M., B. Cope and C. Hughes 1984/5. 'Pluralism and social reform: a review of multiculturalism in Australian education', *Thesis Eleven*, 10/11: 195–215.

Keen, I. 1984. 'A question of interpretation: the definition of "traditional land owners" in the Aborigines Land Rights (NT) Act', in L. Hiatt (ed.), *Aboriginal landowners*, Sydney: Oceania Monograph.

Kelly, R. 1979. 'Why we bother', in *Archaeology resource management in Australia and Oceania*, Wellington: New Zealand Historic Places Trust.

Kendall, H. 1966 (also reprinted 1886, 1890, 1903, 1920). *The poetic works of Henry Kendall* (ed. T.T. Reed), Adelaide: Libraries Board of South Australia.

Kitaoji, Y. 1976. 'Family and social structure among Aborigines in northern New South Wales', Ph.D. thesis, Australian National University, 384 pp.

Land claims in New South Wales 1981. Reprinted by the New South Wales Aboriginal Land Council.

Lane, K. 1978. 'Carved trees and initiation ceremonies on the Nambucca River', in I. McBryde (ed.) *Records of times past*, Canberra: AIAS.

Lattas, A. 1986. 'The aesthetics of terror and the personification of power', *Social Analysis*, 19, 3–21.

—— 1987. 'Savagery and Civilisation: Towards a Genealogy of Racism,' *Social Analysis*, 21, 39–58.

Le Gay Breton, J. 1962. 'An estimate of assimilation rate of mixed-blood Aborigines in New South Wales', *Oceania*, 22 (3), 187–290.

Lévi-Strauss, C. 1966. *The savage mind*, Chicago: University of Chicago Press.

Lippmann, L. 1973. *Words or blows: racial attitudes in Australia*, Harmondsworth: Penguin Books.

—— 1981. *Generations of resistance*, Melbourne: Longman Cheshire.

Lithman, Y.G. 1978. *The community apart: a case study of a Canadian Indian reserve community*, Stockholm: Stockholm Studies in Social Anthropology No. 6.

Long, J.P.M. 1970. *Aboriginal settlements: a survey of institutional communities in eastern Australia*, Canberra: Australian National University Press.

Loos, N. 1982. *Invasion and resistance: Aboriginal–European relations on the north Queensland frontier, 1861–1897*, Canberra: Australian National University Press.

Lumb, R. 1988. 'Aboriginal land rights: judicial approaches in perspective', *The Australian Law Journal*, 62 (4), 273–84.

MacDougall, A. 1900/1. 'Manners, customs and legends of the Coonbangoree tribe', *Science of Man*, 3 (7), 116–17.

McMichael, P. 1979. 'The genesis of settler capitalism in Australia', *Intervention*, 13, 39–78.

McNickle, D. 1973. *Native American tribalism*, New York: Oxford University Press.

Maddock, K. 1983. *Your land is our land*, Harmondsworth: Penguin.

Markus, A. 1974. *From the barrel of a gun: the oppression of Aborigines, 1860–1900*, Melbourne: Victorian Historical Association.

—— 1978. 'Talka Longa Moutha: Aborigines and the Labour Movement 1890–1970', in A. Curthoy and A. Markus (eds), *Who are Our Enemies?*, Sydney: Hale & Premonger.

Martin, J. 1978. *The migrant presence*, Sydney: George Allen & Unwin.

Marx, K. 1963. 'On the Jewish question', in T. Bottomore (ed.), *Karl Marx early writings*, London: C.A. Watts & Co. Ltd.

Massola, A. 1972. *Coranderrk: a history of the Aboriginal station*, Kilmore: Lowden Publishing Company.

Mathews, J. 1977. *The two worlds of Jimmie Barker*, Canberra: AIAS.

Mathews, R. 1894. 'The Kamilaroi class system of the Australian Aborigines', *Queensland Geographical Journal*, 10, 18–34.

—— 1897. 'The totemic divisions of Australian tribes', *Journal of Royal Society of NSW*, 31, 154–76.

—— 1897a. 'The keeparra ceremony of initiation', *Journal of Anthropology Institute*, 26 (99), 320–41.

—— 1897b. 'The Burbung of the New England tribes, NSW', *Royal Society of Victoria*, 9, 120–73.

—— 1897c. 'The Wandarral of the Richmond and Clarence River tribes', *Royal Society of Victoria*, 10, 29–42.

—— 1898. 'Initiation ceremonies of Australian tribes', *The American Philosophical Society*, 37, 54–73.

—— 1900/1. 'The Murrawin ceremony', *Queensland Geographical Journal*, 16, 35–41.

Mathews, R. and Everitt, M. 1900. 'The organisation, language and initiation ceremonies of the Aborigines of the south-east coast of NSW', *Royal Society of NSW*, 34, 262–80.

Mauss, M. 1979. *Sociology and Psychology*, London: Routledge and Kegan Paul.

Meggitt, M. 1972. *The desert people*, Sydney: Angus & Robertson.

Meillassoux, C. 1972. 'From reproduction to production', *Economy and Society*, 1 (1), 93–105.

MHS files.

Mintz, S. 1974. *Caribbean transformations*, Chicago: Aldine Publishing Company.

Mitchell, T.L. 1839. *Three expeditions into the interior of eastern Australia*, vol. 2, London: Boone.

Morgan, G. 1981. 'Class theory and the structural location of black workers', *The Insurgent Sociologist*, 10 (3), 21–34.

Morris, B. 1983. 'From underemployment to unemployment: the changing role of Aborigines in a rural economy', *Mankind*, 13 (6), 499–516.

Morrissey, S. 1970. 'The pastoral economy 1821–1850', in J. Griffin (ed.), *Essays in the economic history of Australia*, Gladesville: Jacaranda Press.

Mulvaney, D. 1975. *The prehistory of Australia*, Sydney: Penguin Books.

Munn, N. 1970. 'The transformation of subjects into objects in Walbiri and Pitjantjatjara myth', in R. Berndt (ed.), *Australian Aboriginal anthropology*, Nedlands: University of Western Australia Press.

Murphy, J. 1986. 'The voice of memory: history, autobiography and oral memory', *Historical Studies*, 22 (87), 157–75.

Neil, M. 1972. *Valley of the Macleay*, Sydney: Wentworth Books.

Neuwirth, G. 1969. 'A Weberian outline of a theory of community: its application to "Dark Ghetto"', *British Journal of Sociology*, 20 (2), 148–63.

Neville, O. n.d. *Australia's coloured minority*, Sydney: Currawong Publishing.

O'Neil, J. 1986. 'The disciplinary society: from Weber to Foucault', *British Journal of Sociology*, 37 (1), 42–60.

Paine, R. 1977. *The white Arctic* (Newfoundland Social and Economic Papers: No.

7), Newfoundland: University of Toronto Press.

Perkins, C. 1975. *Bastard like me*, Sydney: Ure Smith.

Perry, T. 1966. *Australia's first frontier*, Melbourne: Melbourne University Press.

Powell, J. 1978. *The mirrors of the new world*, Canberra: Australian National University Press.

Radcliffe-Brown, A. 1928/9. Fieldnotes.

—— 1929. 'Notes on totemism in eastern Australia', *Journal of the Royal Anthropology Institute*, 59, 399–415.

—— 1930. 'Former numbers and distribution of the Australian Aborigines', *Australian Year Book*, 23, 687–96.

—— 1951. *Structure and function in primitive society*, London: Cohen & West.

Rand, A. 1964. *The virtue of selfishness*, New York: An Nal Book.

Read, P. 1982. 'The stolen generations', occasional paper no. 1, NSW Ministry of Aboriginal Affairs.

Reay, M. 1945. 'A half-caste Aboriginal community in north-western New South Wales', *Oceania*, 15 (4), 296–323.

—— 1949. 'Native thought in rural New South Wales', *Oceania*, 20 (2), 89–118.

—— 1963. 'Aboriginal and white Australian family structure: an enquiry into assimilation trends', *Sociological Review*, 2 (1), 19–47.

Reay, M. and G. Sitlington 1948. 'Class and status in a mixed blood community', *Oceania*, 18 (3), 179–207.

Reece, R. 1974. *Aborigines and colonists*, Sydney: Sydney University Press.

Reynolds, H. 1972. *Aborigines and settlers*, Melbourne: Cassell Australia.

—— 1974. 'Racial thought in early colonial Australia', *The Australian Journal of Politics and History*, 20 (1), 45–53.

—— 1981. *The other side of the frontier*, Townsville: James Cook University of North Queensland.

Roberts, S. 1964. *The squatting age in Australia, 1835–1847*, Melbourne: Melbourne University Press.

Robinson, F. and B. York 1977. *The black resistance*, Camberwell, Victoria: Widescope International Publishers.

Robson, L. 1965. *The convict settlers of Australia*, Melbourne: Melbourne University Press.

Rowley, C.D. 1973. *Outcastes in white Australia*, Harmondsworth: Penguin Books.

—— 1974. *The destruction of Aboriginal society*, Harmondsworth: Penguin Books.

—— 1978. *A matter of justice*, Canberra: Australian National University Press.

—— 1982. *Equality of instalments: the Aboriginal householder in rural New South Wales, 1965 and 1980*, Canberra: AIAS.

Rudder, E.F. 1925. 'Customs and habits of the Aboriginals of the Macleay', *Back to the Macleay Celebrations*, Official Souvenir.

Ryan, L. 1981. *The Aboriginal Tasmanians*, St Lucia: University of Queensland Press.

Sackett, L. 1975/6. 'Exogamy or endogamy: kinship and marriage at Wiluna, Western Australia', *Anthropological Forum*, 4 (1), 44–55.

Sahlins, M. 1974. *Stone age economics*, London: Tavistock Publications.

—— 1987. *Islands of history*, London: Tavistock Publications.

Sartre, J.P. 1972. *Anti Semite and Jew*, New York: Schocken Books.

Schapper, H. 1970. *Aboriginal advancement to integration: conditions and plans for*

Western Australia, Canberra: Australian National University Press.

Shaw, A. 1973. *The economic development of Australia*, Sydney: Longman Australia Pty Ltd.

Sider, G. 1980. 'The ties that bind', *Social History*, 5 (1), 1–39.

Smith, B. 1984. *European vision and the South Pacific*, Sydney: Harper & Row.

Smith, L. 1980. *The Aboriginal population of Australia*, Canberra: Australian National University Press.

Sparrow, The 1914. 'Aboriginalities', in F.A. Fitzpatrick (ed.), *Peeps into the past*, Parramatta: Cumberland Angus.

Stevens, F. 1973. 'Parliamentary attitudes to Aboriginal affairs', in F. Stevens (ed.), *Racism: the Australian experience*, vol. 2, Sydney: Australia & New Zealand Book Company.

—— 1980. *The politics of prejudice*, Chippendale: Alternative Publishing Cooperative Limited.

Sullivan, S. 1978. 'Aboriginal diet and food gathering methods in the Richmond and Tweed River valleys, as seen in early settler records', in I. McBryde (ed.), *Records of times past*, Canberra: AIAS.

Taussig, M. 1980. *The devil and commodity fetishism*, Chapel Hill: University of North Carolina Press.

—— 1984. 'Culture of terror – space of death: Roger Casement's Putamayo report and the explanation of torture', *Comparative Study of Society and History*, 467–97.

—— 1987. *Shamanism, colonialism and the wild man*, Chicago: University of Chicago Press.

Thompson, E.P. 1967. 'Time, work and industrial capitalism', *Past and Present*, 38, 56–97.

—— 1977. 'Folklore, anthropology and social history', *Indian Historical Review*, 3 (2), 247–66.

—— 1982. *The making of the English working class*, Harmondsworth: Penguin.

Thompson, J. 1984. *Studies in the theory of ideology*, Cambridge: Polity Press.

Thorpe, E. 1968. *A historical survey of the Macleay Valley*, Sydney: Wentworth Books.

Tindale, N. 1941. *Survey of the half-caste problem in South Australia*, proceedings of the Royal Geographical Society, South Australian Branch, vol. 4.

Treadgold, M. 1980. 'Aboriginal incomes: an aggregate analysis of the 1976 census results', *Australian Bulletin of Labour*, 7 (1), 31–46.

Turner, B. 1986. 'Personhood and citizenship', *Theory, Culture and Society*, 3 (1), 1–16.

Walker, R. 1962. *Old New England*, Sydney: Sydney University Press.

Ward, R. 1965. *Australia*, London: Horwitz Publications.

Weaver, S. 1983. 'Australian Aboriginal policy: Aboriginal pressure groups or government advisory bodies?', Part I, *Oceania*, 54 (1), 1–22.

—— 1983a. 'Australian Aboriginal policy: Aboriginal pressure groups or government advisory bodies?', part II, *Oceania*, 54 (2), 85–108.

—— 1984. 'Struggles of the nation state to define Aboriginal ethnicity: Canada and Australia', in G. Gold (ed.), *Minorities and mother country imagery*, St Johns: Institute of Social & Economic Research, Memorial University.

Weber, M. 1947. *Theory of social and economic organisation*, London: W. Hodge & Co. Ltd.

—— 1976. *The Protestant ethic and the spirit of capitalism*, Sydney: George Allen & Unwin.

Western, J. 1983. *Social inequality in Australian society*, Melbourne: MacMillan Company.

White, H. 1934. 'Some recollections of the Aborigines of New South Wales in the years 1848, 1849 and 1850', *Mankind*, May, 223–7.

Widders, T. 1977. 'Aboriginal adaptations', in P. Stanbury (ed.), *The moving frontier*, Sydney: A. & W. Reed Pty Ltd.

—— 1979.'Dhan-gadi: an Aboriginal language', honours thesis, Macquarie University.

Wilkie, M. 1983. 'Land rights and wrongs', *Chain Reaction*, 32, 10–12.

—— 1985. *Aboriginal land rights in NSW*, Chippendale: Alternative Publishing Cooperative Limited.

Williams, N. 1986. *The Yolngu and their land*, Canberra: AIAS.

Williams, N. and E. Hunn (eds) 1982. *Resource managers: North American and Australian hunters and gatherers*, Boulder: Westview Press.

Willis, P. 1978. *Profane culture*, London: Routledge & Kegan Paul.

—— 1978a. *Learning to labour*, Farnborough: Saxon House.

Willis, P. and P. Corrigan 1983. 'Orders of experience: working class cultural forms', *Social Text*, 7, 85–103.

Wolf, E. 1971. *Peasant wars of the twentieth century*, New York: Harper & Row.

—— 1982. *Europe and the people without history*, Berkeley: University of California Press.

Wolpe, H. 1975. 'The theory of internal colonialism: the South African case', in I. Oxaal, T. Barnett and D. Booth (eds), *Beyond the sociology of development*, London: Routledge & Kegan Paul.

Yengoyan, A. 1970. 'Demographic factors in Pitjandjara social organisation', in R. Berndt (ed.), *Australian Aboriginal anthropology*, Nedlands: University of Western Australia Press.

Young, E. 1982. 'Aboriginal town dwellers in NSW', in E. Young and E. Fisk (eds), *Town populations*, Canberra: Australian National University Press.

Government Publications

Aboriginal hospital morbidity in New South Wales, 1977, Division of Health Research for the Aboriginal Policy Committee, Health Commission of New South Wales, October 1979.

Aboriginal Quarterly, 1978.

—— 1980.

AWB reports, see under New South Wales Aborigines Welfare Board.

Dawn: a magazine for the Aboriginal people of New South Wales, October 1959, Sydney: Government Printer.

Handbook of Local Statistics, 1975. Sydney: Australian Bureau of Statistics.

—— 1976. Sydney: Australian Bureau of Statistics.

—— 1980. Sydney: Australian Bureau of Statistics.

—— 1981. Sydney: Australian Bureau of Statistics.

Historical Records of Australia, 1838–1850, vols XXII, XXIII, XXIV, XXVI, XXVII and XXX.

Homes for Aborigines, statistical information, Annual reports, 1974–1984. Housing Commission of New South Wales.

National Parks & Wildlife Act, 1974, no. 80 (reprinted 28 February 1985), Sydney: Government Printer.

New South Wales Aborigines Welfare Board. *Reports* for the year ended 30 June, 1940 to 1968, Sydney: Government Printer.

New South Wales Legislative Assembly, 1882. *Votes and proceedings,* Sydney: Government Printer.

—— 1883. *Votes and proceedings,* Sydney: Government Printer.

—— 1885. *Votes and proceedings,* Sydney: Government Printer.

—— 1892. *Votes and proceedings,* Sydney: Government Printer.

New South Wales North Coast Region, *Regional development and employment prospects,* Parts I and II, 1978, Department of Decentralisation & Development.

New South Wales Parliament, 1967. *Minutes of evidence taken before the joint committee of the Legislative Council and Legislative Assembly upon Aboriginal welfare,* Sydney: Government Printer.

Parliament of New South Wales, 1937/8. 'Proceedings of the select committee on administration of the Aborigines Protection Board', in *Joint volumes of papers presented to the Legislative Council and Legislative Assembly,* (1937–1940), vol. 7, Sydney: Government Printer.

—— 1940. 'Report and recommendations of the Public Service Board of New South Wales', in *Joint volumes of papers presented to the Legislative Council and Legislative Assembly,* (1937–1940), vol. 7, Sydney: Government Printer.

—— 1967. *Report from the joint committee of the Legislative Council and Legislative Assembly upon Aborigines welfare,* Part I – Report and Minutes of the Proceedings, Sydney: Government Printer.

—— 1980. *Aboriginal land rights and sacred and significant sights.* First report from the Select Committee of the Legislative Assembly upon Aborigines, Sydney: Government Printer.

Statistical Registrar of New South Wales, 1880–1890.

—— 1949.

—— 1950.

—— 1951.

—— 1952–1953.

—— 1956.

Newspapers

Macleay Argus, 1920–1938
Macleay Argus, 1980
Macleay Chronicle, 1920–1938

Index